Praise for *The Man in the Monster*

"I thought about Malcolm's assertion more than once as I read Martha Elliott's excellent new book, *The Man in the Monster*. As its title indicates, the book explores the gruesome misdeeds of a murderer (and rapist), but it is also an extended reflection on how and why one might write about, and even befriend, such people. On both counts, it is an admirable success." —*The National Book Review*

"Sturdily written and well researched . . . The book will appeal to those curious about why killers kill, and those who can stomach what they learn." —*The Boston Globe*

"A disturbing and multifaceted exposé of both a ruthless killer and the sympathetic, merciful journalist at odds with his capital fate." —*Kirkus Reviews*

"A fascinating, in-depth analysis for true-crime buffs, sociologists, and others grappling with nearly impossible-to-comprehend actions and their consequences." —*Booklist*

"This should be a welcomed volume to both general readers and criminal justice professionals." —*Library Journal*

"*The Man in the Monster* is arresting at every turn." —*BookPage*

"Elliott's harrowing story pulls off something brilliant and new. Elliott peered into the mind of a serial killer by becoming his friend. A narrative that is riveting, honest, and devastating."
—Jack Hitt, author of *Bunch of Amateurs: A Search for the American Character*

"Martha Elliott takes us inside the mind of serial killer and rapist Michael Ross. Elliott spent ten years getting to know the man behind the monster, and the pace of her book is as fast and merciless as a thriller." —Rebecca Tinsley, author of *When the Stars Fall to Earth*

"Martha Elliott has done something no other journalist has done—she devoted ten years getting to know a serial killer, giving the reader a rare glimpse into the mind of a man, a 'monster,' who killed eight women. No matter what your views are on capital punishment or mental illness, this will be a thought-provoking read. You won't want to put it down." —Steven Greenhouse, author of *The Big Squeeze: Tough Times for the American Worker*

"Martha Elliott has written a commanding book about a death row inmate she met as a journalist and talked with at least once a week for ten years. . . . When you read this book, I think you will be overwhelmed as I was and find that Martha Elliott has written a book that makes us look seriously at capital punishment. This is a great read and a must read and I urge it for people in every generation."
—Charles J. Ogletree, Jr., Jesse Climenko Professor of Law, Harvard Law School; Founding and Executive Director, Charles Hamilton Houston Institute for Race and Justice

"Martha Elliott provides us with a rare close-up of the mind behind a serial killer already tried and facing the death penalty. Her meticulous and dispassionate reporting pries open the story behind the series of repulsive crimes the killer has committed against his vulnerable victims. A normal college graduate with girlfriends and, at the same time, an obsessive, demented man stalking young women, the killer reveals himself to the reporter as the complex story of childhood traumas and mental illness unfold. The book is a highly readable contribution both to the debate about capital punishment and the criminal justice system, and, at the same time, journalism as compelling drama."
—Joan Konner, Dean Emerita, Columbia University Graduate School of Journalism

PENGUIN BOOKS

THE MAN IN THE MONSTER

Martha Elliott has been a journalist for almost forty years. She was mentored in graduate school by veteran journalist Fred W. Friendly and became his colleague, producing award-winning television programs and writing three books and numerous articles and speeches. She has run a newspaper and has also taught at Columbia University and at the secondary school level. The recipient of many awards, her most recent is Vassar's Time-Out Grant for 2014–15 to write a novel. She has three children and three grandchildren and lives in Maine.

THE MAN
IN THE
MONSTER

Inside the
Mind of a
Serial Killer

MARTHA
ELLIOTT

PENGUIN BOOKS

PENGUIN BOOKS

An imprint of Penguin Random House LLC

375 Hudson Street

New York, New York 10014

penguin.com

First published in the United States of America by Penguin Press,
an imprint of Penguin Random House LLC, 2015
Published in Penguin Books 2016

THE LIBRARY OF CONGRESS HAS CATALOGED THE
HARDCOVER EDITION AS FOLLOWS:
Names: Elliott, Martha J. H., author.
Title: The man in the monster : an intimate portrait of a serial killer / Martha Elliott.
Description: New York, New York : Penguin Press,
an imprint of Penguin Random House LLC, [2015]
Identifiers: LCCN 2015303334 | ISBN 9781594204906 (hc) | ISBN 9780143109471 (pbk.)
Subjects: LCSH: Ross, Michael (Michael Bruce), 1959-2005. | Serial
murderers—Connecticut—Biography.
| Serial murders—Connecticut—Case studies.
Classification: LCC HV6248.R675 E55 2015 | DDC 364.152/32092 B—dc23

Printed in the United States of America
1   3   5   7   9   10   8   6   4   2

Designed by Lauren Kolm

Names of several people were changed by the author to protect the
identities of those who were romantically involved with Michael
or the survivors of his attacks.

For my children, Hadley, Hannah, and James

And for the eight women whose lives
were so tragically cut short

THE MAN
IN THE
MONSTER

PREFACE

No one in her right mind invites a serial killer into her life. Who would want to know that kind of evil? For more than a decade, this is exactly what I did. I never imagined that I would consider someone like Michael Ross, a convicted serial rapist and murderer, a close friend. But from 1995 until his death by lethal injection in 2005, that is exactly what I did and what he became to me.

I deplore violence, and I do not wish to mitigate what Michael Ross did before his 1984 arrest. He took eight lives, and he ruined many more. Over the course of my investigation into this case, I got to know many of the people whose lives he forever altered. Some of the families of his victims became friends of mine as well. I wrote this book as much for them—and for the daughters they lost—as I did for myself.

The courts and the state of Connecticut have rendered justice in the case of Michael Ross. But until we see the man in the monster, we cannot begin to comprehend why he did what he did or to make a personal judgment as to whether sentencing Michael to death was a just punishment. Many books have been written on the topic of how someone can become a serial killer. This book grapples with the question of why this man, Michael Ross, turned to violence so many times. I hope that what I learned will help identify others like him before they turn down the same murderous path.

Michael Ross was my partner in this investigation. He opened up his life to me so that together we might tell his story. I believe he worked with me for so many years as a kind of atonement for what he had done. His life was full of contradictions. He was a moral man who committed heinously immoral acts, a man capable of great bravery who was also cowardly, an intelligent man whose stubbornness defied reason. All of these facets dwelled within this man.

To the best of my ability, I have told his story.

I became intrigued by Michael Ross's case in the summer of 1995 during my tenure as the editor in chief and publisher of the *Connecticut Law Tribune*. When the Connecticut Supreme Court overturned the six death sentences that he had been given in 1987, he began lobbying to accept a death sentence to spare the families of his victims the pain of going through another trial. I was puzzled by his unusual offer, and I was intrigued by the complexities of mental illness and the death penalty, which I have always strongly opposed. I wrote asking for an interview for an article for the *Tribune*, even though the thought of him petrified me.

The man I met was nothing like what I had expected. He wasn't insane according to the legal definition—someone who lacks the capacity to understand the wrongfulness of an act because of mental disease or defect. Quite the contrary, this sensitive, articulate Cornell graduate was also a devout Roman Catholic who would profusely express his remorse for his crimes to anyone who would listen.

His crimes were horrific. Michael had raped and murdered eight women, and there were other victims of sexual assault as well. To report his story I had to read thousands of pages of court testimony and police reports and interview lawyers, psychiatrists, family members, friends, and the victims' families. I also consulted experts who had evaluated him and cited behavioral, chemical, and psychological origins of Michael's murderous behaviors.

At various times, experts had argued that Michael suffered from a variety of afflictions that might explain his criminal behavior, including sexual sadism, brain lesions, and childhood trauma. I found that his was a case without simple answers—as are so many that involve mental illness. I have no doubt that all of the factors cited by the experts involved in his case contributed to Michael's actions, but I don't believe they tell the whole story. It took a decade with Michael for me to even begin to do so.

My reasons for taking on the assignment were complicated and personal. I was distressed that my home state of Connecticut might be the first New England state to execute someone in four decades. I had been brought up to be strongly opposed to capital punishment, yet even for me, Michael Ross's crimes raised the question of the death penalty. I saw all too vividly the pain and suffering of the parents and loved ones of the young women he had murdered. As a parent, I sympathized with their need to get justice for their daughters. After I met some of these parents and siblings, those feelings became even stronger. Michael's case was not just a daunting task to report on as a journalist, but also to deal with as a human being.

When I filed my article in 1996, I didn't intend to think about Michael Ross ever again. But after it was published, he kept calling, desperate for human contact. I'd been talking to him at least once a week during the nine-month research process, and it seemed cruel to stop taking his calls. I decided that continuing to talk with him was a small effort compared with what it meant to this lonely, haunted man.

Over time, we became friends, something that was very hard for me to admit for many years—even to myself.

Our conversations encompassed much more than the details of his crimes and the legal aftermath; we talked about his childhood, his regrets, his lonely life on death row, and, at times, about my life. Our decade-long relationship had two faces. Sometimes we were focused on the serial killer. We talked about Michael's past, about the murders, about his first trial, about the demons that had invaded his mind. He told me in conversations and letters about the possible origins of his mental illness, "the monster," which began and progressed in college, about the violent fantasies that plagued his mind, and about the murders. After he was convicted and put on death row, he had received medication, hormone therapy, that he said quieted his violent sexual fantasies. Yet the relief also had its costs; it freed his mind so that he had to face his horrific acts. That was the man I got to know. I never actually *met* the serial killer, even though I met Michael face-to-face more times than I can count.

As I became friends with Michael, our conversations became more personal. We joked, talked about the weather or politics. One journalist listening to a tape of a phone conversation between Michael and me commented, "It's too normal. You sound like you're talking to your next-door neighbor." We were talking about an impending snowstorm and whether I'd be able to fly from California to Connecticut to visit him. Michael was worried that the snow would delay my flight and was concerned about my safety. "Promise me you'll drive safely. Don't rush up here from the airport."

Often over the years, I would be at a party when someone would ask what I was working on. "A book." I'd hesitate. As soon as I'd say it was about a serial killer, the questions would ping in rapid fire. Everyone wanted to know who, what, and why. "Why?" was a question I could not answer for many years.

Prior to 1995, I knew nothing about serial killers. But when I began to look into this case, I had to find out where Michael might stand within the context of the history of the serial-killer phenomenon. I began by reading Ann Rule's book on her relationship with Ted Bundy, *The Stranger Beside Me*, published in 1980. Like me, Rule struggled to square the man she knew with the notorious murderer. It's interesting that nowhere in the book does Rule use the term "serial killer," as it didn't become part of the common parlance until about the time that Michael Ross was in the midst of his murder spree in the early 1980s.

Throughout all of my research, I failed to find a striking similarity between Michael Ross and any other murderer. He seemed to stand alone in the annals of serial killers, so I probed deeper into his story.

After his arrest in 1984, Michael was diagnosed as having the mental illness called sexual sadism, a paraphiliac disorder. All of his subsequent doctors concurred with this original diagnosis. According to the edition of the American Psychiatric Association's *Diagnostic and Statistical Manual of Mental Disorders* for that time (DSM-III), sexual sadism required one of the following criteria: "(1) On a nonconsenting partner, the individual has repeatedly and intentionally inflicted psychological or physical suffering in order to achieve sexual excitement. (2) With a consenting partner a repeatedly preferred or exclusive mode of achieving sexual excitement combines humiliation with simulated or mildly injurious bodily suffering. (3) On a consenting partner bodily injury that is extensive, permanent, or possibly mortal is inflicted in order to achieve sexual excitement." As it was written, this diagnosis focuses on the acts and not on the underlying urges or causes of sexual sadism. Although the criteria for the diagnosis have evolved over subsequent revisions of the DSM, based on his crimes, Michael would still meet criteria of the official diagnosis today.

The cause of the disease is not entirely understood; both biological and behavioral factors may be involved. Likewise, there is no universal treatment for the diagnosis. Behavioral therapies may work, and some patients respond to female hormone treatments, as Michael ultimately did. Some of the most renowned experts in the field believe that hormone therapy must be accompanied by psychotherapy.

Much controversy surrounds the diagnosis of sexual sadism and whether it should even be considered a mental illness. Some experts believe that sexual sadism, as well as sexual masochism, are sexual preferences and should not be considered abnormal behavior when the behaviors involve consenting adults. In Michael's mind, at least, his acts of violence were integrally connected to his compulsions; we spoke at length about the connection. He believed, or at least he desperately wanted to believe, that the disease drove him to kill. Part of my investigation was to question whether those who inflict pain or kill are driven by an uncontrollable compulsion or whether it is a choice of sexual preference. In Michael's case, his positive response to Depo-Provera and Depo Lupron drug treatments suggested that his compulsion could be controlled with medication.

Richard Rhodes's 1999 book, *Why They Kill*, is centered on the work of Dr. Lonnie Athens, a criminologist who teaches at Seton Hall University. Athens refutes the classic view that violent killers are mentally ill and do not consciously commit their crimes. From his observation of several hundred convicts, he postulates that after going through four stages (only one of which, possible brutalization and trauma as a child, I could connect with Michael), people actually choose violence as a course of action. During the last stage, he says, the violent person kills because he has come to believe that it is the right way to handle a situation. By the time I read Rhodes's book, I had known Michael for some time, and the idea that he actually chose to be a violent killer seemed impossible to believe. He was consumed with guilt. He insisted that it was shame about his crimes that had kept him from turning himself in, not fear of punishment.

Dr. James Merikangas, a psychiatrist and neurologist who has written about these types of behaviors and who analyzed Michael when he was practicing at Yale–New Haven Hospital, was adamant that each case must be examined individually and that any theory that says that all murderers make a conscious decision to kill is wrong. "Any of the [killers] I have seen are all different. The brain lesions [which Michael also had] are all different. I have not found a unifying thing," he told me. In "The Neurology of Violence," a chapter he wrote for *Brain-Behavior Relationships*, which he also edited, Dr. Merikangas notes, "Violence is not a diagnosis." He points out that "outbursts of rage or verbal or physical aggressiveness" are different from normal behavior and that—like Michael Ross—many people regret their violent acts.

Katherine Ramsland's extensive body of work on the subject supports the caveat against a one-size-fits-all theory of recidivist violent behavior. In *Inside the Minds of Serial Killers: Why They Kill*, she cites more than a dozen reasons for the murderousness of serial killers. She asserts that "when analyzed case by case, serial killers often do not fit into neat categories." In her introduction, she cites former FBI profiler Robert K. Ressler as saying that "too many people . . . try to oversimplify the psychology of these killers, but for every attempt to state a 'truth,' one can find counterexamples that undermine it. . . . Generalizations, Ressler indicated, do a disservice to the subject."

Michael's case did not fit into any stereotype about sexual killers—he didn't dismember his victims or exhibit other antisocial behaviors. After his arrest, he openly admitted his guilt, and he expressed what appeared to be true remorse for his actions and the pain he had caused.

Almost more than anyone else, Michael wanted to understand why he had committed such brutal crimes. That's why he spent thousands and thousands of hours talking to me—and why I listened. It's also why he was willing to speak with almost any psychiatric expert—an opportunity he unfortunately didn't have until it was too late to stop his murderous behavior—and to give me permission to interview them as well. As he told me over and over again, often sobbing, "I didn't wake up one day and decide to be a serial killer. I would have done anything for it to turn out differently."

The more I read, the more I realized that what we knew about other serial killers was based on their crimes, not on a thorough analysis of the person who committed them. It was impossible to draw conclusions about any one of them without a fuller portrait. I spent ten years of my life getting to know a serial killer, Michael Ross, through his eyes as well as those who knew him best.

When I began reporting this story, I was interested in the legal questions raised by the case—whether one could accept a death sentence without a trial and whether those with mental illness should be executed. There were also important constitutional questions involving the right of due process and the definition of cruel and unusual punishment. I hoped the story would start a dialogue about how our justice system deals with a mentally ill person who has committed horrendous crimes. The articles I wrote and this book were always intended to create a "little picture," the term my mentor, Fred Friendly—the iconic journalist and former head of CBS News, who was my professor at Columbia University as well as my colleague—used to describe personal stories that tell an important tale about society.

The little picture I found contradicted all of my own prejudices and fears about serial killers. Although I set out to tell the story as objectively as possible, when I began this process, in my mind, Michael Ross was a monster. Ultimately, writing about this story changed me. Michael

Ross was a brutal rapist and killer, but I also met another side of him—a caring, thoughtful person who exhibited true remorse, perhaps in part because of the Christian faith he had developed from a decade-long relationship with Father John Gilmartin, a Roman Catholic priest who was Michael's spiritual adviser. Father John was the first one to convince Michael that God would forgive him even if no one else would. It wasn't a personal journey, but Michael's faith helped him be firm in his belief that giving up his appeals was the right thing to do.

We are told that the ultimate punishment is reserved for the worst of the worst—those who commit horrendous acts that are cruel and heinous. Yet how do we as a society factor in mental illness when punishments are meted out? Do we show mercy and spare a life? Do monstrous acts make the person who commits them a monster?

I am the only journalist Michael Ross trusted to tell the whole truth, not only to my readers, but also to him. On some level, he wasn't sure what the truth was, and he hoped I would set him straight—even if the truth was something he didn't want to hear. To the best of his ability, he honestly answered and described his experiences—all of them. I learned about the dark side of man, what all of us may be capable of but none of us wants to face. In a sense, it's easier if such violent criminals appear to be subhuman monsters. But that logic protects no one by excusing everyone. To better understand the darkness, we have to see it clearly.

This is not just Michael Ross's story. I hope it also honors the memories of the women he murdered and honestly shows the suffering that Michael caused their families. I am particularly grateful to the Shelley family for all the hours that they spent with me, helping me to understand the tragic human cost of Michael's crimes. I have tried to reflect their honesty and pain in these pages.

This is the story of how I set out to write a story about a monster and met a man.

1

NEW LONDON, CONNECTICUT
SEPTEMBER 28, 1995

It was almost noon when Michael Bruce Ross, convicted serial killer, walked into the crowded courtroom—all 240 pounds of him, the man who had brutally raped and strangled eight young women. He no longer resembled the lanky, bespectacled, nervous-looking young man who had originally gone to trial more than a decade before; sedentary prison life, prison food, and female hormones (Depo-Provera and Depo Lupron to treat his sexual sadism) changed all that. His six-foot frame carried the weight that he jokingly claimed to have gained so that he wouldn't fit into the electric chair, Connecticut's method of execution at the time of his first trial. Oversize prison-issue glasses, a doughy face, and a crew cut gave him a geeky look. He wore the NCI (Northern Correctional Institution) prisoner's jumpsuit and white laceless slip-on sneakers. He was restrained by handcuffs and ankle shackles. As the guards removed the handcuffs at the judge's orders, visible indentations were left by the black box that holds the two shackles together during transport to ensure that there is no escape. The box is standard operating procedure for all death row inmates going to court. They say it hurts like hell.

Ross appeared calm, considering that he was trying to negotiate his own death, and he came armed with a folder full of documents and court decisions. He wanted the court to allow him to accept the death penalty without a new trial, because, he said, he wanted to spare the families of the young women he'd killed from having to go through the pain of another trial.

For the first time since we had started corresponding a few months earlier, we were in the same room, and he was actually able to see me. The reality of being less than twenty feet from a man who had raped and murdered eight young women was terrifying. Michael turned around, smiled at me, and mouthed, "Are you Martha?"

I nodded yes. As a reporter, I was excited. But he knew who I was. A serial killer had identified me. Half of me wished that I could become invisible or crawl under the courtroom bench, though he had four guards surrounding him and leg shackles on. The man couldn't hurt me. *Why did you let yourself get involved in this story?*

Michael had been on death row for almost a decade, but his legal proceedings were starting up again because the Connecticut Supreme Court had overturned his six death sentences and had ordered a new penalty phase because psychiatric evidence had been kept from the jury. As the editor in chief and publisher of the *Connecticut Law Tribune*, a weekly newspaper for lawyers, I could have sat in my office behind a desk, reviewing financials and reading reporters' stories, but I was looking for a powerful story that would demonstrate the problems inherent in the death penalty. What I got instead was a decade of Michael Ross.

2

EASTER SUNDAY 1984

Physically, they were as different as night and day. Leslie Shelley was blond and, as her father described her, "a bean pole" at four feet eleven inches and 85 pounds. April Brunais had brown hair and was chunky at five feet five inches and 160 pounds. No stranger would have suspected that they were less than seven months apart in age. Yet Leslie Shelley and April Brunais were inseparable fourteen-year-olds who had been the best of friends for nearly six years—ever since April had moved into a house two doors away in Griswold, Connecticut. Mimicking the Cabbage Patch Doll craze, they had adopted each other as sisters, even filling out "adoption" papers. Their notes to each other were signed "LYALAS" ("love you always, like a sister").

Typical teenage girls: their world consisted of clothes, makeup, a few select boys, and making sure they never missed a school dance. The parameters of their universe were set by school and their parents. When they hung out at the Shelleys', they'd go down to the basement, where there was a bed and a collection of heavy-metal albums, owned by Leslie's older brother Edwin. They'd play them so loud that it would drive Leslie's father crazy.

April, less than a month shy of her fifteenth birthday, was already a freshman at Griswold High School. Leslie was nearly finished with the

eighth grade at Griswold Elementary School, where she had successfully worked her way through the remedial-reading program. Despite
being extremely shy, Leslie was excited about moving on to high school
and joining her best friend there and had filled out the paperwork during the first week of April.

Although she had been baptized a Roman Catholic, Leslie had gravi-
tated to a local Protestant church, where she rarely missed Sunday school.
On Easter Sunday, April 22, 1984, Leslie had attended church services
before spending the afternoon with April. That afternoon, they were
looking for something to do—something that did not involve grown-
ups. This time they were plotting to go to Jewett City, a town a little
more than three miles away. The trick was getting their parents to let
them go. Ed Shelley was sitting in his living room watching television
when April and Leslie came into the house. April stayed on the landing, a half story lower, as Leslie went up to woo her father. "Can I go
to the movies with April?" she asked.

"Give me a kiss," Ed teased, pointing to his unshaven face. Leslie
leaned over and gave him a peck on the cheek. The girls told Ed that
the Roodes, April's mother and stepfather, were driving them. As they
went to leave, Jennifer, then eight, asked if she could go along, but
sensing that Leslie didn't really want her baby sister tagging along, Ed
decided that Jennifer would stay home.

Ellen Roode was told that the pair was going to meet friends for
pizza and that the Shelleys were giving them a ride. In all likelihood,
the girls cut across a neighbor's yard and hiked over the golf course,
knocking a few miles off the trip and keeping out of sight. Only April
and Leslie know the truth of what they did that afternoon—that is
until they decided to hitch a ride home. When they realized that they
were in danger of missing their 8:30 curfew, they called their families
from the phone booth near a gas station in Jewett City to say they were

running late. There wasn't time to walk home, so they decided to hitchhike. The first car to stop to pick them up was driven by Michael Ross.

At the end of the first quarter of 1984, Michael had been warned by his superiors at the insurance agency about poor job performance. His boss had suggested that he take a vacation to sort things out, and Michael decided to drive to Disney World in Florida with his live-in girlfriend, Diane (not her real name). But Diane's father died unexpectedly while they were in Florida, and they had to cut the trip short by a day—despite Michael's narcissistic pout and complete lack of understanding. The drive home was a 1,500-mile-long battlefield. "It was a very bad drive to say the least," Michael would admit. "I wasn't being very sympathetic or understanding."

Diane's father's wake was Easter Sunday, and Michael assumed that he was not invited because he had been fighting with Diane. Upset about the perceived rebuke, he paced around his apartment all afternoon, knowing that if he went out, someone might die. He tried desperately to control his urge to go on the hunt. Finally, following the pattern of what had already become his sick way of coping with the anger he felt toward a woman with whom he was involved, Michael got into his car. He rationalized it as a way to blow off steam, but he knew he was out looking for female prey. He had already committed five rape-murders and knew his pattern of hunting and stalking. He was only a few blocks from his apartment when he spotted April and Leslie and stopped to pick them up. They asked him to drop them off at a gas station in Voluntown. However, Michael had no intention of complying. When he drove past their stop, the girls became upset, and April startled him by pulling a steak knife from her purse, causing him to swerve and almost drive off the road. Feigning control, but worried, Michael ordered April to give him the knife. She hesitated until Leslie told her to do exactly as he ordered. This was probably a fatal mistake, because if either of them had managed to escape, Michael would have panicked and run.

What happened next is disputed. In 1984, after a day of questioning by the arresting officer, Detective Michael Malchik, Michael confessed to murdering April and Leslie. However, he later contended that Malchik "twisted" the evidence and cajoled him into saying things that weren't true so that he would be not only convicted, but also sentenced to die. Setting the record straight became one of Michael's obsessions after his conviction in 1987.

What follows is what he told me when I first started reporting on the case, noting the discrepancies with his original confession. "I drove to an area in Rhode Island. I never knew it was Rhode Island until [Malchik] showed me a map at midnight on the night of my arrest." Exactly where the murders took place would later become a legal battle between prosecution and defense lawyers; the prosecutors claimed that they had occurred in Connecticut because they wanted to make sure they had jurisdiction to prosecute them.

When he found a secluded spot, Michael pulled his car off the road and out of sight of passing traffic. Out in the woods where no one could come to their rescue, the girls were easily intimidated by his size and followed his commands without hesitation. He ordered April into the backseat as he tied up Leslie with strips of cloth that he cut from an old slipcover that was in the car and put her in the trunk. Then he bound April and pulled her out of the car, telling her to undress. As had become his gruesome ritual, he unzipped his pants and thrust his penis into her mouth, but only long enough to further arouse him. He pulled out before coming close to climax. He pushed her down onto her back and raped her. Flipping her over onto her stomach and using the same pieces of cloth with which he had bound her, he strangled her and then stuffed her lifeless body, naked from the waist down, into the front seat of the car with the back of the front seat lowered.

Michael's version of what happened next differed depending on when he was telling the story. His confession says he took Leslie out of the trunk, then had her undress and "perform oral sex on me." Michael claimed that "she was too small," so he didn't rape her. Instead, he apologized to her and then strangled her. He told Dr. Howard Zonana, a psychiatrist who examined him for the defense but did not testify in court, that "she was the only one who didn't panic. They all fought me and resisted me. She didn't." He said that she "took the excitement out of it" and that he couldn't get hard when he tried to rape her. "She never said a thing, not even when I was strangling her."

However, while on death row, he changed his story. "I tried to rape her vaginally," he claimed, "but I couldn't penetrate her. So I raped her anally." He used the cloth ligatures to strangle her before putting her body back into the trunk of the car. He then looked for a place to hide the bodies, perhaps because the location of the murders was too close to the road and he wanted to make sure the bodies weren't discovered right away; Michael couldn't explain his reasons except that every time he realized what he had done, he panicked. He didn't want to get caught, and the best way to avoid being accused of murder was to hide the bodies. He drove back to Connecticut, toward the place where he had picked up the girls, and disposed of their bodies in a culvert within miles of where they lived. Like a ritualistic wake, Michael returned to that location on several occasions but was always worried that the bodies would be found and "that someone would recognize my car as being in the area. But I had to return to check them. I don't know why . . . I just had to see that they were still there. . . . I didn't stay long," he later told me.

When he was arrested, Michael never went as far as saying that he had killed Leslie to cover his crimes, but because he admitted apologizing to her, it seemed the most likely scenario to many people. He always said that Leslie Shelley's murder bothered him the most. Was any scenario better than another? Either he killed Leslie without sex and therefore may have done it as part of a cover-up, or he tried to rape the poor little girl, couldn't, and settled for anal sex, making Leslie's death more agonizing. Either option was equally abhorrent. That's why Ed and Lera Shelley were present at every hearing and were determined that Michael Ross should be executed.

CONNECTICUT
1994

At the *Law Tribune*, we held weekly editorial meetings in a conference room that overlooked a salt marsh. During a Monday morning meeting in early August 1994, I was staring out the window watching a blue heron lying in wait, standing motionless trying to be invisible to unsuspecting fish, as Joe Calve, the editor of the paper, gave a summary of the Connecticut Supreme Court's opinion that upheld Michael Ross's conviction of guilt but overturned his death sentences.

Michael had been arrested in Connecticut in June 1984 after a three-year killing spree that began just before his graduation from Cornell University in Ithaca, New York, in May 1981. After his Connecticut arrest, he was charged with the rape and murder of six women. Tammy Williams, seventeen, and Debra Smith Taylor, twenty-three, were murdered in Windham County, Connecticut. Robin Stavinsky, nineteen, Leslie Shelley, fourteen, April Brunais, fourteen, and Wendy Baribeault, seventeen, were murdered in adjacent New London County. Later Michael admitted to raping and killing Dzung Ngoc Tu, twenty-five, and Paula Perrera, sixteen, in New York in 1981 and 1982. All of his murders were random. They were vulnerable women who happened to be walking alone along deserted paths or roads.

The Windham County prosecutor did not seek the death penalty.

After consulting with his own psychiatric experts, he concluded that Michael was mentally ill and ineligible for a death sentence under the law. In a plea bargain, Michael was sentenced to two consecutive eighty-year prison terms. However, New London's chief state's attorney C. Robert Satti Sr. did not offer a plea bargain, and after a lengthy trial in 1987, Michael was convicted of the four murders in New London County and given six death sentences—a technicality of the law that allows someone to be charged more than once with the same murder.

Before any death sentence could be carried out, the Connecticut Supreme Court had to review the case. The 1972 U.S. Supreme Court decision in *Furman v. Georgia* required every state to rewrite its death penalty statute because the law was being applied in an arbitrary and capricious manner and thus was a violation of the Fourteenth Amendment guarantee of equal protection of the laws. Some of the justices also said it was a violation of the Eighth Amendment prohibition against cruel and unusual punishment. The decision required that an appellate court in each state review any death sentence to make sure that the Constitution has not been violated, that the application of the death penalty was not arbitrary, and that the trial court did not commit any procedural errors. For twelve years, from 1965 until 1977, there were no executions in the United States while states rewrote their laws to conform to *Furman*. At the time of Michael's sentencing, fewer than one hundred men had been executed—most in the South or West.

It had taken seven years for the Connecticut Supreme Court to reach a decision in Michael's case. The justices upheld his conviction but overturned the death sentences. The court ruled that the prosecutor and trial judge had erred when they kept vital evidence from the jury. In addition, Justice Robert Berdon wrote a scathing criticism of the original prosecutor, Bob Satti, in his concurring opinion. The jury never knew that the state's own expert psychiatrist, Dr. Robert Miller, agreed with the defense expert psychiatrists that Michael was mentally ill—a sexual sadist—and that his mental illness should preclude a death sentence. Dr. Miller had written the letter explaining his position to Satti on February 15, 1987, just two weeks prior to the start of jury selection in Michael's trial. But Satti kept Miller's letter out of the original trial.

In his letter, Dr. Miller said that after ruminating about the case for a long time, he had changed his original analysis of the significance of Michael's mental illness, which he admitted had been based on emotion rather than reason. Dr. Miller wrote that he believed Michael's mental illness played a significant role in the murders and that he could not recommend a death sentence. "If it had been only one or two [murders] I could have held up, but the repetitive nature of the acts as well as past history of assaultive behavior make my (our) position untenable." Michael had attacked, raped, and murdered too many victims for Dr. Miller to deny that his mental illness was linked to his crimes. In Connecticut, under the death penalty statute as it existed in 1987, mental illness was an automatic mitigating factor. A death sentence could not be imposed if there was even one mitigating factor. Yet in part because it never heard Dr. Miller's findings, the jury rejected the psychiatric evidence put on by the defense and imposed six death sentences.

I had recently moved to Connecticut when Michael was first arrested in 1984. I remember being relieved to hear that a suspected serial killer had been apprehended. But I had a sense of dread three years later when I read the headlines announcing that he had been sentenced to die in the electric chair—the first successful capital prosecution since Connecticut had reinstated the death penalty in 1973. I'm not even sure if I knew that Connecticut had a death penalty statute. In New

York, where I had been living, Governor Mario Cuomo had firmly planted himself in front of the executioner's door, vetoing any death penalty statute passed by the legislature. It seemed odd that suburban Connecticut would have tougher penalties than New York. The state I lived in was the first New England state in three decades to sentence a man to death. Even though I knew there would be years and years of appeals, the verdict was unsettling. No one had been executed in Connecticut since 1960. I believed all killing was wrong—not just what Michael had done but also what the state of Connecticut wanted to do to him. Yet on the other hand, as a parent, I couldn't even fathom the pain and suffering of the families of the young women and could sympathize with their need for justice for their daughters.

When the decision was handed down in 1994, I'd been out of the country adopting twins from Paraguay and then was coping with the twenty-four-hour-a-day job of caring for two premature babies, so I missed the newspaper reports. The decision meant that a new jury would determine whether Michael would be sentenced to death or to as long as 480 years in prison—in addition to the 160 years he was already serving. In Connecticut, as in most states, capital murder cases are conducted in two parts. If the jury finds the defendant guilty of a capital crime during the first phase, a second phase with the same jury follows to determine the penalty.

As we walked out of the meeting that day, Joe recounted Michael's personal history. "When he was just a kid, like eight years old or something, his job at the family chicken farm was to weed out the sick chickens and wring their necks. When you read about Ross's life, it's no wonder he was crazy. His sixteen-year-old uncle blew his brains out with a shotgun and left a long suicide note that was written in a spiral, in which he confessed that he was a homosexual and that he couldn't stand to live anymore."

I stopped in the middle of the corridor. "He killed chickens when he was only eight?" I asked.

"He killed the women in the same way—strangling them with his bare hands—after he raped them." Joe had covered parts of the original trial and began to describe the murders in detail. "Ross would be out driving and see some random young girl, pull over, and grab her. He raped them, but he made each of them perform oral sex on him before the actual rape. Then he would strangle her. Sometimes it would take several minutes because his hands would cramp, and he'd have to stop for a moment before finishing them off."

I couldn't take any more. "Okay. I get it."

"But Ross is intelligent. He has a high IQ and graduated from Cornell. He's always sending us articles on why the death penalty should be abolished. And guess what? He used to be for capital punishment, but I guess being sentenced to death prejudices one's worldview on such issues," he chuckled.

"I can see why he might have a change of heart."

"He's not only changed but become a missionary. He is a prolific writer. There's not that much to do on death row, and with all that time on his hands, he cranks out article after article. His pieces are usually pretty good. We'll see what his next move is, but I bet you anything that we'll get a letter from him analyzing the court's decision in a few weeks. Like a lot of people in his position, he's learned a lot about the law."

"Let me know if you hear from him," I added, never really expecting to hear more.

Michael Ross's case could have ended with a life sentence after the Connecticut Supreme Court decision—handed down on his thirty-fifth birthday in 1994. The New London state's attorney now had a second chance to acknowledge that Michael suffered from a mental illness and offer him the equivalent of several life sentences without parole, saving the state the cost of another trial, decades of appeals, and perhaps inevitably an execution. But the prosecutor—"Bulldog" Satti to those who had battled him in court—did not give up so easily.

Satti was barely five feet four inches, but he cut an enormous figure. Michael, at least ten inches taller, feared him. The veteran prosecutor had taken on the case of *State v. Ross* with all the aggression and tenacity his nickname suggested. This had been no ordinary case for the chief state's attorney. When the Ross case came to trial in 1987, Satti had recently failed to secure a death sentence in the Terry Daniels case, involving not only a rape-murder, but also the throat slashing of the victim's two-year-old daughter. Michael Ross's prosecution provided Satti with a second opportunity to be the first Connecticut prosecutor to get a capital conviction under the new statute.

The snowy-haired prosecutor was about to retire after nineteen years of heading the New London State's Attorney's Office and forty-three years of practicing law, but his devotion to this case fueled his effort to stay on part-time as a special assistant state's attorney. There was no question in Satti's mind that Michael Ross was a cunning, manipulative rapist who knew exactly what he was doing when he killed those eight women. He believed that Ross had murdered to ensure that his victims could never identify him and that his mental illness was a sham concocted by Michael to avoid a death sentence. In Satti's mind, Michael should face death because he had committed heinous crimes.

However, the inmate on death row in 1994 was not the same man who had been incarcerated in 1987. Once he was placed on death row, Michael received medication, first Depo-Provera and then Depo Lupron, two drugs that suppressed his production of testosterone. Administered by injection, both were developed as contraceptives for women and contain progesterone, a hormone that prevents egg release. Eventually the medications were used by psychiatrists with considerable success to suppress the production of testosterone in male patients with sexual disorders. It was their belief that overproduction of testosterone might be a root cause of some aberrant sexual behavior. Studies have determined that recidivism rates drop dramatically when the medications are administered in conjunction with psychotherapy for convicted sex offenders who suffer from some paraphiliac disorders, such as pedophilia, exhibitionism, and sexual aggression. Michael was the perfect candidate because he was in a controlled environment where he had mental health personnel checking his medications and state of mind on a regular basis.

When Michael's testosterone production had virtually been eliminated, he said he no longer suffered from the violent sexual fantasies that had constantly played and replayed in his thoughts for more than a decade. He wrote that he had been freed from "the monster within," and returned to being "Michael." Seven years on death row had given him plenty of time to think about what he had done and what he would do when the court finally decided his fate. It also gave him a lot of time to begin a letter-writing campaign to newspaper editors and to write op-ed articles about the flaws in the criminal justice system and why the death penalty should be abolished. His writings also expressed remorse for what he had done.

But Michael had come to a dramatically different conclusion about how his own case should play out. After years in prison and in treatment for his disease, he decided that the only way he could prove to the families of his victims that he was repentant for what he had done was to accept a death sentence. In September 1994, Michael requested that his public defenders hand-deliver a letter to Bob Satti, offering a deal—stop the penalty hearing from going forward, and he would accept a death sentence. He explained that there was "no need and no purpose served in inflicting additional emotional harm or distress on the families of my victims. I do not wish to hurt these people further—it's time for healing. . . . I am willing to hand you the death penalty 'on a silver platter,' on the condition that you will work with me to get this over with as quickly and as painlessly as possible." He asked to be allowed to go into court to admit his guilt and take responsibility for his crimes by accepting the death penalty.

Michael said he would sign a stipulation, a legal declaration, that said his crimes were "especially cruel, heinous, and depraved" (a requirement in a capital case) and that there were no mitigating factors that would preclude a death sentence. In exchange for this deal, Satti had to agree that the state would offer no evidence of any kind to prove its case—no autopsy reports, no gruesome crime scene photos, and no emotional testimony from the victims' families.

However, Michael could not resist editorializing. He said he didn't expect Satti to accept the offer because "I know that you want your circus trial, and that you couldn't care less about how it affects the families of my victims. You want your day in the sun, your day of glory. You want to be the man who sends Connecticut's most hated and despised criminal to the electric chair. And you will probably want to pull the switch yourself. And even though that is exactly what I am offering you with this deal, if you agree there will be no circus trial with you as master of ceremonies. That kind of takes the wind out of your sails, and doesn't make it so much fun, now does it?" He offered to meet with Satti at the prison to work out the details. He said he understood that a meeting would be unpleasant, but that it was necessary to ensure that they were "playing from the same sheet of music."

What he didn't know was that his public defenders, Fred DeCaprio and Peter Scillieri, never delivered his letter to Satti. They later explained that they could not participate in his decision to give up without a legal fight. With no response from the prosecutor, Michael decided that his next best option was to make his offer public. In March 1995, he wrote an article for *Northeast*, the Sunday magazine supplement of the *Hartford Courant*, entitled "It's Time to Die."

Michael's article began with a description of his recurring nightmare of his execution in Connecticut's electric chair. The horror in the dream comes not in the execution itself but in visualizing the crowd outside, counting down the last seconds and cheering as they hear that Michael Ross, the monster serial killer, is dead. He also wrote of life on death row and explained that his mental illness, sexual sadism, had caused him to have repetitive thoughts of rape, murder, and the degradation of women. He was sexually aroused by humiliating and raping women. He claimed that his medication, prescribed by one of his psychiatric expert witnesses, had freed him from those obsessive thoughts and enabled him finally to face what he had done. Over time, he said, he had lost the intense desire to prove his mental illness in a court of law and now wanted to forgo the penalty phase of his trial and accept death, sparing his victims' families the pain of another proceeding. One section of the *Northeast* article suggested that he might be suicidal, making me wonder if his years on death row had made him depressed. I suspected that his real motives might have been state-assisted suicide rather than a selfless act to help give the families closure.

Initially, Michael had been consumed with a desire to prove that he was mentally ill. "When I first came to death row, I was filled with anger at how the prosecution had twisted and distorted facts of my case. I was consumed with an intense desire to prove that my mental illness does in fact exist, and that the mental illness did in fact deprive me of my ability to control my actions and that my mental illness was in fact the cause of my criminal conduct." He said he wanted everyone to "believe that I was sick and that it was the sickness in me that did the killing. I wanted to prove that I wasn't the animal that the state portrayed me to be." But he said he was tired and had "come to believe that any such thinking may be simply wishful thinking." He didn't think anyone would ever believe that his mental illness was the cause of his lack of self-control, so he believed the only logical course of action was to accept death.

Why would anyone opt for death over life? Why was Michael, who was openly opposed to the death penalty and who churned out articles expressing that opinion, willing to accept execution? Was he depressed, as many death row inmates are, and just giving up? Was he actually asking the state to help him commit suicide? Was the prospect of life imprisonment so grim that death became a more palatable option? What did the victims' families think of the offer? To those who had followed Michael's case—his subsequent crusade to establish misconduct on the part of the state, his one-man campaign against the death penalty, and his desire for the world to understand his mental illness—his actions were not only baffling, but also contradictory. Only a few months earlier, in December, he had written, "Executions degrade us all. They are carried out in the middle of the night, in the dark, away from us all to hide what they really are—a barbaric punishment symbolic of our less civilized past." How could the man who had penned that now offer to accept a death sentence for himself?

The *Northeast* article concluded, "Kill me if you must, but please don't let it end there. Learn from this horrible experience." What could anyone possibly learn from executing Michael Ross—or anyone else, for that matter?

I paced around my office considering these questions. Michael's story was both horrifying and fascinating. Was he really mentally ill and the victim of an overzealous prosecutor?

I decided to learn all I could about the case. I gathered up all the documents and articles we had on it in the office. Together, the articles, trial transcripts, court decision, and briefs concerning Ross's case took up a large filing cabinet and three banker's boxes. The most difficult task was getting started, not because of the daunting amount of work, but because opening the boxes was like turning on a horror film. I started with articles that Michael had written, thinking that they would give me clues. Then I began reading the trial transcripts and briefs.

I read some of the documents at work and took some home in handfuls to read at night. I didn't want to bring all of it into my home because it would have been like taking Michael Ross into my house. As I began reading the material—it would take me months to get through it all—two things stood out. First, it was apparent that Michael suffered from mental illness. All five of the psychiatric experts who examined him—even the state's expert witness—agreed that he was mentally ill, a sexual sadist. The second thing I suspected was that in Michael's first trial, the judge, the prosecutor, and the state police's head investigator had, at the very least, made some errors and at the worst, trampled over Michael's rights. As editor in chief and publisher of a newspaper for lawyers, I couldn't ignore a case involving a possible violation of a defendant's Fifth, Sixth, and Fourteenth Amendment rights.

Woven within this legal morass was also a story of horror and suffering—of young women who were brutally raped and then literally had the life squeezed out of them and of their families, who had been waiting for some sort of closure for more than a decade, waiting to know if Michael Ross would pay the ultimate price for killing their sisters and daughters.

I wrote a letter to Michael, in the late summer of 1995, introducing myself, expressing my interest in what he was doing, and asking if he'd be willing to be interviewed. It was only a matter of days before I received his reply in a handwritten envelope with his return address clearly printed on the front. I held the envelope and hesitated before I opened it, afraid of what might be inside. I think that I feared that the serial killer, the monster, would reveal himself to me, jumping out in front of me. I stared at the hand-printed letter, thinking about the man who had written it, trying to imagine him—not in a physical sense but as a person, his soul, if he had one. What type of man would commit such brutal acts?

"I would be happy to grant you an interview but . . ." he began. Death row had been transferred into the state's maximum security prison, Northern Correctional Institution, and access to the press had been cut off. Only immediate family members were allowed to visit death row inmates. The policy seemed Draconian, as families often don't always support relatives on death row. But I could understand the state wanting to keep journalists out; they give the death row inmates a mouthpiece and threaten the state's veil of secrecy about what happens behind the prison walls. So I called the Connecticut Department of Correction to try to set up an interview and was told that it was not possible. I wrote a letter appealing to the commissioner and to the attorney general of the state, Richard Blumenthal, who was known in the journalistic community as accessible and open to reasonable requests. With time, Blumenthal approved my request, but it took even more time to get through the red tape. It would take almost six months just to get on Michael's phone list, to hear how he answered questions rather than see written, thought-out responses about what was making him offer to give up his life. In the meantime, I started attending the court proceedings.

A few days before the first hearing I attended, a second letter from Michael arrived. Parts of the letter were almost lawyerly, yet it was also passionate and, at times, contrite. He seemed remorseful, but there was also an underlying anger and frustration with the system. Michael accused Satti of being willing to do anything to sway the jury's emotions, including using "crime scene photos, autopsy reports, and, most important, the victims' families. He will put them on the stand and tear open old wounds. If he can get them to break down on the stand he will do it. He doesn't give a damn about them." He also was reneging on his willingness to cooperate. He was afraid that an article by me would "piss him off." He expected that the stipulations would be full of lies but that he would sign them anyway to stop Satti from hurting the families of his victims further. "That's what is most important at this time. Not my life, not justice, but my victims' families' well-being. . . . I owe my victims' families the world. I can never even begin to repair the damage that I have done to them. Reconciliation is impossible. I can't even ask their forgiveness. How could I?"

Repeating what would become his mantra, he insisted that it was his duty to prevent the families any harm. "How can I justify putting the families of my victims through that again? Especially for something as intangible as a principle of 'justice.'" In order to prevent a new trial, he said he would sign anything, "including something that says I'm the biggest scumbag in the world, that I knowingly and willingly killed my victims in cold-blooded ecstasy, and that I deserve to die, I will do so. For they are only words that won't change the ultimate truth." Michael said he didn't expect me to understand what he was trying to do, but he hoped I would understand why he couldn't grant an interview at that time unless I promised that none of it would be printed until his negotiations with Satti were completed.

I read it over and over, concluding that Michael had a motive beyond sparing the families more pain. In some twisted way, he was attempting to shift the blame of pain from himself, the killer, to Satti, the prosecutor. Somehow in Michael's mind, the pain didn't come from his horrific acts but from the fact that Satti would revel in the gory details of his crimes in court. It was a convenient rationalization. How else is a prosecutor going to prove his case? The question remained as to whether he, depressed and feeling hopeless about his chances of receiving a life sentence at a new penalty hearing, might actually be trying to get the state to help him commit suicide, seeing it as an easy way out. It also could be an insincere move to get attention in the media.

The Ross case was not first on the docket in that courtroom the day I first saw him. I sat waiting while the judge dealt with other cases, from parole violations to petty larceny.

Upstairs in the New London court, Michael and Satti were debating the details of their unprecedented alliance between defendant and prosecutor. This was the third time they had met to negotiate Michael's death—and there would be many more meetings before they had agreed on all the details of the stipulation.

The stipulation was to say that Michael murdered Wendy Baribeault, Leslie Shelley, April Brunais, and Robin Stavinsky, that the murders had been especially cruel and heinous, that there were no mitigating factors that required mercy, and that the proper penalty was death.

"Do you know what it is like to sit at a table with a man who despises you? Who wants you dead? . . . You cannot imagine what it is like to sit across a table, and have to listen to that arrogant bastard speak of justice," Michael wrote to me later. "He speaks of how, as the state's attorney, he not only represents the people of Connecticut, but must protect my rights! He speaks of my rights after all the twisting, distortion, deception, and out-and-out lies that he has orchestrated over the last decade in my case! And I have to sit there, smile and be courteous, and bite my tongue because I'm scared to death that I'll say something to anger him and that he'll say, 'The hell with this, we start picking a jury tomorrow.'"

Later, Bob Satti would confide in me that it was also difficult for him to sit in a room with Michael, negotiating his death. Satti never publicly wavered in his resolve to secure a death sentence for Ross, but privately he admitted that his negotiations with Ross had somewhat tempered his opinion of him. At the time, I did not appreciate the meaning of what Satti had said: Michael Ross the serial killer was a scary concept, but Michael Ross the man was not. Face-to-face, it is difficult to tell a man that you think he should be executed. Perhaps that's why the executioner always wears a hood to hide his identity. It may be part of the reason why those who were hanged, electrocuted, or shot were also hooded. The hood creates a barrier. No one wants to see the panic in the face of the condemned or the gruesome, distorted face of the corpse. Both the executioner and the condemned were anonymous, hiding their humanity.

While negotiations continued upstairs, I looked around the sparsely filled courtroom at that first hearing for the usual journalists or lawyers. Across the aisle from where I was sitting and a few rows back sat Ed and Lera Shelley, the parents of Leslie, the youngest of Michael's victims. At least one of them attended every court proceeding, generating ten years of missed workdays and irritated bosses. "We wanted to be there for our daughter," they had explained to reporters over and over again. No one had to point them out, because it was obvious that Mrs. Shelley found it painful to be in court. As soon as Michael's case was called, she dabbed her eyes with a tissue. Ed was stoic, but it was clear that he regarded Michael as pure evil. His steely-eyed expression almost cried out that he not only wanted all of this to be over, but that he also would have liked to offer to personally pull the switch at Michael's execution. Ed later told me that during the first trial, he and a father of one of the other victims sneaked a gun into the courtroom with the intention of killing Michael. In the end, neither could bring himself to do it. Neither could risk hurting someone else or getting hurt himself. Perhaps the fleeting sensation of being in control of Michael's fate as he had been in control of their daughters' lives was enough to assuage their urge to kill him.

When Michael and Satti finally appeared in court that afternoon, they reported that they were making progress but that there was more work to be done. Satti outlined for the court what had and had not been agreed to in minute detail. They would report back to the court in a month.

My immediate concern was to report on the hearing. I had been there not just to write a future article, but also to report for the *Law Tribune* on each hearing I attended. From the tone of Michael's magazine article in the *Northeast*, I believed that he was so tired or depressed that he actually wanted to die, so the lead of my story about the hearing read, "Convicted serial killer Michael Ross wants to die, but in volunteering to waive a new death penalty hearing, he unwittingly may be delaying his execution."

Within a few days of the article's publication, Michael sent a letter with a number of enclosures, including his competency report and a gentle upbraiding, saying he had sent the competency report "to show that I'm not incompetent and well aware of what I am doing, but, more importantly, to show you that I have very concrete reasons why I am doing this. When reporters write 'Michael Ross wants to die,' they are incorrect. I have no death wish and would much prefer to receive an effective natural life sentence." However, he said the cost to achieve that would be too high.

Michael was becoming even more of a contradiction: He was against the death penalty but willing to accept it for himself. He wanted to live but felt that he could not fight for his own life because it would hurt the families.

Michael continued to send me more and more information about his case. He was clearly obsessed with "getting" Satti, and I sensed that there was more to the story than Michael's offer to die. Did Michael get a fair trial in 1987? Were there mistakes or acts of misconduct by officers and prosecutors? Was Michael really mentally ill, or was that a mere excuse for his murderous conduct? Did his drugs change him? Had he changed significantly since committing the murders? Answering those questions was going to require an interview not only with Michael, but also with the few people who really knew him.

4

NEW LONDON COURTHOUSE
NOVEMBER 9, 1995

While I was waiting for *State v. Ross* to be called in the New London Courthouse several weeks after the first hearing I attended, a man with a clerical collar sat down a few rows behind me on the other side of the aisle. In a letter, Michael had informed me that he had a few friends who sometimes attended court and that his spiritual adviser was Monsignor John Gilmartin. He urged me to contact him. With that as my introduction, I sat down next to Father John—Michael had told him to talk to me.

Fiftyish and graying, Father John's blue eyes radiated kindness. After introductions, we exchanged information about court procedures and Michael Ross. Father John introduced his companion as a lawyer from his parish who had come to help him understand what was happening in the courtroom. I was astonished by Father John's friendliness and willingness to share his thoughts and information. Usually, journalists have to work a bit harder to gain trust.

In his work as diocesan director of Catholic Charities of Rockville Centre, Long Island, Father John did not share in responsibilities involving prison ministry. Michael had come to him. "Michael was sending out articles to every Catholic publication that existed, and he found us listed," he explained. Catholic publications like Father John's *Passage* magazine were Michael's best outlet because they were pleased to receive thoughtful columns about capital punishment. The Roman Catholic Church is one of the few denominations that had taken a stand against the death penalty.

Michael sent a letter asking them to publish one of his articles. "I read the article, and it was very compelling," Father John explained. "When I looked at the bottom and realized that he was on death row, I said that I have got to be careful publishing this thing. I've got to find out who this guy is and what he did." John Gilmartin took the ferry across Long Island Sound and drove to Somers, Connecticut, to meet Michael, a convicted serial killer. Michael had not been given any formal religious training as a child and had assumed that he was a Lutheran like his Ross relatives. It wasn't until he began working with Father John that his father informed him that he had been baptized in the Roman Catholic Church. If his parents had told him, he had forgotten.

While we waited for Michael to appear, Ann Cole, Michael's former jury consultant, whom he had also mentioned I should meet, stomped into the courtroom. I suspected that Ann was suspicious of me because of her years of courtroom experience with nosy journalists. I was lucky that Father John was there, or she might not have spoken to me at all. Short and blond, Ann Cole's speech was staccato. She was direct and openly skeptical, not just about me, but also about what she perceived as the injustices in Michael's case.

If Michael Ross had not become a serial killer, he and Ann Cole would never have crossed paths. Ann committed herself to helping him as an anti–death penalty activist and joined several abolition groups devoted to the cause. Because of her reputation in the legal community, she was often sought out in hopeless cases, such as Timothy McVeigh's. Tending to Michael was not only part of her fight against capital punishment, which she regarded as barbarous, but it was also personal.

During his 1987 trial, Michael had regarded Ann as his only friend. His lawyers were too busy preparing the case, and Michael's family did not attend the trial except to give testimony during the penalty phase. Dan Ross had explained to his son that he thought he would be insulting the victims' families if he showed up. Michael confided in Ann during noontime breaks and wrote to her at night from his jail cell, pouring out his pessimism and shame. Ann and Michael lost touch for a number of years after the original trial, in part because Ann became concerned that Michael was developing romantic notions about her. She stopped answering his letters and eventually lost contact.

Father John brought them back together in 1994. During the previous winter, just as Michael was beginning the process of negotiating his death, Ann met Father John at an anti–death penalty benefit. They found they had a serial-killer friend in common. From that evening on, the Catholic priest and the Jewish psychologist joined forces to give Michael Ross emotional, spiritual, and legal support. Both would eventually have professional and personal commitments that for long periods of time took them away from supporting Michael, but they were my first guides in my long journey to understanding who he was. Without them, I don't think I would have ever been able—or would have wanted—to get to know Michael Ross.

In the weeks since the last hearing, Michael and Satti had come to terms on the agreement. While we sat there, they were going over the final details to work out before coming into court. Everyone assumed that they would sign the stipulation that day in open court, but Michael's friends were still holding out hope that he would not sign his life away.

When the case was passed over until the afternoon, I followed Ann to lunch at the Radisson Hotel, a block away from the courthouse. I wanted to find out as much as I could about Michael Ross's mental illness, his offer to die, and what had happened at the first trial. Father John was given permission to briefly visit Michael in the jail buried downstairs beneath the courtroom. They were locked together in a small holding cell so that they could speak privately, but Michael was almost too upset to talk. As they hugged, he started to sob uncontrollably. After a brief prayer, Father John tried to persuade him not to sign the stipulation, to give it more thought. Michael was adamant. "I have to do this. I can't turn back now," he said, choking back tears. "I owe it to the families. It's the least I can do."

When John caught up with us at lunch, he reported on Michael's state of mind. "He was crying because he doesn't want to sign it, but he says he has to." I would later understand that if Michael was unsure about something, he wanted to commit to it quickly—in an article, in a public statement, or by signing an agreement. Then he wouldn't have to think about it anymore. There'd be no turning back.

As we ate our tuna sandwiches, Ann made it clear that she thought Michael's first trial was a travesty. It had been her first case as a jury consultant. There was circuslike media exposure, and the judge, G. Sarsfield Ford, she said, seemed prejudiced against Michael. During testimony, she saw Judge Ford open his mail, balance his checkbook, and file his nails, acting as if the whole proceeding was a waste of his time. She remembers him rolling his eyes during psychiatric testimony, as if to mock what the doctor was saying. It took the jury only eighty-seven minutes to decide Michael's guilt on six counts of capital murder. A month later, after the penalty phase, the six death sentences arrived in four hours.

Ann appeared to feel responsible that the jury in Michael's first trial was a defendant's nightmare. In truth, she didn't have much to work with. The trial had been moved from New London because the defense had argued that it would be difficult for Michael to get a fair trial so close to the places where the victims had lived. It was up to the chief administrative judge of the state to pick the site of the new trial, and Bridgeport was selected. A blue-collar town, it was not the kind of place where people gave much credence to mental illness in 1987.

They both explained that getting to know Michael was both easy and impossible. He was lonely, completely approachable, and brutally honest to the point that he gave you the sense that he didn't know how to lie. Yet he was also capable of incredible denial and deflection. He used jokes to cover his true feelings. In many ways he seemed like a needy child, compulsive and immature, desperately wanting affection and attention. Michael found it both satisfying and mystifying that Ann and Father John would take the time to visit him and try to help him. Almost everyone in his immediate family—with the exception of his father, who had been mildly supportive with occasional visits or calls—abandoned Michael in shame and disgust by the time he got on death row. If his family members were disgusted with or ashamed of him, why should strangers care? What did they want from him?

"Why do you care?" I finally asked.

"Michael is not the person I met back in 1987," said Ann. "He has completely changed." She said that during the trial Michael appeared cold and unfeeling, but now he acted like an emotional human being, albeit sometimes immature or narcissistic. In pictures of Michael during the times of his arrest and trial, he is always expressionless. His eyes are empty. The Michael Ross of 1995 was different; he joked, cried, and was at times even introspective, even if he still viewed the world like an eight-year-old focused on his own needs.

Father John concurred, adding that even in the short time he had known Michael, there had been a profound change in him. They both theorized that this was in part due to his medication and in part due to his need to accept responsibility for what he had done. He had survived the trial by shutting down emotionally and pretending that nothing bothered him, but the truth was that sitting through the trial had torn him apart and made him face a side of himself that he had long avoided. He was shamed by the evidence of what he had done. He was humiliated by the psychiatric testimony and mortified listening to the pain of the victims' families. Yet in 1987 he was incapable of accepting the pain that he had inflicted not just on the women, but also on their families. He deflected reality by joking with the people around him, a habit that made him seem callous and unrepentant to jurors and spectators. Michael would later explain to me that his behavior came from a lesson he had learned well as a child: Do not show feelings unless you want them beaten out of you.

The first time they met was in the big visiting room at Osborn Correctional Institution where other prisoners had visits. A female guard escorted Michael, and Father John thought, *This can't be Michael Ross if he's being escorted by a woman.* John remembered Michael being cautious at first, listening but saying almost nothing. "When I saw Michael the first time, he was very nervous, his hands were sweating, and I did an awful lot of the talking. After the first five minutes there, he finally said, 'I know why you are here.' So I asked him why he thought I was there, and he said that I wanted to talk to him about forgiveness. I said that was not on my agenda, and I asked if that was on his." Michael didn't respond, but after that visit, forgiveness became the focal point of their dialogue. It was also the one thing he wanted more than anything.

"That first time I saw him, he didn't want to touch it." John theorized that forgiveness was what scared him most and what he struggled with as a person. "It's the whole question of the families of the victims. Will they ever forgive him?" he explained. "And I think he knows that they won't, but he desperately wants to do something to gain some kind of recognition that he is sorry. . . . That's why he's [offering to accept death]."

While Michael wanted to gain forgiveness and to avoid inflicting more pain, he also feared death. On one of Father John's early visits, he broached the subject. Michael had been moved to the supermax prison next to Osborn, so instead of a large visiting room, they met in a small room, usually reserved for lawyers and their clients. Sitting face-to-face, he hardly knew Michael at all, but he was compelled to ask what he saw as an important spiritual question. "What are you going to say to those eight women when you meet them in heaven?" To Michael it was like a sucker punch. "Don't you ever ask me that again. Don't ever ask anyone that again," he snapped back. Yet Michael wanted and even needed Father John to come back, because he knew that he needed someone to tell him that God would forgive him.

Father John's arrival in Michael Ross's life was Michael's first close encounter with someone he regarded as a truly spiritual person. Although he had been brought up to believe that there was a God, he had not gone to any particular church or Sunday school. After his trial, he even began to question the existence of a supreme being because he felt that if there were a God, he would have prevented him from raping and killing the women. Father John opened his mind to the possibility that God would forgive him. He also began schooling Michael in Catholic theology and having him read books on the topic of forgiveness, particularly those written by Henri Nouwen. It was not long before Michael asked to receive first communion and be confirmed, and he became a devout Roman Catholic.

Ann looked out for Michael. That meant taking his phone calls each week—even when she was thousands of miles away tending to a sick family member—or making copies of his articles in her office or even counseling him to be cautious about strange women who wrote to him. Until her own family obligations became too time-consuming, Ann was his clearinghouse—for monetary support, for distribution of the newsletter *Walking with Michael* that he sent to about a hundred people who followed his case, and for his outside purchases—as well as his supportive friend doing whatever he needed. It was a huge undertaking, but she did it willingly, even lovingly.

Their support was not just part of their fight against the death penalty, but was also for this man. They could see past the horrible things that he had done. Something about Michael Ross made him likable. Their affection gave him humanity. Until then it was much easier to stick to labels.

I was surprised to find that they shared a lot of Michael's views. In Ann and Father John's world, this serial killer had become the victim of a sinister and unpredictable prosecutor who was out to get a death sentence at any cost. I had heard many stories about Bob Satti's courtroom style, but it didn't make sense to me that someone who had devoted his life to prosecuting criminals would be willing to compromise all his principles just to be the first to secure a death sentence.

Michael was brought into court promptly at 2:00 P.M. It was as if we were about to witness an execution. Satti presented the nine-page document to the court, reading it aloud. Michael sat at the opposite table, listening to Satti go through the same legal language that he had heard in the upstairs conference room. Satti said he was ready to sign the stipulation but that he could not speak for Michael, who might want to delay his decision. Michael snapped back that he would sign it right there and then. *He* was not going to be the one who caused any delay. Satti and Michael penned their names to the agreement, and Judge Joseph Purtill, who was the judge hearing the pretrial motions on the stipulation, formally accepted the stipulation and agreed to send it to the state high court to answer "reserved questions" to clarify the law. It happened so quickly and efficiently, it was surreal. Michael had signed what could become his own death warrant—if the high court agreed to answer and the trial court accepted it.

At this point, I still hadn't interviewed Michael in person, and it was not clear whether the Department of Correction would ever allow me to visit him. The next best option was a telephone interview. However, securing a spot on a prisoner's phone list also takes time. Michael explained the process in a letter. First, the prisoner has to request that your name be added to his list. To make this happen, you have to write to the prisoner. Letters in prison are not delivered in a timely manner—those incoming are censored, and sometimes so are the prisoners' responses. On Connecticut death row, prisoners could add or subtract only one name once a month, and the request had to be submitted just before the first of the month or it wouldn't be considered until the next month. Then it would take a few more weeks for the name to be cleared and placed on the list. The DOC has to make sure that prisoners are not calling convicted felons or conducting any illegal business from prison. It took more than six months from our initial correspondence before Michael was able to call me.

At that time, death row inmates made calls in the evening, and all calls had to be made to a residence, not a cell phone. That meant that I'd have to give him my home phone number. He said he'd understand if I didn't want to give it out. I hesitated because I had a teenage daughter and twins who were not yet two years old, so I was extremely anxious about what I felt was the same as inviting a serial killer into my home. I rationalized that it would be okay because I gave him the fax line number to avoid the possibility of my children answering the phone by mistake. Yet I remained terrified that my children might somehow be compromised by being only one beep of the fax machine away from a serial rapist and murderer.

I wanted to speed up the process, so I asked Ann Cole if I could talk to Michael when he called her. She agreed, and we made a date for January 30, 1996. Ann Cole Opinion Research was at the time on the eighth floor of an old prewar building just off Times Square in New York City. It's one of those buildings with long, winding hallways that house hundreds of little businesses in small offices behind stenciled doors. I arrived well ahead of the scheduled 6:00 P.M. call.

As we waited for the phone to ring, my anxiety level rose. It was the same bogeyman fear that his letters had provoked—I worried that he would say something bizarre or threaten me. I had just watched a parole hearing for Charles Manson on Court TV, so I was convinced that Michael Ross was more likely to reveal his sadistic mind over the phone than in a letter. It didn't matter that Ann and I could easily hang up. It didn't matter that we were literally hundreds of miles away. I was petrified.

"Hello. This is the MCI operator. You have a collect call from"— Michael's recorded voice briefly stated his first name, and the male operator continued—"who is an inmate in a Connecticut correctional institution. The state has recorded this call and may have recorded your telephone number. To deny charges hang up now, or to accept charges press 5 now or say yes after the tone." Ann said yes.

"Hello," announced the upbeat voice on speakerphone.

"Hi, Mike. It's Ann."

"This is Martha," I said.

I did *not* want to talk about the murders yet and wasn't sure I ever could. I immediately steered the conversation toward why he thought his trial was unfair.

He reiterated his position that he didn't want his complaints about Satti and Michael Malchik, the state trooper who arrested him, to come out until the judge had accepted his deal to forgo another trial. He believed that Malchik had deliberately distorted evidence to secure a death sentence. "For example, they testified that when I was strangling one of the victims, my hands cramped and I stopped and I had to massage my hands and then the victim started moving and I strangled her again. That never happened," he insisted. He said his proof was that Malchik and Satti had invented a crime scene in Connecticut so that the Leslie Shelley and April Brunais murders would not appear to have been perpetrated in another state—especially one without a death penalty. Michael wanted to get Malchik on the stand; Michael Malchik was the liar, not Michael Ross. He would not rest until Malchik and Satti had been "exposed." Getting "the truth out" was more important to him than living. I could not comprehend why sparing his life wasn't more important than what appeared to be his need for revenge.

When we hung up, my hands and arms were shaking. I was soaked in perspiration, although I was sitting in a drafty building in the dead of winter. As Ann began to talk more about Michael's family history, I started to calm down. Putting him in the context of a family made him more human.

Ann told me that Dan Ross visited or called Michael on his birthday and at Christmas. "His father seemed to care about him during his first trial—buy clothes for him. His mother, Pat, had nothing to do with him. She changed her name—disavows that she's his mother." At the first trial, evidence had been introduced to show that Pat had been psychologically abusive, but she couldn't stand the fact that everyone was trying to blame her for Michael's problems. As Michael would later tell me, she said she "didn't want to be the goat" at the trial. Ann said that during the penalty phase Pat even helped the prosecution refute testimony of the other family members about her.

After such a close encounter with Michael, I was soothed by the cold winter air as I left Ann's office. I wasn't sure whether I felt sorry for Michael or thought he was just a prisoner trying to manipulate me.

Throughout my career, I had encountered many self-proclaimed inno-
cents who wanted to tell me how they had been framed by the system.
I knew from experience that one had to be cautious about whom and
what to believe. Yet two distinct pictures of Michael Ross were emerg-
ing. One was a ruthless killer, and the other was a very sick but sorry
man. It was my job as a journalist to try to reconcile the two. It's a process that has always reminded me of the story about the blind men and
the elephant. Each of the blind men describes a different part of the
elephant—the trunk, the tail, the leg, etc. All of the descriptions are accurate, and yet all are also wrong because no one has the big picture.

5

NEW CANAAN AND SOMERS, CONNECTICUT
WINTER–SPRING 1996

Two weeks after the first phone call with Ann, I was placed on Michael's phone list and received word from the Department of Correction that I would be allowed two visits and an extended phone call from a phone that was not tape-recorded by the state. It had taken more than six months to secure. Beginning on February 15, 1996—oddly enough, my birthday—Michael and I began what would become weekly and, by the end, daily phone conversations. Before the first call, I was even more fearful. Now I was alone. No Ann to protect me.

Michael's openness was eerie. He talked of the murders with detachment, almost as if someone else had committed them. But he sounded on the verge of tears when talking about issues he deemed important, such as his remorse, his concern for the victims' families, the unfairness of his first trial, or proving his mental illness. Yet he never allowed me to forget his crimes. In one of our first telephone conversations, he said, "I don't want you to start to feel sorry for Michael Ross. Think about how you would feel if one of your daughters had been one of my victims." I had thought of that, and I knew my instinct would have been to wring his neck myself. "Whenever you look at me, you have to remember that there are eight bodies behind me. I killed those women, and I did nothing to stop myself for three years. And because of that,

I'm guilty. When you write your story, I want you to have pictures of all of them on your desk."

The only topic off-limits was his religious views. He explained that he had discussed his religious feelings once with a reporter, and the conversation had been distorted. "He said that I said, 'God made me do it,' which is totally not true."

"I'd never say that God made you do it. Hell, no," I said. "I'd say the devil made you do it." Michael laughed. It was my first successful stab at tearing down his wall of defenses. It would take years before he would ever talk about his faith with me—other than reports about his visits with Father John—and he did so first through a journal he started keeping. Some of those discussions would not come until we were literally sitting a few feet from the execution chamber. I eventually realized how desperately he wanted to believe that God forgave him for what he had done, in the same childlike way that he wanted some tangible proof that he was mentally ill.

In our first phone call, I did not press him about the details of the crimes because he still scared me. But there were a few questions I had to ask about his mental state when he killed. Michael had written me that when a killing was over, it was like walking through a door, so in an early telephone conversation I asked him if he could explain what he meant. "After they were dead, it was a very distinct feeling that all of a sudden I realized what had happened. I mean I knew what was going on when I was killing them. I never blacked out or anything like that. It was on a different level. It's hard to explain." He told me that the door analogy wasn't accurate but that it explained how quickly he would become aware of what he'd done. He'd realize "my heart was pounding, really bad, really beating in my chest. And the next thing I remember was my hands were cramped, and they actually hurt. And the next thing I remember is that I felt fear because I was realizing there was another body."

It didn't make sense to me that a man of his intelligence—an IQ of 122—hadn't realized that what he had done was wrong and that he needed professional help after he had killed someone.

"At some point when you were having these urges and then raping and killing women, didn't some part of you say, 'This isn't normal'? Why didn't you get psychiatric help?" I asked.

"I kept telling myself that it would end, that I could control myself. Plus, you don't understand how I was brought up. People didn't go to shrinks. That showed weakness. Psychiatric problems were just an excuse. You just sucked it up and went on—and I was too ashamed to tell anyone what was going on inside my head. It disgusted me. What would anyone else think?"

"Didn't you know what you were doing was wrong?"

"Yes, but I kept telling myself it would never happen again. I was in denial."

This was not the whole truth. I later learned that Michael told Dr. Howard Zonana, the psychiatrist who evaluated him for the defense in 1985 but who was never called by the defense, that he actually forgot about some of the killings. It wasn't that he forgot *about* them because he could remember them if prompted, but that they were completely gone from his conscious memory. As Michael later told me, "I don't know how, but I really forgot about some of them. I know it doesn't make sense, but it's true."

Soon Michael began calling me on an almost daily basis. He regarded reporters as a lifeline. The courts had rejected his mental illness, and the only way he was going to get his story out was to tell it to people who could write about it. I was not the first reporter to whom he had told his story, but I was his current hope. He was powerless without help, and to get help, he had to surrender his mistrust. I understood this vulnerability, but I also didn't want to be manipulated by him.

Most of our telephone conversations began with his current legal issues and what happened at his first trial, but after a while I'd steer him in other directions. "If this were a perfect world, what would happen to you?" I thought he'd say he would want to be released. Instead he said he thought he should be at Whiting, the state hospital for the criminally insane, for the rest of his life. "I can never be set free, but I should be in a mental hospital setting rather than a prison setting."

I had never thought of a place like Whiting as better than a prison, because institutions for the criminally insane are often fraught with problems. "Why do you want to go to Whiting? Is it because you think that you'd get therapy?"

"Well, actually, I don't even need that." I rolled my eyes at the suggestion that he didn't need therapy, that his medication, Depo Lupron, was all he needed. He said it stopped the violent sexual fantasies that had caused his criminal behavior. "The thing is that I don't think I should be locked up in a prison and treated like a criminal when I had no control over what I did. I am dangerous and can never be released, but I should be locked up in an institution." Michael explained that the staff at the mental health units understood he was ill and didn't treat him like a killer. However, he felt the staff at Northern, the maximum security prison where he was incarcerated, was cold and unsympathetic. "In here I'm the biggest piece of shit there is. You know? And I get guards coming by all the time, just making little comments." He said that none of the guards believed he was mentally ill. A few months after he had been put on death row, he had been stabbed by a prisoner with a makeshift knife, but that physical attack didn't bother him as much as the judgmental snipes of the guards. "They treat me like I woke up in the morning and went out and raped and killed because I didn't have anything better to do." In Whiting, he said he would be just another sick man who had committed a crime.

Invariably our telephone conversations would cover his offer to forgo another trial. It didn't make sense to me that he didn't want to fight for his life under almost any circumstances. "I don't think I'd fight even [if I thought I would win] because beating the death penalty is not what I care about," he tried to explain. "I already lost. My issue is that my mental illness drove me to do what I did. That's not the issue I'm going to court for now. The issue I'm going to court for now is whether I'm going to live or die."

"But that is partially the function of—"

"No it's not—" he interrupted, apparently knowing what I was going to say.

"—whether or not your mental illness caused you to do what you did."

"No, because I'm going to be locked in a prison for the rest of my life. I'll be Michael Ross, that scumbag who should have gotten the death sentence but got life through a loophole."

His explanation made me even more confused. "What's the difference? If you got life, they'd be saying, in effect, we recognize you didn't have control because you were mentally ill."

"It ain't worth fighting for that."

"I don't understand the difference between being found mentally ill in the trial and the penalty phase."

"Because I'm not winning anything."

"You're winning your life!"

"But that's not important to me. You know, I really don't care about that." It was shocking that when he spoke about whether he would be executed, he seemed to be devoid of affect. "That's never been an issue. All I was interested in was proving my case. I didn't care about the penalty phase. . . . I wanted to prove to people that I didn't have control over what I did and that maybe I needed to be locked up, but I'm not a criminal. And that's all I cared about. So, now I'm a criminal, and all we're deciding is what punishment I'm going to have. See what I'm saying? To me there's not a hell of a lot of difference." He said he would have been happy with a verdict of "insane, but fry him anyway." Living wasn't the issue. Making people understand was all he cared about.

He thought for a moment and then continued to try to make me understand. "They were laughing in the jury room. I heard them. I knew they were coming out. I could hear them laughing in there when they brought me back up. You know, it was a joke to them," he said, his voice cracking. "And it didn't take them very long to convict me—eighty-seven minutes. And it took them less than a day to give me the death penalty. It was all a big joke." I was beginning to understand why he thought the criminal justice system was stacked against him.

"But this time Dr. Miller's letter will come in as evidence," I said, referring to the evidence that had been withheld from the jury in the first trial—the fact that even the state's own psychiatric witness confirmed Michael's mental illness and agreed that he should not be given a death sentence.

"It's not important. You know what's not important? Justice is not important. Perceived justice is important. If I got sent down to Whiting, it would be in all the newspapers about how I beat the system and how this murderer should have gotten the death penalty," he said, sounding defeated. He was also pouting by this point, feeling sorry for himself that he would be condemned no matter how his case came out—either condemned to death or condemned as a fraud.

"You truly don't care whether you live or die?"

"If they came to me and said, we'll give you a life sentence, no more hearings or anything, then great, that would be fine. I can live with that." He mused that he might be able to get a teaching job in the prison school as a tutor because of his college degree—if he ever got off death row into general population. "I could make something out of my life, but I'm not going to fight for that if I know I'm going to hurt other people," he said, referring to the victims' families.

"Do you know what it's like to wake up in the morning and be sad that God didn't take you during the night? That's how I feel every day." I couldn't imagine.

As I delved deeper into his case, Michael Ross made even less sense to me. He wanted to expose the flaws in the criminal justice system that led to his being put on death row, but he didn't want to do it to get off death row. He didn't care if he was executed. He just wanted people to believe that he was mentally ill, a sexual sadist, and that he couldn't control his impulses to rape and murder.

Sexual sadism was not a psychological disorder with which I was familiar, so I needed a medical expert who had studied Michael to explain the mental illness. At least five psychiatrists had evaluated Michael before his first trial, one for the prosecution and four for the defense. All had agreed that he was a sexual sadist.

I contacted Dr. Fred Berlin, who was the chief defense witness for Michael Ross during the penalty phase of the trial. He heads the National Institute for the Study, Prevention and Treatment of Sexual Trauma at Johns Hopkins University in Baltimore and is a widely renowned expert on paraphiliac disorders that include sexual sadism. He is also the doctor who prescribed Michael's medication after he was on death row. Dr. Berlin became my guide to understanding Michael's mental illness and his medication.

He was adamant from the very beginning that the diagnosis of sexual sadism was correct. He explained that a sexual sadist is someone whose sex drive is attached to the wrong type of behavior—in this case inflicting pain and injury on someone else. Having a paraphiliac disorder means that there is something different about a person's sexual makeup. It can be either the kinds of partners that one is attracted to sexually—children, corpses, animals—or it can be the sexual behaviors one craves, for example, exhibitionism. In Michael's case, it was "recurrent erotic urges and fantasies that drive [the sadism]," Dr. Berlin explained. "[The urges] are driven by a powerful biological drive." His ultimate climax resulted from degrading and killing a woman.

I asked Dr. Berlin how a person can become a sexual sadist. "The question is really how do any of us develop the sexual desires that we have." Dr. Berlin said. "How is it that some people are recurrently attracted to children, a diagnosis of pedophilia? Why is it that some men are aroused by dressing up in female clothing?" He said there are three reasons that are sometimes intertwined. The first is that none of these desires are voluntary. "No one as a little kid sits down and weighs their options of what kind of sexual desires they are going to experience as they grow older. People discover the nature of their own sexual makeup, and in the case of Michael Ross, he discovered that he was afflicted with intense recurrent sexual fantasies and urges about causing others to suffer and even causing their death." There's also nature versus nurture. In some cases, children have been warped in their sexual development because of traumatic sexual experiences during childhood. A significant number of pedophiles were sexually abused as children. But recent research data has also shown in some cases that abnormal sexual cravings may have resulted because something went wrong at a biological level. "No one is interested in having sex because we read a book and decide it makes sense. Those feelings well up inside because of our biology, because of chromosomes and hormones and areas of the brain that are clearly relevant to sexuality." Dr. Berlin helped me understand the possible explanations for Michael's condition, but he could offer no easy answers.

Researchers have discovered that there are differences in the brains of a significant number of sexual sadists. In Michael's case, lesions were discovered on his brain that might help explain his loss of control—although Dr. James Merikangas, the neurologist and psychiatrist who examined him in the 1990s, could not explain how or why those lesions could actually produce murderous behavior. Someone may have lesions but not be violent. He explained that doctors don't understand how the lesions result in loss of control, but they do know that there is a connection between the two. The brain scans of sexual sadists often appear different from those of normal patients' scans.

Dr. Berlin's and Dr. Merikangas's explanations only made me more curious. What was Michael's childhood like? Had anyone else in his family been diagnosed with similar mental illnesses? How do lesions affect self-control? Some of my questions had easy answers that would just take some additional reporting, but others only led to more questions.

Over the course of the next few months, I found that Michael was easy to talk to, and slowly I began to realize that the serial killer was never going to jump out and grab me. The man who emerged was soft-spoken, self-effacing, and even funny. He was sometimes articulate and sometimes slipped back into a farm-boy dialect with faulty grammar. It came out most when he was angry or when he was using humor to deflect discomfort. He had a charm that was either disarming or manipulative and cunning. I wasn't sure. Michael and his psychiatrists acknowledged that his highly developed defense of denial sometimes hid the truth from him. Yet he seemed almost incapable of lying intentionally. When asked a question that he found difficult to answer, he would deflect it with an inappropriate nervous laugh or joke. How had he managed to keep his sense of humor after so many years on death row? "I don't know. I must be crazy."

This openness was also apparent in the months just after his arrest.

In nine hours of taped sessions with Dr. Zonana, Michael appeared to answer every question as truthfully as possible, even when his answers might not be in his best interest legally.

The first time I remember him speaking about the monster as a separate person was in a telephone conversation in which he was talking about how his medications had helped him. I was startled at first. I knew he blamed his mental illness for the killings, but I had not heard him refer to it so specifically as a separate person over which he had no control. "He was cunning. He would be satisfied and go away for a while after I stalked someone or killed someone, and then I would realize what he had done and feel like a total piece of shit. But he was always there waiting to take control. My medication changed all that. He was caged. He didn't go away completely, but he was under control."

He saw his decision to accept death as his way of conquering the monster. He wrote, "The one great consolation is that I will get the last laugh. I may die, but I find it quite satisfying to know that the bastard of my mind will die with me. . . . And he hates that because he knows that finally, only in death, will we be separated from one another. I will go to the light and understanding, and he will go to darkness and truly be alone—forever."

It was disturbing that on some level he didn't consider himself personally responsible for what "the monster" did. "I couldn't control him. He controlled me, and I never knew when he would reappear and take control." Michael could live with himself by blaming his murderous behavior on an alter ego.

Dr. Merikangas and Dr. John Cegalis, who examined Michael six times and testified as one of his psychiatric witnesses at the 1987 trial, theorized that he suffered from some type of dissociative disorder. In a dissociative disorder, a person goes into a fuguelike state and adopts a different personality. Sometimes one is aware of what is going on but feels like an observer of the action; at other times, one has no memory of what occurred. Michael Ross was totally aware of what the monster had done and, I would later find, had experienced the pleasure that the monster had experienced when he was doing the killing. But because he saw himself as a good person—or desperately wanted to believe that he was—he could not accept that he was a lustful rapist and murderer, so he named the bad part of himself the monster.

In addition to talking with Michael, Dr. Cegalis gave him a battery of psychological tests to aid in making a diagnosis. One such test, the Thematic Apperception Test (TAT), consists of a number of ambiguously drawn pictures about which the test subject is asked to convey his feelings: What is the person in the picture thinking and feeling? What is happening? What will happen in the future? From Michael's responses, Dr. Cegalis concluded that he had difficulty relating to other human beings and that he had a lot of anger pent up inside. The Rorschach or inkblot test revealed he had "evident psychopathology," meaning he was mentally ill. Cegalis said that Michael had difficulties "modulating or controlling strong emotions like aggression, like violence, like fear, like sexuality." He said at times Michael could even have difficulty in knowing what was real and what was not.

Based on all of his testing, Dr. Cegalis found that Michael was "immature, egocentric, manipulative, driven to a kind of sexual satisfaction that fuses aggression and sexuality together in a highly abnormal way." He said that Michael was also paranoid and unable to control his emotional impulses and that he acted out his anger in violent ways. His overall diagnosis concurred with that of Dr. Berlin's; Michael suffered from sexual sadism.

In my early conversations with Michael, I got a sense of how complex a person he really was. He was compulsive and had frequent mood swings. One call would be upbeat and positive, and by the next week, his defeatist attitude would have taken over. "Why bother?" he would ask rhetorically. "There is no way I'll get a fair trial. Nobody wants to know the truth."

"Be careful about making such big pronouncements," I cautioned. "I'm not a nobody, and I did and do want to know the truth. You have to stop feeling sorry for yourself—at least if you want me to listen."

Sometimes he would call and the first thing out of his mouth would be "Got a pencil?" The next words out of his mouth would be instructions about whom I should call or what I should look up. He would give me the names and numbers or the general instructions about where I could get the information. He'd also want to know if I had read the latest installment of documents he had sent. Often they were things that had come in the mail the day before, and I would have to tell him that I couldn't drop everything to read what he sent me. I had a job and a family.

In this initial stage of our dialogue, it became increasingly obvious that Michael wanted to forgo another trial not only because it would be too painful for the families, but also because it would be too painful for him to listen to a litany of what he had done. I had a lingering suspicion that his offer to die was a suicidal act, the result of depression from living on death row, although Michael denied that he was suicidal. For a time, I stopped pushing him on the suicide issue. In retrospect I know that he could not have been honest with me at that point, because he did not trust me yet.

6

BROOKLYN, CONNECTICUT
1958–1966

Michael Ross's hometown of Brooklyn, Connecticut, is nothing like the borough of New York. A rural community of about six thousand, located in eastern Connecticut, Brooklyn seemed poor and provincial— much the opposite of Fairfield County, where I lived, the New York suburb in the western part of the state. When I visited in 1996 and 1997 to learn more about Michael's past, many of the farms that dotted the countryside seemed to be eroding with the landscape, victims of a changing economy. The Ross family farm was no exception. Once a thriving business, it was then dormant except for a few apartments and a trailer. Some of the coops had been torn down, and the area had the look of a makeshift junkyard. In the state it was in, I had a hard time understanding why Michael wanted to return to it after Cornell.

In 1995, Brooklyn was essentially a crossroads where three state highways—Routes 6, 169, and 208—converge. The biggest landmark in town is the county fairground that comes alive once a year and is situated on a side road off Route 208. There's a church, a nursing home, a town hall, firehouse, and even a jail scattered along the three routes, but no town center.

Brooklyn's biggest claim to fame, or infamy, was that a serial killer grew up there. Most people did not want to talk about Michael. None of Michael's family and very few of the people who had known him growing up would speak with me. At that time, his arrest and trial had been too painful, and with the prospect of another trial, most refused interviews because they felt I was the first of many reporters who would be knocking on their doors. Over the course of a decade, I asked Michael about his childhood, interviewed psychiatrists who had talked with family and friends, and pored over trial transcripts, psychological evaluations, and police reports to try to reconstruct his early years.

When they started going out in the fall of 1958, Pat Laine was seventeen and a senior at Killingly High School in Danielson, Connecticut; Dan Ross was a slightly older man who had already been through two years of college and a stint in the U.S. Marine Corps, serving as a guard at the brig in Pensacola, Florida. He went back to his hometown of Brooklyn unattached and began chicken farming. According to Frances Wolak, a neighbor and one of several women who served as mother figures for Michael during his teenage years, Pat made it clear to everyone that Dan Ross was going to be hers.

Within months, their romance resulted in a pregnancy. Dan Ross did the honorable thing, and the two were wed in February 1959; Michael Bruce Ross arrived on July 26 the same year, a healthy eight pounds. With his birth, Pat settled into farm life and the duties of motherhood. She worked in the egg business, picking up eggs by hand at the coops that the Ross family kept on rented property on Route 205 in Brooklyn. Little Michael accompanied her to work, his baby buggy covered with cheesecloth to keep off the flies. Dan worked for Pierce Egg Farm, the business that he and his father would soon buy with two other partners.

But Pat's infatuation faded quickly. She soon found that she actually didn't want to be a farmer's wife, tied down with a baby. She hadn't envisioned her entire future in Brooklyn, Connecticut. Faced with the unromantic realities of being a wife and mother, Pat found a former classmate, her boyfriend from her teenage years, more appealing. She began to see him secretly.

When Michael was two, a sister—Donna—arrived, and the Ross family moved from a rental into an old farmhouse on Tatnic Road, just down from where Dan's parents and younger brother Ned lived. It was small and primitive, with no indoor bathroom, but there was plenty of room on the lot. By the fall of 1964, after nearly six years of marriage, Pat Ross, twenty-three, had given birth to another son, Kenny, and another daughter, Tina. With each child, her misery and her mental health worsened, probably the result of untreated postpartum depression, according to medical and court records. In the months after her youngest child's birth, she began talking about suicide. She severely punished her children, according to medical reports. It was common for her to threaten to leave the children, and she would occasionally storm out of the house, only to return a few hours later, acting as if nothing had happened.

As the oldest, Michael was seen by his siblings as his mother's favorite. Yet according to Dr. Walter Borden, a forensic psychiatrist who assessed him for more than a year after his arrest and testified at his first trial, Michael was the source of all of Pat's misery. Because of him, she had to marry, and because of him, she wanted to run away. She called him a bastard and told him she hated him. "Michael became the scapegoat, the person upon whom anger, disappointment, rejection, and failure in the adult relationship between mother and father were placed," said Dr. John Cegalis in court testimony. "He lived in the netherworld of being his mother's favorite, most devoted child and also her favorite target. It was a very close, very complicated and hate-filled relationship."

Shirley Grenier, who had worked packing eggs at the family farm when Michael was six or seven, testified that Pat "would hit him, calling him a little bastard, I hate you, I never wanted you in the first place." Sometimes Michael's hyperactivity set her off, but sometimes she slapped him for no reason. Grenier said that Pat treated Michael worse than the other children, but that Michael never showed any emotion when his mother made the verbal attacks. Even Michael's father later observed that he took the brunt of his mother's anger. As an adult, however, Michael either couldn't or wouldn't accept that he was treated any worse than his other siblings. "Only one of us became a serial killer. I never felt more persecuted than the rest of them."

Unable to deal with her life, Pat ran away to be with her longtime boyfriend, only to be dragged back to Brooklyn by her father. Trapped again, Pat treated her children with such hostility that Dan had to take her away from them. Scared and helpless, on October 6, 1964, he admitted her to the state psychiatric hospital at Norwich. In hospital records, Pat was described as "cooperative and slightly seductive, with a history of being emotionally upset, acting out towards her children." Doctors at the hospital gave her a diagnosis of "personality trait disturbance," virtually meaningless without specifying what type of personality trait she exhibited. Nevertheless, they pronounced her emotionally unstable. "Presently, we are dealing with a patient who feels tremendous hostility against her husband, stating that he is lazy and not worth a penny. Patient is not depressed, but it is felt that the patient . . . has been manipulative with many people around her including her husband, by threatening to walk out and never come back, and threatening with suicide," wrote Dr. Michael Eligenstein, the attending physician who wrote Pat's evaluation. After a month at the hospital, Pat was released to Dan's custody with the recommendation that she and Dan receive marriage counseling, but there was no recommendation of any therapy or counseling to help her better deal with her four small children.

"You were dealing with a woman with at minimum a mental illness occurring during a postpartum period," said Dr. Borden of the treatment she received at Norwich. "That should have been followed up. . . . They were treating a broken arm with a Band-Aid when they talk about group therapy. There should have been a much more assertive therapeutic approach."

For the next three years, the family limped along, coping with Pat's mood swings and volatile temper. Then in October 1967, Pat's old boyfriend made a surprise visit to Brooklyn and phoned. It was the first time they had spoken in three years, and the call immediately rekindled her dream of leaving Dan and the children. Pat ran off to North Carolina, where her former boyfriend was now living, only to be brought back again to Brooklyn by Dan. On November 5, 1967, she was readmitted to Norwich hospital as a psychiatric patient. In less than thirty days, she was discharged with nothing more than a recommendation for group therapy for married couples.

Although he was eight at the time of his mother's second hospitalization, Michael didn't remember either of her absences. "To be honest, I don't think I would have missed her really." It's not as if she were the type of parent who tucked him into bed and kissed him good night.

Pat Ross's precarious temperament made her unpredictable. Even if she was in a good mood, she could fly into a rage without warning. There were times when she was charming and happy, when she would seem to enjoy doing simple things with her children, like ice skating or chopping wood. But there were also times when, according to elder daughter Donna's testimony during the first trial, "Something would inflame her and make her angry and you never knew where you stood." She said Pat was never happy because she felt "she missed out on her young adult life in her early 20's." She said Pat blamed Michael and Dan for her misery.

Michael's sister Tina, the youngest of the Ross children, also testified at the trial. She described her mother's moods. "We used to say that she had a short fuse. She could flare up without any notice . . . I tried to behave myself as best I could . . . You had a 50/50 chance. [If you showed emotion] she would either get madder at you or she would back off you. Usually she would get madder." And when she got mad, she got verbally abusive. "She swore . . . a lot. She tried to humiliate us a lot." Tina said her mother was cruel and cold and verbally abusive to people and animals. Tina told of coming home from school one day and finding out that her mother had thrown the cat out a second-story window. On other occasions, she said, she vacuumed the cat because it shed too much. "She also made us declaw the cat. She said if we didn't declaw the cat, she would put a rock around its head and throw it in the lake."

During the penalty phase of the trial, both sisters testified about their mother and their home life. They also talked about Michael. Tina said that she and her two other siblings were very close friends, but they were not close to Michael, so they shunned him from their play. Donna said that Michael didn't have many friends and that when he had tried to date, there had been a big blowup between him and Pat. She didn't want him to date.

I tried to interview Dan Ross and Michael's two sisters, but they made it clear through Michael that they did not want to be interviewed for any article or book. In fact, Michael gave me a copy of a scathing letter from Donna in response to his request; she accused him of wanting to be in the spotlight and having no concern for what his notoriety had done and would continue to do to his family. Later I did speak with Dan several times at the prison, during which I got most of Michael's stories confirmed and some insights about the family dynamic—especially concerning Pat—but I was never able to formally interview Dan for the book. Most of what I know about the family comes from Michael, neighbors, a videotape made during Dr. Zonana's assessment of Michael, court testimony, medical reports, and Dr. Borden, who had done a thorough investigation of Michael's past.

Dr. Borden devoted a tremendous amount of time to the case because he believed that it was one of the most important of his long career; he said he never spent as much time and effort on any other. At one point he called me to tell me that "Michael Ross should be studied" to help the world better understand sexual sadism and what had caused him to kill. He said that Michael's mental illness was "off the charts"—that his sexual sadism was so extreme that it went beyond the criteria that the DSM-III and DSM-IV used to identify and classify mental disorders at the time of Michael's arrest and first trial. Dr. Borden was convinced that because Michael was articulate and intelligent, he could help professionals understand his complex mental disorder. Michael also was willing because he wanted answers.

As they got older, the Ross kids learned that the best way to handle their mother was to try to avoid doing anything that might set her off. Each morning they had to wonder, *What's mom's mood like today?* Rather than risk her wrath, they developed what Michael called "mom drills." They took turns going downstairs first and testing her reaction. The other three would listen from upstairs as they finished dressing. If things were quiet, they would follow. If she began screaming in what seemed to a child like a violent rage, they would immediately begin the drill, which they executed with precision. Each had a job—squeezing orange juice, getting wood, setting the table—designed to distract and

pacify their mother. There was almost no conversation. They just bus-
ied themselves until it was time to eat and run to the bus.

"Some days she'd be in a hell of a mood," said Michael. "I remember one time that Tina went downstairs first. She was unloading the
dishwasher so that we could set the table. Since there were six of us, she
picked up the orange juice glasses, three in each hand. As she carried
them to the table, the glasses made a clinking sound. 'What the hell are
you doing?' Mom started yelling. 'Are you trying to break those damn
glasses?' Then we all knew to be on guard. You did what you had to do."

The Ross children knew that for their own peace of mind, there
were certain rules to follow: Never show weakness. Never let her know
what is important to you because she will take it away. What hurt you
most would be used later to taunt and tease you. "She would go for
the emotional jugular," Michael explained. "One time she dumped
some red dye on my sister's favorite blouse. My mother claimed she was
going to dye some curtains. She said she didn't know," he said in a tone
that meant he didn't believe a word of it. "She could be very sweet,"
he said. "It was like a spider luring a fly into her web. You had to be
careful."

Pat might have been the judge, but Dan Ross was the purveyor of
punishment. If Michael got into trouble with his mother, he knew that
Pat would instruct Dan to carry out her sentence when he returned
home at dinnertime. Michael would be sent to the woodshed to pick
a switch for the spanking, knowing that the switch had to be strong
enough not to break. "It was of utmost importance to take your punishment like a man. The main thing was not to make any noise. If
you screamed or showed any weakness like crying, you were beaten
more," Michael reported without emotion. Dr. Borden said Dan was
the punisher. "But it was the mother who called the shots. . . . She ran
the children, she ran the relationship—she ran the house." Michael agreed.
"I never blamed my father. I thought he was as henpecked as we were."

As Dr. Cegalis explained, Michael "had poor nurturance from his mother and his father. He had a minimal relationship with his siblings; he was treated in a brutal, violent way by both of his parents . . . verbally, psychologically as well as physically." He added that Michael was humiliated, degraded, and continually criticized by his parents. Because of his treatment by his parents, Dr. Cegalis testified, Michael was unable to form attachments to other people. "It is important in human relationships to establish what is called 'object consistency.' That is seeing another human being as a human being, relating to another human being with empathy," he explained. He said Michael could not understand "that other people have feelings." This was certainly true of how he regarded his victims. Dr. Cegalis said this lack of empathy comes "from brutality and violence perpetrated on him and . . . from abuse in general from the family."

Michael was not close to his father as a child and teenager. According to those who worked at Eggs, Inc., Dan was always busy, distant, and cold. Michael lamented that he could only talk about farming to his father but could not confide in him. He said he wanted to be more like his father, except he told Dr. Zonana that Dan "don't show feeling at all. I can't remember the last time he said, 'I love you.' I know he does, but he can't show it." He told Dr. Borden that his father was unreadable. "He was a rock . . . you might as well talk to a rock. . . . There was no way to read him."

However, Michael later told me, "My father's changed a lot since I've been in here. He used to seem so distant and unable to show emotion, but I think that was because he was married to my mother. Since he married Carol [Dan's second wife, whom he married a few years after he and Pat divorced], he's really changed. He's happier and more at ease with me. Carol has been good for him."

Another message of Pat Ross's behavior was that her children should never stand up for themselves. At age six, Michael was the constant target of a neighborhood bully named Johnny. One day Johnny chased Michael all the way home, and in an uncharacteristically bold act, Michael picked up a stick, turned around, and started to hit Johnny. Startled at Michael's newfound courage, Johnny turned and ran.

Hearing the commotion, Pat came to the window and observed the entire episode. "Bring me that stick," she called to her son. Obediently— and proud that he had finally had the courage to defend himself— Michael picked up the stick and took it to his mother. It was a rare occasion when Pat carried out the beating herself. When he got inside, Pat grabbed the stick from Michael and proceeded "to beat the hell out of me," Michael remembered. "She was so mad, and she beat me so badly that I needed a butterfly bandage for the cut on my forehead." Confused and hurt, Michael knew that from then on he was powerless against Johnny or any other bully.

"It's emotionally castrating, to do that to a little boy; the message is very clear: You can't stand up for yourself," charged Dr. Borden. "It had to do with her total control of him, that he couldn't stand up to anybody, that he could not assert himself. And any kind of self-assertion was attacked; especially having to do with being a boy, being male."

The result, said Dr. Cegalis, was that he was chronically malad-justed. He described Michael as "a person who is paranoid, a person who is capable of manipulativeness, distance, lack of attachment in his relationships with other people; a person who is incredibly angry; a person who is capable of acting out that anger in a rather direct way on other people."

From his earliest years, Michael became confused about the mean-ing of love. His parents' relationship was hate filled, and Dr. Cegalis suggested in his psychiatric evaluation that sometimes there was even violence between his parents—although Michael had no memory of this. Almost everyone who knew her reported that Pat was often cruel and verbally abusive but that it was Michael's father who punished him with beatings in the woodshed. These were the people who were supposed to love him, nurture him, and love each other, and yet there was little love in the Ross household. Dr. Cegalis, who had died by the time I met Michael, testified that Michael's lack of parental nurturing "resulted in a kind of fragile ego, a damaged ego, one in which Mr. Ross' sense of self-esteem is extremely weak, extremely inadequate with evidence of problems of sexual potency, sexual identity, self-worth, self-competence."

7

BROOKLYN, CONNECTICUT
1967–1977

Eight-year-old Michael Ross trudged a hundred yards up Tatnic Road, from the modest white house where he lived, through the snow, up the hill toward the chicken coop on his grandfather's property. It is a quiet side street where a young boy could easily be distracted. But Michael didn't dawdle on that snowy afternoon. It wasn't the cold that kept the tall, skinny boy focused: He had an important assignment. He was on his way to get instructions from Grandfather Ross about taking over some of the former chores of his sixteen-year-old uncle Ned.

A few weeks earlier, Ned had shot himself in the head with his father's .22-caliber rifle. His suicide note, written in an inward spiral, explained exactly why he killed himself: He was a homosexual, not an accepted sexual orientation in Brooklyn, Connecticut, in 1967. The troubled teenager saw only one possible escape. When Dr. Borden mentioned that Ned had written a suicide note in the form of an inward spiral, Michael immediately responded, "That's me. He exploded inside and I exploded outside."

The family's official story to the Ross grandchildren was that Ned had died by accident when a bullet ricocheted off a stone wall during target practice. *Who'd be so stupid as to have target practice on a stone wall?* Michael wondered at the time, but he instinctively trusted the explanation of his parents. Michael was not allowed to attend Ned's funeral. No one was to speak of Ned, because it would be too hard on Karl and Louise Ross, Michael's grandparents—perhaps because Karl's own father had committed suicide in a similar manner. Ned was gone. Talking about him wouldn't bring him back.

The loss had been particularly great for Michael. He and Ned had been close. Ned and Michael wrestled with each other on the lawn, Ned often ending the play with a "Chinese shampoo," otherwise known as a Dutch rub. Michael enjoyed the mixture of pain and pleasure. In private, their play might have been much different. Dr. Borden said that he suspected that Ned, the occasional family babysitter, was sexually abusing his nephew from the time Michael was four because of symptoms he exhibited. Michael's father rejected the theory, and Michael said he had no memory of any such behavior.

At first a hired farmworker named Ray took over Ned's responsibilities, but when a snowstorm prevented Ray from reaching the farm, Michael had to assume Ned's chores—tending the chicks. The prospect of farmwork was not troubling to Michael. In fact, tending the chicks elevated him to a new level of adult responsibility. He would be paid fifty cents an hour for his labor. It was a chance for the eight-year-old to gain his father's love and respect. "That was the most important thing to me," Michael explained.

Michael idealized his father and wanted nothing more than his love and attention. He knew that there was nothing his father loved more than farming. If he became a good farmworker, Michael thought, he just might be able to please his father and win his approval. He would work twice as hard as anyone else. Having spent time with Ned while he was working, Michael already knew much of the routine, but his grandfather went over all the details of tending the coop, which housed about five thousand chicks. At one day old, each flock was delivered from the hatchery and raised as floor birds for five months, and then they were moved over to be layers at Eggs, Inc., the family's newly acquired seventy-nine-acre chicken farm situated about a mile down the road from their home.

Day-old chickens do not have feathers and must be constantly monitored and kept warm with gas stoves inside coops until their feathers grow in several weeks later. Michael learned to check the temperature by the behavior of the birds. If they were huddled close together under the stove, it was too cold; if they were spread out away from the stove, it was too hot. The first few days are the most critical because the young chicks don't know how to find the heat. During that time, they must be checked again after dark to make sure they aren't bunched together in the corners away from the stoves.

Three times a day, morning, noon, and late afternoon, the birds needed to be checked, watered, or fed. On school days, his grandfather would make the noon rounds. Each morning Michael was to be at the coop by dawn to turn on the birds' drinking water. He would walk through the building, checking to make sure everything was in order and pick up any birds that had died during the night, since it was not unusual to lose 200 to 250 birds from each flock of 5,000. After school, he would feed the birds, pick up any more dead, and dump the carcasses into a pit in the field. Before dark, he would make one final check and turn off the water for the evening to prevent any chance of flooding.

"I did it on my own even though I hated getting up that early in the morning," Michael admitted. "I guess I kind of got used to it. It's a lifestyle, farming. There's a lot of satisfaction from raising a good flock of birds. I got a batch of baby chicks, and I got to raise them for five months before they went into the henhouse. And I knew that the birds that went into that henhouse were better birds than we could buy anywhere else. That's farming."

While most of his job was caring for the birds, the flock also had to be culled. Weak or sick birds don't grow into productive hens and are an expense that needs to be eliminated as soon as possible. Michael understood that killing the birds was a necessity, even if it was unpleasant.

"Okay, now Michael, pay attention," said his grandfather. "You've got to break its neck. Hold their feet in your left hand and hold their neck with your right hand. The trick is to break the neck without pulling off the head," he instructed. "That can get pretty bloody," Michael told me. "You pull the neck until you feel the bone break, then immediately stop pulling."

Michael, immature and uncoordinated, tried to repeat the procedure that his grandfather had demonstrated but pulled the neck off the bird, wincing as blood spewed all over. He worried that if he didn't do his job properly, the responsibility might be taken away. But as time went on, he got better. Soon he bragged that he could kill chicks in his sleep.

The first flock he tended was already a few months old when he took charge. Later, when the next batch of day-old chicks was delivered, Michael needed to learn other methods of culling. For the first four or five weeks, the chicks are only four to five inches long, so small that it is virtually impossible to break their necks. For these birds, his grandfather explained, there are two methods of killing—"The way I like to do it is to just squeeze the lungs until the bird suffocates." But Michael didn't like this method because it took too long. It was difficult for his small hands to exert enough pressure for any length of time, especially with the chick squirming, desperately fighting for its life. Sometimes it would take him two or three tries to kill a chick.

The second method is quicker, but, Michael felt, "more overtly brutal. You take the chick in your hand and smack its head against a post. If you do it right, the chick will die on the first whack and not make a bloody mess." Learning exactly how hard to hit the bird against the post takes experience. He didn't particularly like this method either and was always glad when the birds were big enough so that he could break their necks because "it seemed more humane."

At times Michael would get in trouble for not killing the birds, especially the older ones. Sometimes Marek's disease struck the birds at twelve to sixteen weeks, paralyzing one side of the bird so that it couldn't get to food or water. Having raised them from the first day of their lives, Michael would feel sorry for the afflicted birds and individually feed and water them by hand. Some survived and gained partial use of their limbs, but they were irrevocably damaged and never would grow into productive hens. Whenever his grandfather found a bird that Michael had spared, he would scold him. "Michael, these birds are suffering and have to be put out of their misery. Besides, they will eat our feed, but they'll never lay an egg. They've got to go. Period." It was pure farm economics.

Ever obedient, Michael did what he was told—even unpleasant things. That also included learning how to turn off his feelings, how to separate himself from what he was doing. "Very early, killing became an accepted pattern," Dr. Borden testified at Michael's 1987 trial, "a kind of brutalized killing of animals, chickens . . . became his thing."

"I learned how to do unpleasant things that I didn't want to do, but had to be done," Michael remembered. "I guess that's when I learned how to turn off my feelings."

Even in high school, only Michael was given the job of culling the chicks; Michael's mother wouldn't let the others kill the birds because they found it too upsetting. As he got older, Michael was also the butcher of young roosters in the flock. Although the day-old chicks are sexed at the hatchery, some male birds were always mixed in—as many as 2 percent when the sexing got sloppy. At about ten to twelve weeks, when the roosters' combs would start to grow, they were singled out and killed. Michael would round them up on a weekend and bring them home to butcher for the meat. "Dad was usually at work, so I had to kill them. I'd skin them, cut off the legs and breast, and cut out the heart and liver. . . . I got pretty good at it. I could kill and butcher a rooster so fast that I could take out his heart which would still be beating in the palm of my hand," he bragged.

"[Michael] was the designated killer of the family. No one else wanted the job. His sisters were spared; the brother avoided it," Dr. Borden asserted. "That became so much part of his life that he didn't make anything of it. He was beyond repulsion."

I was haunted by the idea of an eight-year-old boy killing the chickens he had been caring for. Dr. Borden suggested that learning to kill without emotion was a skill that would later allow the young adult Michael to separate himself from the murders he was committing. It was the monster who raped and murdered, not Michael the man. Almost all of the psychiatrists I talked to brought up the chicken culling as significant, but none of them could definitively say that this early experience caused him to kill the women. Dr. Berlin noted the similarities in the way the women and the chicks were killed and ruminated, "So the question is did [killing the chickens] eroticize him? He doesn't say that himself. Did it simply desensitize him to the idea of taking life by doing that? Again, we are left with more questions than answers."

Like the psychiatrists who evaluated him, Michael also didn't know the answer. "There could be a connection. I honestly don't know." Yet he was tempted to accept it or any other reasonable hypothesis as proof of his mental illness and theorized, "I think it came in handy later on when I killed. I turned off everything inside of me and allowed it to happen." He wanted to understand how he became a killer. As he reminded me several times, often sobbing, "I didn't wake up one day and decide to be a serial killer. I would have done anything for it to turn out differently."

Michael worked on the farm while his elementary school class-mates were playing Little League and building tree houses. Although it was easy for him to focus on his farmwork, he was hyper-active, impulsive, and disruptive at home and even worse at school. He wet his bed until he was twelve, walked in his sleep, and suffered from nightmares and night terrors.

This behavior, while distressing, may not connect directly with the violence of Michael's later life. "There's a depressive rage in children which is expressed in hyperactivity," explained Dr. Borden. "The child feels mad and bad. The feelings, the impulses get expressed in a more disorganized way, in emotional behavior, in distractibility, in restless-ness. It's discharged in action. That's what little kids are: they are action. They don't think." Many other biological differences have been identi-fied as contributing to hyperactivity since Dr. Borden explained his diagnosis to me, and some psychological experts would now disagree with Dr. Borden's characterization of hyperactivity as being attributed to a depressive rage.

There were aspects of his play that were possibly more relevant. By the time he was ten years old, Michael had developed an active fantasy life. In it, he was a Superman-like character, disguised as Clark Kent, who would rescue damsels in distress and then take them to his harem (a barn on the farm). There in his private lair, all the women would sur-render to him and worship him. Michael said "there was nothing overtly sexual" in the fantasies he had as a young boy. "I don't know when it changed—probably around puberty when I started to masturbate."

Dr. Cegalis said that from this early age, Michael had an aberrant fusion of aggression and sexuality. The result was violence. He said this stemmed from his need for approval and love from his mother. Rejection by his mother or a girlfriend "precipitated enough rage, enough anger for Mr. Ross to act out those impulses."

At twelve, he began undressing and fondling young neighborhood girls. Teresa Cross (not her real name), who was six years younger than Michael, lived near his grandparents' house. "I would lure her into the woods between my house and my grandparents'." Once out of sight, he would get her to take off her clothes and "I would undress and rub my penis against her, but I never attempted to penetrate her or anything." Teresa eventually told her mother, who confronted Pat Ross with the crime. Mortified and angry, Pat and Dan marched Michael over to the Cross house and offered him up for a beating, but Teresa's parents didn't want to take part in the punishment. Instead, Michael was sent to the woodpile to find a stick so that Dan could carry out the sentence. "I got the tar whipped out of me." Perhaps more painful to Michael than the beating was that he was also forbidden to go near the Cross house or his grandfather's coops, because his parents felt he could not be trusted anywhere near the little girl. That was the end of his job minding the flock at his grandfather's farm; he began working on the main farm, where his father could keep an eye on him. "That job meant a lot to me, then, because I was responsible for taking care of the chickens. I was downgraded to flunky, and I had to rework my way up. I think it was taking away the responsibility that hurt the most."

Resentful toward Teresa and her family, he "snuck over to their house after dark and cut their clotheslines. . . . I know it don't make any sense. They didn't do anything, but in my mind, they deserved to be punished too." At twelve years old, he didn't think what he had done was wrong, but his embarrassment about both his molestation of

Teresa and his revenge on her parents was apparent when he recounted the story.

Pat took Michael to the family doctor, who suggested that his hyperactivity was a large part of the problem. Michael had often been in trouble for "impulsively blurting out inappropriate (often angry or lewd) statements and jokes." In elementary school, he had a reputation for being disruptive and unruly. He recalled that his fourth-grade teacher, Mr. Post, met him at the bus on the first day of school and marched him down to the classroom, where he was shown his assigned seat and told what was expected of him in terms of classroom decorum. "I was a big troublemaker in school until I started taking Ritalin. I had a short attention span and was a smart aleck, not a bad dude. . . . I got into very few fights because I'd get in trouble at home. As punishment, I split a lot of wood, and I got my bottom tanned a lot."

The doctor assured Michael's parents that they shouldn't be concerned about the fondling, because Michael, who was at the beginning of puberty, was just going through a phase. The pediatrician prescribed Ritalin, a mild central nervous system stimulant widely used to help children with attention deficit disorder (now called attention deficit hyperactivity disorder, or ADHD) or minimal brain dysfunction. His grades improved from Cs and Ds to mostly As. However, according to Dr. Cegalis, he also had "marked mood changes during that period including depressed periods." Both can be side effects of Ritalin.

Taking Ritalin embarrassed Michael. He took a dose three times a day, at home and at school, for six years. Trying to make light of it, he would joke, "Gotta take my uppers and my downers," as he popped one of the pills. But to Michael taking Ritalin was an admission that he was weak.

"The Ritalin was introduced at a critical point and kind of sealed things over. . . . It provided control of these underlying problems, these impulses," said Dr. Borden. "So you couldn't see it from the outside. You had Ritalin and you had a very controlling mother—both of those factors, strong factors—concealing what was an evolving mental illness." Dr. Borden said that the Ritalin hid Michael's underlying impulsivity and psychological problems and allowed them to go untreated and even get worse.

The *Physicians' Desk Reference* at the time recommended that Ritalin, or methylphenidate, periodically be discontinued under a doctor's care so that the condition can be reassessed. "Drug treatment should not and need not be indefinite and usually may be discontinued after puberty." However, for reasons he couldn't explain, Michael had taken the drug long after puberty and had neither been carefully monitored nor periodically taken off the medication.

Ritalin is a stimulant. It increases the levels of dopamine and noradrenalin, both natural chemicals in the brain, in parts of the brain that control the area of attention and behavior but are underactive. The International Center for the Study of Psychiatry and Psychology has urged the FDA to restrict the use of these drugs on children due to a bevy of problems—overprescription, addiction, and various neurological and cardiovascular side effects.

Michael's doctor was correct about the calming effect of Ritalin but wrong about its effects on Michael's sexual fantasies. He masturbated obsessively, sometimes several times a day. "My first recollection of masturbation was in seventh grade. I had a crush on my homeroom teacher, Mrs. Penny," who taught home economics. "I used to hold my pillow between my legs, and rubbing against the bed, I would ejaculate on the pillow. After a while, my mother noticed the yellow stains on the pillowcases after the wash," he said. She was so angry that "from then on I was only allowed to use the old set of sheets for my bed." Pat began to try to sneak up on Michael if she suspected he might be masturbating.

"If I was upstairs in my bedroom too long, she would try to tiptoe up the stairs to catch me in the act," he recalled. However, the old farmhouse's creaky stairs gave him fair warning.

Michael's obsessive masturbating was surpassed only by his mother's obsession to stop him because it was the one part of his life that she couldn't control. While he was at school, she found a pair of his stained underpants hidden under his bed. Michael told psychiatrists that she met him at the door with the pants in hand. "'Found these in your room,'" she said with "a tone that meant she was going for the emotional jugular. I knew I was in trouble. She made me wear them on my head all afternoon. But it didn't bother me as much as she had hoped," primarily because his siblings and even his father thought the stains were from his bed-wetting.

When the underpants punishment didn't work, Pat berated him. She ridiculed him in front of everyone. She made his proclivities the subject of dinnertime conversation. On his birthday, just before his senior year in high school, his sister Tina gave him a T-shirt with OFFICIAL CHICKEN CHOKER printed on the front. "I'm sure that she wasn't aware of the pun to masturbation, but I suspect that my mother was and helped her pick it out." Michael pretended to like the present but quickly burned the shirt in the garbage. Yet no name-calling and no amount of humiliation could stop his fantasies and his need for sexual release. He couldn't fall asleep without masturbating, and so it continued to be his nightly ritual.

"I hated my mother in high school. I remember during the summer after my senior year, I was counting the days. I had ninety-three days, ninety-two days, and I was crossing them off the calendar. I couldn't wait to get away from her."

Michael said "the climax of [his] mother's obsession" came after he left for college. She pulled the mattress off his bed, dragged it out of his room and down the stairs, and threw it into the backyard. "She doused it with gasoline and burned it. I wasn't there to witness the grand event, but I understand that she made quite a show of it," Michael told me, but he also said that his siblings may have made up the story to tease him.

Dr. Borden said that the combination of Michael's symptoms— hyperactivity, bed-wetting, sleep disturbances, and fantasies associated with compulsive masturbation—indicates "a substantial mental illness, mental disturbance in a child."

Besides doing household chores, the Ross children worked on the farm, and their hours and hourly wages increased as they got older. Every day after school, they walked to Eggs, Inc. directly from the school bus and worked until dinner. On weekends and during the summer, they worked from eight until four or five. "I worked the most hours," Michael proclaimed proudly, "a minimum of thirty hours per week and sometimes as much as seventy hours a week in the summer."

Eggs, Inc. consisted of four buildings, each housing twenty-five to thirty thousand chickens. The buildings were divided into four rows of cages, five birds to a cage, and designed to make egg collection fully automated. After an egg was laid, it would roll down the slanted floor of the cage onto a conveyor belt and at the end of the room to a cross belt. At the end of the conveyor belt was the egg room, where the eggs were packed, stored in a cooler, and sold.

Every day, the one hundred thousand birds at the farm ate eleven tons of grain, drank eight thousand gallons of water, and produced sixteen tons of chicken manure—two truckloads. V-shaped troughs with chains running through pulled the grain along the cages so that the birds could eat anytime. The manure was collected below the cages in pits about a foot deep. A cable system of scrapers pushed the manure out to the end of the buildings, where it was dumped into barn cleaners and then loaded into a dump truck.

As a rule, the girls worked in the egg room, a rather pleasant place to work by agricultural standards. It was air-conditioned and clean. They helped with egg collection and did minor chores, such as replenishing supplies. The boys took more responsibility for the daily care of the birds and did the dirty work of cleaning out the coops. "We would sweep the aisles and generally keep the indoors clean," Michael said. "You had to dust off the lightbulbs regularly because the light stimulates egg production because there are no windows in the building. We would keep the motors of the fans clean so that the air kept moving and the birds didn't suffocate. And there was always something breaking, stuff that needs to be repaired like fan belts or the feeders. If the scrapers broke in one of the manure pits, you'd have to climb in and fix it." Michael learned carpentry and electrical wiring. "I could fix almost anything. It might not look pretty, but it would work."

Michael laughed when he described fixing the belts. "One time I had to get into one of the manure trucks up to my waist to find a missing part," he said boastfully. "You just do what you have to do." Pete Wolak, a neighbor who was a plumber by trade but also farmed, told Michael that "the first thing you should do when you went into a barn was to pick up some manure and rub it on your hands. Then you won't worry about getting dirty."

The demands of their daily work schedule left little time for anything else. "The Ross kids didn't play; they worked," said Frances Wolak, Pete's wife. The Wolaks were the only two people in Brooklyn who would talk to me or any other reporter about Michael. They said that the Ross children's only extracurricular activity was Future Farmers of America. Michael never played any team sports because he didn't have time for them. They rarely went to movies or other normal high school activities. Pat made sure that they did their homework and worked hard in school. It was a nonnegotiable fact of life.

"None of us was able to have friendships. We couldn't have friends over to the house and stuff like that," said his sister Donna at Michael's first trial. Both Tina and Donna testified during the penalty phase, trying to explain Michael's home life so that he might not get the death penalty. "[Mom] made it clear that we were not allowed to have friends over. She would humiliate us in front of them, and it just became a lot easier not to have friends. . . . When I had a friend over one time when I was nine or ten, everything was going fine. We were outside [in] the front yard, and all of a sudden my mom just changed and told us that [my friend] was going home and put us in the car and brought the girl home." Dating was a virtual impossibility. During his four years in high school, Michael went out only once or twice and never to a dance or prom. Pat made borrowing the car or meeting curfew too difficult. "I was under my mother's thumb. Dating wasn't something I could do."

In his 1985 report for the defense, Dr. Cegalis concluded that this isolation, coupled with Michael's "incredibly poor nurturance, including extreme physical harshness, constant criticism, and rejection by parents" led to a deep-seated paranoia. Michael did not have an ally inside or outside the family and did not receive parental acceptance or reward. His internalized images of childhood were harsh, if not brutal, and "formed the basis of Michael's tortured and torturing adult personality."

Pat has never spoken publicly about Michael since his arrest. Her need to control her children may have resulted from her desire to make sure that her children got more out of life than she had; she didn't want them to make the same mistakes. Or maybe she was simply bitter about her own life. Maybe feeling trapped on the farm drove her to imprison her children as well. We cannot know for sure.

Despite all of this, Michael thought he was happy, but that was because he had no other reference point. He didn't know what it was like to be a part of a loving family. He looked up to his father, and so, like his father, he became totally absorbed in his work at the farm. While still in high school, Michael was made a vice president of the corporation and given a 10 percent share in the business. Farming was to be his life, as it had been his father's and grandfather's. After college, his plan was to return to Brooklyn to take over Eggs, Inc., make it state of the art, and become the "main rooster," as he called it. He reminisced. "I thought Brooklyn was a great place to raise a family. It was kind of rural. It was just a good place. I thought living on a farm was good for children; it teaches you values, like hard work. I liked the lifestyle. It's a hard life, but I think it taught me a lot of good things. Like you have to get up and feed the chickens every day. Just because you don't want to get up in the morning, you can't stay in bed. You got to get up and do what has to be done. And if a piece of equipment is broke, and it's four o'clock in the afternoon and it's quitting time, and the chickens ain't been fed, that means you're gonna miss your supper because you got to be sure the chickens get fed before you get fed." He considered himself indispensable. "My dad knew that if he took a weekend off and was going somewhere, I would make sure that the eggs would be packed, and the chickens would be fed, and everything would get done. No matter what happened, I would be able to take care of it one way or the other. And there've been some times"—he chuckled—"when I've come up with some very creative solutions. But he knew he could count on me."

Pete Wolak was a father figure for Michael. He kept about forty head of cattle, some on his farm on South Street in Brooklyn and some on the property adjacent to the Ross farm. In his spare time, Michael would help Pete with farm chores, from plowing, planting, and harvesting corn and hay to butchering cattle and hogs. Pete tried to give him money—even stuck cash into his pocket or truck, but Michael would always put it back in the jar in the kitchen where the Wolaks kept cash. Pete and Frances would treat him to a roast beef dinner a couple of times a month.

Pete is a man of few words, but it was clear how much he loved Michael even after what he had done. "Michael was the perfect all-American farm boy. Any father would have been proud to call him son," he said, his eyes welling up with tears.

More than a decade after Michael had been arrested, Frances still couldn't understand how Michael had raped and murdered anyone, never mind eight women. "I remember the day he was arrested," she said. "I went out to get the paper and couldn't believe it." She said she ran in to tell Pete. "I thought, 'It could have been me that he killed.'"

I told her that he never killed anyone he knew and he certainly would never have hurt her, because they were so close. "I didn't think so, but you never know. Who would have ever thought that someone like Michael could have done that?" Michael wrote to them often from prison, and they wrote back when they had time.

"I still don't believe it," Frances said. "He was such a nice boy."

DECEMBER 1976

Pat Ross pulled her car up close to coop three at the farm. She had arrived at 4:45 P.M., fifteen minutes before quitting time, and Michael was still inside cleaning out the coop. She hurried inside, out of the December dark and cold.

"You're here early," Michael said trying not to make eye contact or upset her as he continued sweeping. He never knew whether to start a conversation with his mother or to ignore her, because either was just as likely to set her off. But this time he'd decided to speak to her to make sure she knew he had a few more minutes to finish his chores.

"Got something for you," she said, holding up an envelope with a return address from Cornell University.

He grabbed it and sighed. It was thin. It wasn't even a regular letter-size envelope, and he could feel that there was nothing but a card inside. Every high-school senior knows that a thin letter is a rejection letter, so Michael shoved the unopened letter into his overall pocket, trying not to show his disappointment. He had dreamed of going to college to study agriculture. It had been in the back of his mind at every livestock fair, at Future Farmers of America meetings, and every time he had gone to the bank to deposit his farm wages into his college fund, which then totaled more than ten thousand dollars. He had saved his first hundred dollars by the time he was eight years old and his first thousand by ten. "Everything went straight into the bank. We weren't allowed to use our wages for spending money," Michael explained.

Applying himself just as much at school as on the farm, Michael had quietly impressed his teachers. "Ross was an exceptional student for two reasons: First of all, he was an academically gifted student; second of all, he was a hard worker. He really liked to be the number-one person in class," said Richard Colson, the vocational agriculture teacher at Killingly High, in court testimony. "He was quiet, shy, withdrawn to some extent. But he related very well to his teachers, more so than perhaps his peers."

During his junior year, Michael decided that Cornell, the alma mater of his uncle Quentin, was his first choice and that he would apply early to the College of Agriculture and Life Sciences. Given his good grades and decent board scores, he dreamed that he just might have a chance of getting accepted. Now he imagined he would have to apply to other schools, like Penn State or, if worse came to worst, settle for the University of Connecticut at Storrs, which, in Michael's mind, was too close to home.

"Aren't you going to open it?" asked Pat impatiently.

"What's the use? It's obviously a rejection."

"You don't know until you open it," she insisted, not telling her son that she had already held the envelope up to the light and knew he had been accepted. "Open it and read it to me."

Grudgingly, he opened it and soon let out a cry of joy as he read the news announcing that he had been admitted to the school of agriculture as a member of the class of 1981. Pat Ross was pleased with her son and actually allowed him to openly celebrate his acceptance to Cornell. Maybe she was sharing in his glory. She was the one who kept him home working on the farm and doing his homework rather than wasting time on dates or dances—and it had paid off.

Now that he was about to go to college, Michael wanted to rid himself of his crutch, Ritalin. Convinced that he didn't need it, he took himself off the drug during the winter of his senior year in high school—without consulting his family physician or his parents. What he didn't know was that the potential consequences of discontinuing the drug after such a long time were significant. He would have less internal control of his feelings, of his thinking, of his ability to concentrate and study, of his organizational ability, and of the overall maintenance of his life. Without the Ritalin, the areas of the brain that control attention and behavior would be underactive because there would be lower levels of dopamine and noradrenalin produced. Michael should have been weaned off the medication and monitored, because he had been taking it for six years. He had no idea how he would feel without it. On the eve of attending college, he released himself from both Ritalin and his mother's dominance.

After interviewing Dr. Borden and Dr. Berlin several times, watching hours of psychological evaluation by Dr. Zonana, reading the psychological reports of several doctors and the trial testimony, there was little doubt in my mind that Michael was mentally ill. In all of the psychiatric testimony that had been introduced at innumerable hearings, the prosecution had never put on any witness or introduced one report refuting Michael's diagnoses. Prosecutors had tried to challenge defense witnesses, but there was not one expert who had ever disagreed that Michael was a sexual sadist with other personality disorders. The question that remained was whether his mental illness alone was enough to cause him to murder eight women. It took several years of piecing together all the information for me to decide. The answer did not lie solely in his childhood.

NORTHERN CORRECTIONAL INSTITUTION
MARCH 1996

On March 21, 1996, I met Michael Ross face-to-face for the first time. By then I had talked to him many dozens of times on the phone, and he had recounted details about his arrest and trial and was beginning to open up about his upbringing and his time at Cornell. Although I had become comfortable talking with Michael on the phone, I was wary of meeting him in person. Originally I had been told that I would have a contact visit, which meant that he and I would be locked in a room together. It's one thing to be told that someone is taking medication that prevents him from having violent sexual fantasies and suppresses his urge to rape and murder. It is another thing to be absolutely sure that the medicine works when you are about to be locked in a room with him. I was nervous but tried to quell the anxiety with the knowledge that Michael had never killed anyone he knew, only strangers. And when I got to the prison, I learned that we would be talking on phones and be separated by a wall of glass and concrete.

Death row is in a cement fortress known as northern Connecticut's maximum security prison in the town of Somers—the prison capital of the state, where six other correctional facilities of medium or minimum security levels are located. Until 1995, condemned men were housed across the parking lot in the facility originally named Somers but now known as Osborn. Northern is nicknamed "the birthday cake" because the structure looks as if it is stacked in several layers. Standing in the parking lot on the corner between Osborn and Northern, you might mistakenly judge Osborn as the higher-security prison. It is surrounded by a high fence and double rows of barbed wire. But that impression changes when you enter Northern. The sound—or rather lack of it—is ominous. When you enter an older prison, what strikes you immediately is the noise. It's deafening. Your ears ring with the slamming of barred gates and cell doors. Voices echo not only up and down the tiers, but also throughout the building. At Northern there is no sound. The cells have no bars but metal doors with small, thick-paned windows that are sealed shut by remote control, burying the sound with the men behind them.

A visitor enters through a door controlled from a command center inside. After passing through metal detectors, you approach a guard station whose officers are invisible behind impenetrable darkened glass. You pass your photo ID through a metal drawer. If your name is on the visitor list, a visitor's badge is pushed out in the drawer. After a few minutes, an officer opens another steel door by remote control, allowing you to enter a large, austere waiting room that consists of several cold cement benches. Eventually—and sometimes this can be a half hour or more—a guard appears to escort you to your visit. You must first take an elevator—again controlled by the command center—to the second floor. Then you walk down a long windowless corridor, divided in the middle by a riot gate. To pass through, the guard must call on his walkie-talkie and wait for someone to respond. Northern is divided into six pods, three to a side. Each pod contains separate rings of cells that surround a bubbled command center.

It was so clean that the hall floors sparkled. The silence was deceptively peaceful. As an outsider, it may be easy to think it isn't so bad.

They have three square meals a day. It's probably better than where many of these guys lived before they got here. But these inmates are sealed in their cells twenty-three hours of the day, seven days a week. The lucky ones have jobs mopping the floors of the tier. Even after an hour or so inside, I began to feel trapped.

At that time, death row was located in 1E at the far end of the corridor. However, the location of death row changed several times during the years I visited Michael. For you to enter the visiting area off the row, an officer in the bubble inside the tier must open the door electronically. Once you're inside, the door is sealed shut, and you have to wait in a cubicle that consists of a cold cement cylinder to sit on, a cement slab connected to the wall that serves as a sort of desk, and a two-way phone. The inmate is escorted into a similar booth on the other side of a virtually soundproof glass window. You are unable to leave the less than four-by-four-foot hermetically sealed cubicle without the permission of the command center.

Yet despite the setting and his yellow prison jumpsuit, the man across from me did not look like a serial killer. Michael looked like the type of person who would offer to carry my groceries. New London *Day* reporter Karen Clarke had commented to me at the trial, "If I were walking down a dark alley and I heard footsteps behind me and turned around and saw Michael Ross, I'd be relieved."

Once more he made sure to remind me of his murders. "I have a mental illness, and I couldn't control myself. But whenever you look at me, I want you to remember that I killed eight women."

I'm buried in a cold prison. How could I forget? I thought but didn't say. "I told you before, if you killed one of my children, I would want to kill you with my bare hands. I have a teenage daughter."

"That was my target age," he said in an almost statistical way that made me shudder.

"But I would hope that I wouldn't want the state to kill you or any-one else," I said. "Even though I might personally have the desire to go and get a gun and shoot the person who hurt my child, I can't imagine getting to the point where I would kill or want the killer to be exe-cuted. Two wrongs don't make a right." I was being honest, but the con-versation unnerved me.

Michael had come to the visit with a stack of folders. Periodically he held up a couple of documents to the glass for me to read. I asked a few questions, filling in details on topics raised in earlier conversations. The purpose of the visit was more for fact-checking than it was for an interview. I wasn't allowed to tape-record the conversation because recorders are not allowed in the facility, and talking on the wall phone made writing difficult. But I watched him closely as we spoke.

When he took out the papers from the collapsible folder, his hands shook. He was nervous, but I don't think it was because he was worried about what I would write about him. It was apparent that he desper-ately wanted me to like him. He was paranoid about having our con-versations taped by the prison, so he had me write some questions on a piece of paper so he could see and answer. He tried to lighten the con-versation whenever it got serious; he continually joked—usually gal-lows humor—trying to make me laugh, trying to put me at ease. "So how do you like my place here?"

The concrete cylinder that I was sitting on was not only hard, but also cold. "Your decorator seems to be trying to discourage guests. This is the most uncomfortable thing I ever sat on."

"My room's a little homier, but I doubt that they'd let us visit in there," he joked.

He wanted to chat about my life, deflecting attention away from his own. "How are the twins?" "How was the drive?" "Did they give you any trouble getting in here?"

"They aren't a very friendly lot downstairs. Hardly anyone speaks to you with more than a syllable or two. I felt like I was being fitted for a cell."

"Tell me about it. I live with this 24/7."

I knew I would have only a short time, so I finally had to steer the subject back to his reasons for accepting a death sentence. The mood suddenly changed, and he began to cry. He repeated the reasons. "I have to do it. There's no other way. I owe it to the families of my victims."

"What about your family?" I asked. Other than reading court documents and letters he wrote me, we'd never really discussed his relationship with his family. I knew they didn't visit him or call, but he hadn't told me much about his relationship with his parents and siblings.

"For the most part, I don't think they'll miss me."

"Won't your father and your aunt miss you? They visit."

"I see my father maybe once a year at the most, and my aunt only comes once in a while, but it's not like they are here all the time. I don't even talk much. It would probably be a relief to them to not have me around." I thought about all the years that virtually no one called or visited. He'd been in jail for twelve years and on death row for nine. His sisters had come to visit at first, but they had stopped after the trial. He had only one real friend on the row, Bob Breton, who had been convicted of killing family members. Bob was not well educated, but he was friendly and depended on Michael, whose loneliness was painful to witness.

Having visited a few supermax prisons, I could understand his feelings about the oppressiveness of Northern. The first time I visited a supermax was in Waynesville, Pennsylvania. I was startled by the sense of being inside a tomb. The few windows don't open. It made me think of Edgar Allan Poe's story "The Premature Burial," in which the narrator finds that he has been buried alive by mistake.

At Northern, Michael was locked up for twenty-three hours a day in an eight-by-ten-foot cell. He was allowed out to shower two or three times a week and for a few hours of recreation in what he referred to as a cage or dog run. At Somers, death row inmates had been allowed to be together for meals and recreation. Although death row was deep inside Somers, multiple riot doors from the entrance, it was not a hermetically sealed tomb like at Northern. There were bars on the cells rather than solid doors with small windows, so prisoners could talk to one another and—if no one noticed—pass things to one another. The tier of death row cells at Somers faced large windows to the outside, bringing in lots of light—as well as cold in the winter and heat in the summer. Probably the most notable difference was the staff. Even to the visitor, the guards at Northern were intimidating and surly; the guards at Somers were much friendlier and, according to Michael, treated the inmates like human beings. I was beginning to understand why death would be a relief.

On another visit to Northern, I arrived late in the day, near the end of a shift, and after the visit, I was left locked in a concrete and glass visiting room for a couple of hours beyond the time I was scheduled to leave. My only communication was a buzzer to signal that I wanted to leave, but it was ignored for one long, excruciating hour while the guards fed the prisoners and conducted a prisoner count, as they did every day at shift change. I didn't know why they were ignoring me. I began to experience total claustrophobia.

As I stood waiting by the sealed door, I began to panic. I waited, beginning to think that the guards were ignoring me on purpose. In my mind, they were sitting in the command center laughing at me. I imagined being trapped in that visiting area for hours, days. The air-conditioning made it uncomfortably cold, yet I was sweating. Finally the door swished open and a guard led me out.

Michael later explained to me what had actually happened. There had been a shift change, which meant a prisoner count, followed by dinner, so they didn't have anyone to escort me out. He told me the daily schedule, and I made sure I never again made the mistake of visiting when I might get trapped inside. I never forgot the feeling of freedom that I experienced when I was outside the prison and in my car.

In the hour we spent together that first day, Michael and I began to develop a rapport. I had a sense of what John Gilmartin and Ann Cole saw in him. Michael did not seem like the beast that Satti had described at trial. He did not seem evil. He showed empathy when he sensed that I felt awkward. He often asked about my family. I had told him about them because there was no way I could talk on the phone at home without him knowing I had toddlers—even when I tried to shut the door to my little office, because it was right off the playroom.

"What's all that racket?" he had asked.

"That's Hannah and James playing."

"They make a lot of noise. I don't think I ever made that much noise."

"You weren't a twin."

He laughed, he cried, he was friendly. There was no sign of the "monster." The serial killer would never be revealed to me in person—only on paper. The Depo-Provera had caged the monster somewhere deep inside the man.

CORNELL UNIVERSITY
EARLY SEPTEMBER 1977

The Ross family—Michael, his mother, and grandfather—arrived in Ithaca, New York, the night before Cornell's freshman orientation after a five-hour drive from Brooklyn. They stayed in a motel on the outskirts of the city until Michael could move into his dorm.

University Hall number four was the cheapest dorm, located down the hill from the agriculture school on the southern edge of the campus. Michael's saved farm wages were paying his college tuition and his room and board, so he took extra care to pinch his pennies. U-Hall-4 was a four-story building with alternating floors of men and women. The two top floors were designated study floors with strict rules about noise. Michael had always been a dedicated student and requested the third floor, the men's study floor.

After he had unloaded all his luggage, he started to look through all the piles of papers that he had been given when he checked in. "I guess that I got tied up with the papers, because later I looked up and noticed that everyone was gone. My grandfather would later say that I couldn't wait for them to go, and I totally ignored them. The truth was that I was excited and was reading about registration, classes, books, and a million other details of campus life." For the first time in his life, he was free. Free of farm chores. Free of rules and restrictions. Free of his mother.

Yet another part of Michael found it difficult to separate from the people who were important to him—*especially* his mother. Without her iron-fisted rule, he sometimes felt lost. If he found himself lonely or faced with a problem, he would call home, and she invariably would be the one who answered the phone. He feared, even hated her at times, but he also loved and needed her. As much as he wanted to get away from her when he was home, he got closer to her while he was in college. "It don't make sense, but especially at the beginning of freshman year, I felt like she was the only one I could talk to." Because of the control she had exerted over him, she had forged the boundaries of his whole world. In many ways, he felt he owed her because she was the one who was responsible for demanding that he do well in school. She could be cruel, but he needed her to be good and loving because she was his mother, and on some level, according to Dr. Borden, he worshipped her.

Tall and lanky at six one and 150 pounds, Michael looked the part of the farm boy. He had an affable manner and a conservative outlook on life. Gun control was un-American. Only lazy people were on welfare. Death should be the penalty for murder. Drugs were for losers, and criminals should not get off on legal technicalities like the exclusionary rule or the insanity plea.

His conservative views, however, were in no way going to impede his social life. He was eager to finally get the chance to have fun and date, something he had never been able to do at home. High on Michael's list of activities was meeting women. A few days after arriving, he took a grocery bag and sneaked around campus snipping flowers from the various gardens, ignoring the prominent signs prohibiting picking. He brought the full bag back to the dorm and passed the flowers out on the women's floors. In the space of a few hours, he was able to meet most of the women in his dorm and received many grateful pecks on the cheek.

He particularly liked a woman named April, whom he dated on and off during the first semester. She lived in a single on the second floor, and he could see her room from his third-floor window.

After their first meeting, Michael asked April to meet him the next day, at the annual Fun in the Sun festival held on the arts quad. He also had a placement math exam scheduled that afternoon but didn't realize that the exam was supposed to take three hours until he arrived at the test site. Worried that he would blow his very first college date, he rushed through the exam and finished it in an hour, not even attempting to answer the more difficult questions. He was on time for his date with April but misjudged the importance of the exam. He was placed in a noncredit remedial math class.

Michael worked at dating as compulsively as he did everything else. Excited about the possibility of having a real girlfriend, he would watch from his window and wait for April to return to her room. As soon as he saw her light go on, he would be on the phone, wanting to plan an activity or just talk. April soon tired of Michael's obsessive calling and even stopped turning on her light when she entered her room in order to avoid his phone calls. Finally he took the hint and moved on to other dates. To his delight, he found that it wasn't difficult to find someone to accompany him to go dancing or to a movie, and there were weeks when he would see as many as four different women. But none of these first dates ever developed into anything serious.

One of the biggest challenges for Michael in developing relationships was his total lack of social skills and empathy. The Ross household had left him clueless in the realm of interpersonal relationships. He never had anyone he was close to or in whom he could confide. Growing up, he was friends with the Wolaks and to some extent his sister Donna, but he never really shared any intimate thoughts with any of them.

I tried to imagine the eighteen-year-old Michael arriving at Cornell, unsure of how to make friends. That person had come from a home full of people who functioned as a farm business but not as a family. They worked together and ate meals together but not much more. That boy was nothing like the person I had met, who was remorseful, funny, and had spent more than a decade trying to sort out how he had ended up on death row. The Cornell freshman from Brooklyn would never have poured out his shame and allowed himself to show his vulnerability—especially not to a woman.

Michael also felt that everyone at Cornell was wealthy, and he was extremely insecure about his working-class farm background. "I felt like I was deprived, and I didn't want to be the country bumpkin." Although he had been known at home as a shy and unassuming boy who didn't take on airs, he compensated for his insecurity at Cornell by bragging about Eggs, Inc., the family farm. Some people began to avoid him to be spared of his boasting. He would spend money ostentatiously and binge-drink on the weekends. A few times, he woke up lying in a snowbank where he had collapsed on the way home from a fraternity party. "I went a little wild when I wasn't under my mother's scrutiny," he admitted.

For Michael, living with a roommate was especially difficult. He masturbated at least once a day. He had promised himself that he would stop when he got to college, but he couldn't resist the sexual cravings.

At eighteen, he no longer dreamed about his seventh-grade homeroom teacher, Mrs. Penny, but of young women who could be love slaves in his imaginary harem. Michael's fantasies were becoming more sexual, but not yet violent. In his fantasies, he told me, he would forcibly abduct women—ostensibly to protect them from some evil—and whisk them back to his lair. The frightened women might be uncooperative at first, but they would soon relax, eternally grateful that he had saved them, and fall madly in love with him. Waiting each night until he was sure his roommate was asleep, Michael would masturbate to his fantasies of sexual domination while in constant fear that he would be caught and humiliated as he had been at home.

College board was expensive, and the food left a lot to be desired, so at the start of the second semester, when one of Michael's friends asked him if he would like to join a cooking group, he quickly agreed and changed his meal plan. Five or six of his dorm mates got together for Saturday and Sunday dinners, sharing the cost and chores. Michael didn't cook, but he was an old hand at cleaning up. From the very first dinner, he was drawn to a freshman named Rachel (her name has been changed), an attractive, diminutive engineering student from New York. Just talking to her excited him. After a few meals together, he gathered up enough courage to ask her out.

"I still remember our first date. We met at eight P.M. and went to Ithaca to go dancing—disco was big then. The dancing stopped at one or two A.M., and we spent the rest of the night walking all around Ithaca and talking. We walked by the gorge in the middle of the night, coming up in Collegetown. It was crazy." After eating breakfast at a diner, he got back to his room at noon the next day and went to sleep after a sixteen-hour first date.

For the next few weeks, they continued seeing each other frequently. In February, Michael's roommate went home for the weekend. Michael and Rachel began a date at the disco, but this time, rather than walking the streets of Ithaca, they returned to his dorm room.

"I didn't know at the time—because I didn't ask—but Rachel was sexually experienced," Michael said. "I, on the other hand, was about as inexperienced as they come. I was a virgin. I was nervous and apprehensive. I rushed things a bit, which didn't lend itself to a romantic lovemaking session. I got frustrated and lost my erection. As you might imagine, it was very embarrassing. And though I didn't say anything to Rachel, I began questioning my manhood."

Embarrassed, Michael got out of bed, pulled on a pair of cutoff jeans, and left the room. At the end of the hall, he stopped, opened a window, and gasped for air. "Though it seemed like an eternity, I don't think it was more than a minute or so before Rachel came out of the room. She stood in the doorway, naked except for a sheet she had wrapped around her," he remembered. "I will never forget how she looked as she held out her hand to me and beckoned me to come back to her." She took his hand and led him back into his room. It was clear to Rachel by then that Michael was not only a virgin, but also a scared virgin. He didn't remember what she said, but she gave him confidence, and he said he wasn't afraid or nervous anymore. "And the rest of the night and throughout the rest of the weekend, we made love several times. She totally owned my heart then, and she was the first woman whom I was truly in love with, and one of only two that I seriously considered asking to marry me."

Michael had never felt as good about himself. Just as new and exciting as sex was the communication he had with Rachel. For all of his eighteen years, he had never had a friend or family member with whom he could talk. Rachel knew how to put him at ease, whether at the library or taking a walk by Beebe Lake or in bed. She loved him for who he was, not for how much work he could do. He could trust her with his dreams; she never went for his emotional jugular as his mother always did. Rachel had a ready-to-please nature that put Michael in total control.

For sophomore year, Michael moved into the Alpha Zeta fraternity house, and Rachel moved to a one-bedroom off-campus apartment with a roommate. Michael and his friend Bob Davenport had rushed two agriculture fraternities in the fall of their freshman year and received invitations from both. Alpha Zeta is an honors fraternity on most campuses, although not at Cornell at that time. Michael was a member of the local chapter, but not a member of the honors fraternity. About forty men lived in the house, just off campus on Thurston Avenue. "They had to take me," he chuckled. "My uncle had been in the same fraternity at Cornell, and I was a legacy."

Every Wednesday was date night at the fraternity house. The brothers dressed in jackets and ties, and dates ate for free at a sit-down dinner. Rachel was always there, and although it was against fire-code regulations to sleep in the main fraternity house (the brothers were supposed to sleep in the dorm attached to the house), the two would routinely spend the night in Michael's study room. During his sophomore year, they spent three or four nights a week together. "We would normally make love before going to sleep and once again when we woke up in the morning. Rachel also had a habit of waking me up in the middle of the night to make love to her—the only woman I'd ever been with on a regular basis who actually woke me up to make love to her!" Michael wrote me.

That December he was dealt two blows. First, he was put on academic probation because his grade point average had slipped to 1.7. His active love life had dramatically cut into the amount of time he devoted to schoolwork. Just before Christmas break, Rachel had asked him to come over. As he left the house, a fraternity brother who was on the phone and standing near the front door teased him, "What'd ya do? Go and get her pregnant?"

Michael laughed. But when he got to Rachel's apartment, he realized that there was nothing funny about it. Rachel's roommate hurried out the door and gave him an accusatory leer. But even then, he was too naive to suspect what was wrong until Rachel sat him down in the living room.

"I'm pregnant," she announced.

"Are you sure? I don't get it. We used condoms. How could this happen?" She reminded him of a weekend they had shared when her roommate was away; they hadn't used contraceptives as religiously as usual. "I handled the entire situation very badly. I guess I was scared. I don't really know." He was concerned and told her they would work it out, but "like I did with all of my problems, I ignored it and pretended that it would go away." The news came just as they were about to go home for the holidays, Rachel to her family, in New York, and Michael to Brooklyn. In the back of his head, he had the notion that he might drop out of school. "I had prepared myself all my life for not dealing with things, locking things out, pretending they didn't exist."

There was no one in his family to whom he felt he could turn for advice. He certainly wasn't going to tell his mother. So he went to Pete Wolak. As usual, at Christmas Michael offered to give Pete a hand with some of his chores. He desperately wanted to tell Pete about his problem, but he was too embarrassed and ashamed to explain the situation. What would Pete and Frances think of him if they knew that he had gotten a girl pregnant?

As the two crossed the parking lot at the Ross farm on their way to the fields where Pete kept some of his cattle, Michael couldn't hold it in anymore. "I'm thinking of dropping out of college," he blurted out.

Pete stopped and looked at him. "Turn sideways," he said, motioning to Michael to show him his profile. Michael thought it an odd request but shrugged and obliged his friend.

"No. I don't see a hole in your head," Wolak said.

Michael laughed. "I knew then that I had to go back, but it was never the same with Rachel."

In January when they returned from break, Rachel announced that she had had an abortion. They had agreed it was the only alternative, but he had not expected her to do it over break. On one level, he was relieved. The problem had been solved; there were no more choices to make. But on another level, he was ashamed because he had run away from the situation and left Rachel to fend for herself. "I should have been there for her. I should have helped her financially. But she never asked, and I never offered," he told me. He felt he had not done the honorable thing, as his father had.

It was more than the two nineteen-year-olds could handle. Although he loved Rachel, he felt awkward around her and started to avoid her. "I can only imagine what she thought of me. Our relationship was never the same after that. She was the best woman I ever had, and I screwed it up big time."

Rachel and Michael didn't officially break up until the beginning of their junior year, but he soon was seeing other women on the side. "She wanted to join the Air Force and had to sign her four-year commitment papers," he said. "I told her that I didn't want to wait four years for a wife." It was just an excuse, because soon Michael was dating three or four different women at once but not telling Rachel. He suspected she was seeing other men as well, but neither of them confessed to the other. "I always have to wonder what would have happened if I had married Rachel. She was good for me." But he rationalized the outcome: "My only consolation is that because we didn't get married, she didn't know anything about my sickness."

In the nine months between the abortion and the breakup, Michael's sexual fantasies had taken a darker turn. They became more and more aggressive and coercive. "Although I wouldn't hurt anyone, the theme was basically the same," he told me. "I would get a woman into a situation where I was in control, convince her—sometimes using aggressive behavior—to have sex with me. She would struggle at first, but I would win her over in the end, and she would give herself willingly to me because of my sexual prowess." Eventually, degrading the women became more important than winning them over. These were probably his earliest true rape fantasies. Michael wondered whether the unwanted pregnancy and the tension it created in his relationship with Rachel might have been enough to induce his aberrant fantasies.

During the next two years, his noxious fantasies increased, and by the second semester of senior year, he couldn't get them out of his head. They filled his mind when he was awake, and they became his ugly dreams when he slept. The urges grew even stronger and more frequent. Even masturbation provided only a minor relief to the turmoil in his mind and his constant need for sexual release.

SUMMER 1978

When summer came, Michael headed back to Brooklyn to work on the farm. His relationship with his mother had improved while he was away; he no longer hated her as he had in high school. But their relationship quickly deteriorated to what it had been as soon as he moved back into the house.

Other than Pete and Frances Wolak, Michael actually felt closest to Charlie Brown, the family dog. She had been Michael's best friend since Ned had died when Michael was eight. Charlie Brown was technically Kenny's dog, but each of the Ross men claimed the dog as his own. Kenny, the sibling to whom Michael was least close, had named the female dog after the cartoon character because, as Michael remembers, Kenny was obsessed with him. Dan Ross felt the dog was his because when the kids were in school, she followed him around the farm. But Michael was sure that he was the dog's best friend. When there was a thunderstorm, she would go into his room. "I was the only one who would comfort her. The rest of them would kick her out of their rooms."

Whoever the rightful master was, when Michael was around, he and

Charlie Brown were inseparable. She would even help him with his work, herding escaping chickens, gently catching them in her mouth, and dropping them at Michael's feet. When Michael had a free moment, he and the dog would walk in the woods or go to his grandfather's pond to hunt frogs. She didn't eat them; she just caught them and then let them go. As she got older and started going blind, he would point out the frogs, and she'd catch them when they jumped out.

By the time Michael went to Cornell, Charlie Brown was also going deaf, and when he returned home the next summer, he was shocked to see how much she had aged. So when his mother told him that the dog was very ill, couldn't keep food down, and needed to be put out of her misery, Michael believed her. There was actually nothing wrong with Charlie Brown except old age, but Michael later believed that his mother must have decided to punish him for some unknown transgression. Perhaps it was simply a reminder of who ran the house or that she was just tired of the poor old dog. Thinking back, he couldn't come up with a reason why she wanted to be rid of the dog, but "I can't figure out the reasons why my mother did a lot of things." Whatever her motivation, Pat ordered Michael to take Charlie Brown up to his grandfather's house, get his shotgun, and shoot her. Dutifully, Michael trudged up the familiar hill on Tatnic Road, but his grandfather had more sense and refused to turn over the gun. He told Michael he was a fool for ever considering such a thing. "I don't think I could have done it anyway," Michael admitted.

Not to be defeated in her mission, Pat had another solution. "Take the dog up to Dr. Sherman's and have him put her to sleep." Michael could see that she was rapidly losing patience. Again, he complied, believing he was doing the right thing. He didn't want the dog to suffer. It wasn't what he wanted, but like culling the chicks, it was his job. It also was an eerie foreshadowing of the future.

Occasionally while in high school, Michael had worked at the vet's, and so he was allowed to hold the dog as Dr. Sherman gave her the fatal injection. "She died in my arms," he remembered sadly. When he arrived home, he found his father and siblings furious. "You idiot," they screamed accusingly. "There was nothing wrong with Charlie Brown. You killed the dog for no reason." Instinctively, he knew they were right. His mother had duped him into killing the pet he loved.

Devastated, Michael wanted to bury his friend in the backyard, but his mother would not allow it. She told him to throw the dog in the pits where dead chicken carcasses were thrown. Not wanting to incur his mother's wrath, he obeyed, but returned every day for weeks to be with the dead dog and watch as her body decomposed. It would become his ritual of penitence.

FALL 1979

Within days of his final breakup with Rachel, Michael had found someone else. It happened the following Thursday night at a Future Farmers of America meeting. As he sat on a bench, working on a farm appraisal assignment, Betsy (her name has been changed), a petite brunette wearing glasses, came in and sat down next to him. "I was immediately attracted to her beauty. I don't know if I truly believe in love at first sight, but I felt a strong attraction to Betsy from the first time I saw her. I had just broken up with Rachel, so I was open to the idea of a new relationship." As he sat next to her, he tried to look busy working with the written formulas that he had learned only a few hours earlier. "I had no idea what I was doing, but I pretended to know exactly what I was doing." He told her he was estimating the value of a farm. She lived on a dairy farm and immediately became curious. "Betsy asked me some questions about my calculations, and I answered with confidence, though I suspect now that my answers, while sounding good, were complete rubbish. It didn't matter, because it gave us something to talk about."

At nine o'clock, when the meeting ended, Michael asked if she would like him to walk her home to her dorm on the east side of the campus. After realizing that she was a freshman, he also offered to give her a tour of the huge campus. Taking advantage of the clear late-summer night, he took her over to Beebe Lake. On the far side of the lake is a stone footbridge where they paused to watch a group of divers snorkeling beneath them.

It was dark, but they could easily see with the aid of the full moon. Because Betsy was in no hurry to get back to her dorm, Michael took her down Thurston Avenue to the Alpha Zeta fraternity house, but they didn't go inside. Instead they turned left and walked to the suspension bridge high above the fabled gorge with its waterfalls flowing into Cayuga Lake. Halfway across, he paused to tell her the famous myth of that bridge, one of several that spans the famous gorge. As the story goes, the bridge was designed as a class project by a Cornell engineering student whose professor failed him, claiming the bridge was of such poor design that it would never stand. The student eventually graduated and became a successful engineer, never forgetting the sting of the failing grade. Eventually he came back to Cornell with the original design and built the bridge on his own. The mystery professor allegedly swore that the bridge was unsound and refused to set foot on it. Cornellians have created the tradition that any man and woman who cross the bridge together must kiss in the center, lest the professor be right and the bridge collapse.

"Betsy, completely understanding of the importance of tradition, granted me our first kiss—and several more throughout the course of the evening," Michael remembered. The next night they went out to dinner and dancing. Around 1:00 or 2:00 A.M., they went back to Michael's room in the fraternity house. "She seemed nervous, and I asked what was wrong. It took a little prodding, but finally she told me. The previous year she had worked in Washington, D.C., as an intern for a representative from her home district. One night, on her way home to her apartment, she cut through a dark parking lot where she was attacked by a man. He made her perform oral sex on him. I didn't press for any more details because she was quite upset. She felt that she was damaged goods and that no man would want her once he found out what had happened to her. She thought that I wouldn't want her. I felt so sorry for her, and I just held her and talked to her. I told her that it didn't matter and that as far as I was concerned, she was still completely a virgin and would remain a virgin until she decided to give herself to a man. Shortly thereafter, she chose to give herself to me."

The relationship moved quickly. "My junior year with Betsy was, I believe, the best year of my life. I loved her completely without reservation, and she loved me the same way," Michael told me. In a matter of days, he had forgotten Rachel and had fallen in love with another woman.

Just before Thanksgiving, Michael had to be hospitalized to remove a cyst in his saliva gland. "The doctor messed up, and I was bleeding into my cheek, which swelled up like a grapefruit. I was in tremendous pain and vomited blood. I had to go back into the operating room to stop the bleeding. I don't remember much of the day besides the pain, and when I woke up later that night, I was in the intensive-care ward." Although his pain was gone, the nurses told him that he would have to spend the night in intensive care because he had been operated on twice in one day, and they needed to keep a careful watch over him. Because she wasn't a relative, Betsy couldn't visit him, but she was upset and frightened. She wanted him to know how she felt, so she wrote a note and asked the nurse to deliver it. "I wish that I had the actual note now. I carried it in my wallet until 1984 when I was arrested—long after we had broken up and there was no chance of us ever getting back together. It was a love letter, actually. In it she told me how much she loved me and how we would get married, have children, and have our own little farm. It was a blueprint of what our life was supposed to be. I cherished it greatly."

Touched by the letter, Michael wanted to reciprocate in some way. While he was home for Christmas break, he went to a jewelry store in neighboring Danielson and bought a pre-engagement ring for about $150. After some protracted negotiation with his parents, he was allowed to drive the pick-up truck from the farm to Vermont to visit Betsy. "I gave the ring to Betsy as a Christmas gift. We didn't actually get engaged or anything. It was just assumed that we would be married."

That visit to Betsy's home was the first time that Michael realized how dysfunctional his own family was. "My family wasn't close at all. In fact, the only person I was close to was my sister Donna. I didn't understand what a family was until I visited Betsy's." He said in his own family, Christmas lasted about an hour. "We opened presents and then it was all over. At Betsy's it was an all-day thing." They would open a few presents, do chores, and come back and open some more. It took the entire day. They didn't give one another big presents. In fact, he remembered that one of Betsy's mother's presents was a year's supply of deodorant. Before Christmas, he had gone down to the Agway store with her mother. "I picked up a little cowbell and said, 'What's this?' and then was laughing and ringing it. Her mother snuck back and bought it for me." He choked up. "That little bell was given with more love and meant more than anything my family ever gave me." He put it on a chain and hung it from his rearview mirror.

Michael and Betsy spent more and more time together. Because Betsy had a roommate, the only place they could sleep together was in the fraternity house. Before long they began spending three or four nights a week there, which soon caused a confrontation between Michael and a few of his more conservative brothers. No sanctions were taken against him, but the incident convinced Michael that it was time to move out. In February he and Betsy began looking for an apartment. Off-campus housing was tight in Ithaca, but in March they found an apartment at 109 Wyckoff Avenue and signed a lease for a fall rental.

Sometime in that second year, Betsy changed. Michael later suggested that perhaps both of them began to become more secure—or entrenched—in their personalities. "I think she outgrew me," he admitted. No longer was Betsy the impressionable freshman who had written the love letter describing their shared dream of life on the farm in Brooklyn. Marriage, kids, and the farm were not enough. She began to think of their future in terms of her own career. She constantly complained about the prospect of being "stuck in Hicksville," her sardonic term for Brooklyn. The more they talked of marriage, the more she felt that Michael was tying her down. And Michael was no longer the teenage boy infatuated with love. His goal was less about pleasing Betsy and more about protecting what he saw as his vision of a perfect future.

Betsy pushed Michael to agree that after she graduated, they would choose where to live based on who made the highest salary. Half joking, half serious, she'd refer to him as her future "house hubby." Michael would laugh and shrug it off, but the thought of being forced to follow her career infuriated him. He didn't want to give in to her competitiveness; he wanted to go back to Brooklyn and take over the farm, while Betsy wanted to become an executive in agribusiness. "If she had said, go with me or we go our separate ways, I would have gone. But I was afraid if I told her, I would have given her the upper hand. That's what I was afraid of. I didn't want her to know how much power she had over me, how much I cared. I was madly in love—or I thought I was. Now I think it was infatuation, sexual attraction, and nothing else," Michael decided. "The problem was that she was too much like my mother. She was too controlling, too competitive.

"I had always dreamed of returning to the farm. It's all that I had ever wanted. I had no big dreams. I was going to be the next genera-tion. I was going to build new buildings and make the farm state of the art, as it had been when we started building in the sixties." But to sat-isfy Betsy, Michael began interviewing during the fall semester.

Adding to Michael's turmoil was news that his parents had decided to separate and were in the process of divorce. Michael never knew ex-actly what prompted the decision but assumed that they just couldn't stand each other anymore. Both Pat and Dan were telling Michael not to come back to Brooklyn to work at Eggs, Inc. after graduation. "My Dad was pressing me to interview. He said he wanted something better for me, maybe because he was proud of me. I don't think he under-stood that I didn't want anything more than to go back to Brooklyn and settle down and raise a family like he had done." By Christmas Michael had landed a job with Cargill, Incorporated, one of the largest agricul-tural conglomerates in the country, in the poultry products division in North Carolina. Betsy was happy. Pat and Dan were pleased. Only Michael was miserable about his success.

Police reports from the time of Michael's arrest in 1984 reveal that a relative of Pat's and a few neighbors saw a change in Michael after the divorce. They said he appeared even more hostile toward Pat and blamed her for the divorce, but later he claimed to have no memory of an abrupt shift in his feelings toward her. He simply felt he was twenty-one years old and didn't have to answer to her anymore. However, the divorce proceedings later became even more upsetting. Pat wanted 50 percent of the farm even if that meant selling it. The prospect of losing what he saw as his future added to the strain on his relationship with Betsy. Now both Betsy and his mother were destroying his dreams.

Michael became increasingly withdrawn. During his junior year, he loved going out and dancing. But more and more by his senior year, he wanted to stay home in their apartment. Betsy resented the change.

The pressure of living together was overwhelming. Soon he would graduate, and they would be separated by hundreds of miles. A sense of loneliness and abandonment haunted him. He even began to suspect that she was seeing another man on the side. "Betsy was a flirt," he said, "and I got suspicious when she said some guy wanted to take pictures of her, but she wouldn't let me go. She said it would be awkward. But I never did see any of those pictures."

They fought as the relationship unraveled. On one occasion, Michael was drunk but determined to drive home to Connecticut. Trying to protect him from himself, Betsy hid the car keys. Unbearable anger welled up inside him. He wanted to hurt her, but she had too much power over him. Her love helped to define him; losing Betsy would be like death. So instead of force, he used words, trying to tear at her emotionally, going for the emotional jugular like his mother. "I fantasized forcing my penis in her mouth, making her relive her demons." Finally, the fight over the keys became so nasty that Betsy got scared and called one of the Alpha Zeta brothers to come to the apartment to help her. It made me uncomfortable knowing about his fantasy—not because of the mention of forced oral sex, but because it was the first indication that he consciously wanted to hurt a woman who was important in his life.

During another fight, he said he actually hit her with an open-hand slap to the face, hard enough to knock off her glasses. "I remember feeling so rotten—angry at myself that I hit her, angry at her for getting me so angry—that I left the apartment and walked around campus," he told me, ashamed of even remembering the rage. "I think that was one of the first times I stalked a woman."

In a police interview after Michael was arrested, Betsy said that he had a "violent temper." She told them that he got so angry on one occasion that he "violently choked her and on another occasion he struck her with his fist across the face." Another time he got mad about something "petty" and tore their apartment apart. Michael couldn't remember all his fights with Betsy but conceded that "if she said it happened, it happened."

In an effort to salvage the relationship, before Christmas Michael secretly purchased an engagement ring for several hundred dollars. "We had looked at engagement rings weeks before and I purchased a ring that she liked," he remembered. He had given her the impression that he needed more cash to be able to buy the ring. Michael said she expected a ring, but not right away. The drive from Ithaca to Brooklyn took six hours, and he knew that Betsy would often get kind of grouchy during those long drives. "So I put the ring in the glove compartment. Three or four hours into the drive, when she started to get a bit testy, I had her open the glove compartment and find the ring. Needless to say, her mood improved greatly, and we found a secluded place to pull over and make love. I suppose that doesn't sound very romantic, no formal proposal during a candlelit dinner, but the ring was just a formality. It was my way of hanging on to our relationship. I wanted to do something to hold us together. We got engaged, but we weren't honest with each other."

Betsy was aware of the growing problems in their relationship, but she did not know that there was an even greater problem growing within

Michael. His fantasies had become increasingly aggressive and sadistic since Rachel's abortion. Despite his active sex life, he continued to masturbate to the growing violence in his head. "Rape became incorporated into my fantasies after I met Betsy my junior year. I knew firsthand how the rape in Washington had affected her, how she still could get frightened even months and years after the attack," he remembered. Knowing her fears gave him both a physical and emotional power over her.

Most of the time, sex for Michael was an expression of love, but it also became a power game. He used it to control Betsy. She said he demanded sex from her twice a day. When he was angry or displeased, he would force sex on her. It was his way of punishing her, his way of gaining the upper hand in their relationship. "It was wrong and I wish now that I could tell her that I am sorry," he lamented. "On occasion, I used sex to hurt her. In my fantasies, sex became a way to degrade a woman. And while I was never as aggressive with Betsy as I was in my fantasies, some of that spilled over into our relationship. There were times when I was angry and wanted to hurt her, more emotionally than physically, but I would only go so far." He depended on her and needed her, yet she was making him miserable.

As Michael's anger and frustration with Betsy increased, the fantasies and the urges became a constant torment. Now the fantasies were not only of degradation and rape, but also of murder. "The best way for someone who is not plagued with this problem to understand the obsessive and repetitive nature of these thoughts, urges, and fantasies is to remember a time when you had a song or some catchy tune stuck in your mind, playing over and over and over again, driving you crazy. Even if you like the melody, its constant repetition becomes more than merely annoying. When this happens, the harder you try to push that melody out of your mind, the louder and more persistent it becomes, driving you almost to the point of madness," he told me. However, it wasn't a catchy tune playing in Michael's head, but noxious images of physically and mentally degrading women, of raping and strangling them—images that are nearly impossible for the average person to imagine.

"In my fantasies I did not have to hold back like I did with Betsy, so they continued to grow. Somehow, and I don't really know how it happened, fantasy spilled out into reality. Stalking was the first step." Stalking relieved the internal pressure when his relationship with Betsy was tense.

"When I was very agitated, stalking relaxed me. It started out as a game—to follow a woman without her knowing. Afterwards, the incident would feed my masturbation fantasies. Slowly, the game developed into how close I could get to the woman without her knowing. There were times when I got so close that I could have easily grabbed her. Then the game became to see how close I could get to her while thinking of what I could do to her. Then there were times that I deliberately let the woman know that I was following her, and it was such a rush to be able to feel her fear." All these incidents would later be incorporated into fantasies that he masturbated to. He began to feel as if he were separated from the act of stalking, almost as if he were watching it all happen. This sense of separation from the actual acts might have been the first indication of what Dr. Merikangas would later describe as a fugue-like state or depersonalization disorder, in which reality testing remains intact but one feels as if one were outside oneself or watching a movie rather than participating in the action.

Michael had been in denial about the seriousness of his desire to stalk. He was convinced that it was just a harmless game and that he would never hurt anyone. He said he had no fear of being discovered or recognized. Somehow taking off his glasses and being one of six thousand students made him feel unrecognizable. "As time went on, I had to get closer to them. Like a drug, I needed more and more to gain the same release. From then on, it wasn't enough just to follow them. I had to frighten them. When I was stalking or masturbating, I craved that feeling. It was as if I could feed on their fear."

"Finally, I actually grabbed one," he admitted, although he wasn't exactly sure when it happened. "It was after dark but probably before midnight. I felt an irresistible impulse to stalk. A young woman left the Agriculture library alone and walked into the parking lot behind the building. I followed her and grabbed her from behind as she turned between two parked cars. I covered her mouth and dragged her to the ground. I remember being frightened at what I had done. I hadn't planned on grabbing her. I was only supposed to follow her and maybe frighten her by making my presence known. So when I had her on the ground, I didn't know what to do. I became frightened and ran off into the night." Although Michael did not rape the woman, he had begun to re-create the scenario of Betsy's attack.

In court testimony, Dr. Borden said that becoming sexually active was the initial trigger for Michael's "core personality" to come to the surface. "There were serious problems in his . . . psychological structure that has to do with relationships." Michael had acted out when he reached puberty at thirteen and fondled his neighbor, suggesting that there was "an underlying personality disturbance core." Dr. Borden said that when he became sexually active, the underlying personality core took over. "It comes out in relationships. It comes out in the interaction, because that provokes and stimulates feelings. That can set the whole thing in motion." He explained that if a woman was accommodating and "let him dominate her" in the way Rachel did, his mental illness would be controlled and pacified. She was "sexually comforting and built his ego."

Michael's fear of losing Betsy was important in understanding his mental illness. "We have a honeymoon period where [Betsy] serves to control him. That relationship keeps him together. Just like his mother kept him together." He might have resented it, but his mother kept him under her thumb. "A woman can keep him together for a while. If she's . . . basically accommodating, it can be for a longer period of time. If she's more like his mother, that's like a fuse or a trigger for him. It's like a grenade and the woman is the pin. It arms him, but it controls him. When that pin is pulled, leaves, separates, he's going to explode." Betsy was the pin.

The "monster" was strong and powerful, capable of controlling women. Michael, on the other hand, felt weak because he was losing control of Betsy and his future life in Brooklyn. The frustration, powerlessness, and rage that he experienced as his world slipped away only fueled his need to keep the monster alive. He had the same push/pull relationship with the monster that he had with his mother.

Although Michael was becoming aware that he and Betsy were mismatched, he would later object to Dr. Borden or any psychiatrist or observer describing Betsy as any part of the problem. He said he was the problem and insisted she had nothing to do with it.

A few weeks after the first attack, Michael was again in his stalking mode when he followed a woman off campus and down Thurston Avenue toward the Alpha Zeta house. "I grabbed her from behind and dragged her into a grassy area just across the street from the fraternity. The thrill was in the pursuit and in seeing and feeling her terrors as I pulled her off the path. It all happened so quickly." Almost immediately, he let her go, again without hurting or raping her, and ran off through some nearby woods. These attacks were reported to the Cornell police, who filed reports and did some investigation, but not until after Michael's arrest in 1984 did they know all had been committed by the same man.

The third attack that spring was even bolder and more aggressive. It was a warm night after dark when Michael felt the urge to stalk. "I followed a woman as she walked towards the Pancake House, a campus eatery in a secluded part of the campus, towards the dorms. As she walked up a slight rise, I grabbed her around the neck, dragged her over a wooden fence, down a hill through some woods to the footpath along Beebe Lake. I walked her along the lake going towards a stone bridge on the far side of the lake, but got frightened when I heard others approaching. I pushed her down a small embankment towards the lake and ran off. If I hadn't heard the voices, I think I would have raped her."

10

NEW YORK CITY
WINTER 1996

A few months after I met Michael Ross face-to-face, my husband and I were having dinner with our friends Steve and Michelle at the restaurant in the Metropolitan Opera House. Steve and Michelle were familiar with my work. Hearing that I was now having telephone conversations with a serial killer, Michelle asked why I liked talking to murderers.

This was the conversation I was always trying to avoid. It wasn't that I liked talking to murderers; it was more that I was willing to listen. "I guess once you do a story about prisons or crime, someone is always calling or writing you about some injustice. It becomes impossible to escape doing more prison stories."

"If a murderer called me, I'd have no problem hanging up the phone," Michelle responded.

"It's probably also because this is a death penalty case, and I'm opposed to capital punishment. I was brought up to think that all killing is wrong." My father, a clergyman, had been brought up with Quaker ideals and was a conscientious objector in World War II. He often repeated a quote attributed to Gandhi: "An eye for an eye and the whole world is blind."

I suspected that Michelle was in no way opposed to the death penalty for serial killers. I might have said more before my husband interrupted.

"She's chasing her own demons."

"What are you talking about?" I asked.

"You're confronting your attack in college."

I was dumbstruck. I hadn't thought about the incident for nearly twenty years. I had buried the memory for years, but now he had put the attack squarely in front of me, and I had to deal with it. I also had to explain it to our friends.

"During my junior year at Williams, I was attacked by a stranger who had come looking for a friend of mine. I thought he was going to kill me. But honestly, my motivation for doing this story doesn't have anything to do with it."

The more I considered it, the more I began to suspect that on some level my husband was right. I hadn't thought about the attack for more than a decade. Until that night at the opera, I'd thought I had gotten past it.

It was a Sunday. I had been working out for the crew team in the tanks in the gym and was exhausted, but there was the never-ending homework to do. I didn't even have the energy to eat dinner; I went straight to my room, put on a nightgown, and started to work. Then the phone rang. It was my friend Katie's mother asking me to give her daughter a message. Katie had just gotten back from a semester in India, and her phone had not yet been installed. Over Christmas break, an old high-school classmate had been hanging around Katie's house, and there were signs that made her family believe that he was not stable. "David's been acting strange. We think he might be on his way up to Williamstown. Please tell Katie that if he arrives call campus security. He could be dangerous."

"Sure," I said, thinking she might be overreacting. Because Katie lived in the next entry, all I had to do was put on enough clothes, go out into the cold, go out one door and into the next, give Katie the message, and go back to my environmental geology. I pulled on a pair of corduroy jeans, tucked in my Lanz nightgown, slipped on hiking boots and a warm sweater, and ran next door. I knocked on the door, but there was no answer. Katie, like me, lived in a two-room double. Her roommate had the larger, outer room; she had the inner one. The door was unlocked, so I let myself in and went into Katie's room to leave her a note, not bothering to turn on the light in the inner room. As I scribbled down the warning, I heard a noise behind me and spun around. A man was standing in the doorway of Katie's closet. Worried that Katie was in the closet, I stepped forward to see past him. In hindsight I should have run out of the room and called for help. I feared that Katie was injured, tied up, or worse, dying in the closet. My mind shot back to the note I'd just written. So I made sure I was clear of the desk.

"Hello," I began. "You must be David. Have you seen Katie?"

"No, I came to marry her or rape her depending on what she said, but you'll do."

Katie obviously wasn't there, and I saw my chance to exit. "Okay, I guess I should go back to my room to do my homework."

"Wait," he said, lunging toward me. I stepped back to avoid his grasp, forgetting that there was a large ottoman in the middle of the room. I lost my balance and found myself in a prone position. David, a former New Jersey state wrestling champion, now had control, but at that point, he didn't terrify me. I thought I could handle myself because I was strong from rowing crew. I remembered someone saying that the best thing to do is to not resist. *What turns rapists on is fear, so don't be afraid. They get off on the resistance. Act like you aren't the least bit upset.* So I smiled and tried to talk my way out of the predicament. I argued that I had a steady boyfriend, that I was not on the pill, that I didn't even know him—anything and everything that I could think of to persuade him to leave me alone.

Every so often I yelled, "Help!" *There are dozens of guys in the dorm; one of them is bound to hear my cries for help.* However, those cries made things much worse. David responded by hitting me every time I yelled. As my resistance to him became more intense, so did his physical response. He started slamming me against the walls, which made me yell louder and more frequently, but that only made him hurt me more. By that time, I was panicked, but I didn't want him to know it. He had given up on any type of cooperation and was trying to rip off my clothes. Something changed. His eyes were angry; he no longer responded to anything I said. My heart began to pound in my ears. *Oh shit. Now what are you going to do, smart one? You obviously can't get away or fight him off. No one is hearing you or at least no one has come to your rescue. You need to come up with something—quickly.* I was totally panicked. I had run out of ideas and I knew that I was running out of time.

Soon it didn't appear that rape was his motive—he wanted to hurt me. Finally he picked me up and threw me down on Katie's bed. *He's going to kill me. He is actually going to kill me. Why the hell didn't I just let him rape me and be done with it?* But of course that solution doesn't come naturally to anyone in this situation. I could persuade myself not to resist for a while, but the instinct to fight back and protect myself was far too strong. I used every ounce of energy to fight back, but my strength was running out. My arms felt weighed down. *No one is going to help you. But you can't give up. Keep fighting.* But by that point I was having trouble even blocking the blows, never mind fighting back. *God, please don't let me die. I haven't even finished my homework.*

By that point I was beyond being scared. It's hard to explain, but I didn't have the strength to be scared. I don't know why, but the panic subsided. Maybe it's a natural grace that allows us to live our final moments without excruciating fear.

Then came my miracle. Katie's roommate, who was much larger than I in height and weight, arrived. I managed one last weak "Help!" and she rushed into Katie's room. What happened next was surreal. David regressed, acting like a small child who had been scolded by his mother. He released me, grabbed his raincoat, and ran out the door half dressed. I was in a state of shock. I couldn't feel anything. I got up and pulled my clothes back on. I was paralyzed. Karen must have called campus security, because they arrived almost instantly, catching him as he tried to escape. Williamstown police also arrived within minutes and questioned me about what had happened. *Thank you, God. Now this is over. Just let me go back to my room and get away from all of this.*

David was indicted by a grand jury, but before the case went to trial, he was killed in a car accident. For years afterward, I couldn't walk into a dark room without feeling a sense of panic. I couldn't go to bed without checking underneath it and in the closet. When I finally lived alone in my first apartment, I got triple locks on the door. But after I was married, I was able to bury it deep enough that I never thought about that night.

My husband's assertion unnerved me. Was I unconsciously going through some cathartic exercise, trying to understand why a man would rape and possibly murder? Was I looking for some sort of closure in my own past, some sort of inner peace or sense of forgiveness? Had the college attack really had that much of a long-term effect on me?

I began to feel vulnerable again. I had nightmares. When I was alone in the house, I went through the bedrooms checking the closets. I was reliving the ordeal all over again—except this time it was worse, and I didn't know why.

I was not sure whether to tell Michael about the attack. I didn't want him to find out later and think that I had misled him. On the other hand, I was terrified to tell him. It would turn me into a victim. It would give him power.

The next time Michael called, I gathered up my courage and said, "When I was in college I was the victim of an assault and attempted rape. I don't think that has anything to do with why I am writing this story, but you should know. I don't want you to think that I have some ulterior motive."

There was an agonizing silence, but his reaction was considerate. "I'm sorry," he said. "You know that getting this story out is important to me, but if writing about this is too painful, you should stop. I've caused too much pain already. I don't want to be the cause of any more pain."

I assured him that he was not causing me any psychic pain (a lie), and that was the last time we ever spoke about it. I think knowing Michael actually helped me to get over the trauma once and for all. I realized that David had not hurt *me*; I was just a convenient object, something I later learned from talking to Michael. I didn't have to take it personally. David probably wouldn't have even recognized me if he ever saw me again. Perhaps more important, after the first six months, I wasn't afraid of Michael. If I could be comfortable talking with a serial killer and believe his remorse, I could stop being afraid.

11

CLERK'S OFFICE, NEW LONDON, CONNECTICUT
1996

I knew I might never meet the monster, but I had to face the horror he had caused, and it was important to do it by looking at evidence that had been presented in open court, to see what Michael feared having to sit through again.

To read the transcripts of the taped confessions and to look at the evidence in Michael's case, I went to the New London Judicial Department clerk's office and carefully sifted through the box of documents and photographs that survived the first trial. I knew that the crime scene photos were grisly—photographs of partially decomposed bodies, autopsy pictures, ligatures used by Michael to strangle the girls—but I needed to see the reality of the damage that he had done. I wasn't prepared for the impact that the evidence would have on me. I was overwhelmed by the sheer gruesomeness of seeing corpses and autopsy pictures. I thought of how a mother and father would have felt looking at these photos of their dead daughter, and I wondered if Michael had ever *really* looked at the pictures. I knew I had to look at them.

I was almost done with my article and I knew I could no longer avoid some of the hard questions I had to ask him. When he called a few nights later, Michael knew that I had carefully examined the evidence, and he asked if I had looked at the autopsy photos. "Did it look like they had been beaten up?"

"Yes. There were bruises." I couldn't tell what had caused all the bruises, but Wendy Baribeault had two black eyes. There were bruises on the face that looked like they were the result of punches.

"I don't remember hitting anybody. I can't believe I did that, but if it's in the pictures, I must have," he conceded reluctantly.

I realized that he was more upset about hitting the women than raping and killing them. He was whining. And in some odd way, he wanted sympathy. He wanted me to say, "Don't worry about it, Michael. You didn't know what you were doing. It was the monster, not you, hitting those women." He had struck a raw nerve. I exploded. "I really don't get you. You murdered them. What the hell could be worse than that? Believe me; I'll take a good punch any day over death." It was the first time I had actually screamed at him, and it startled me as much as it did Michael.

"I know it doesn't make sense," he admitted.

"You're being kind to yourself. It's totally insane."

"I know. I know; it's just, I was brought up to think that hitting a woman was wrong."

"And you were brought up to think that raping and killing was right?" I stopped because I was afraid he'd hang up on me—and because I realized that by dwelling on the hitting, Michael was avoiding the killing. Or maybe he couldn't tuck the act of hitting a woman neatly into his mental illness. He couldn't control the raping and killing, but on some level he thought he should be able to stop himself from hitting a woman.

I changed the subject to the taped confessions he made on the day of his arrest. Michael had always insisted that when he was making his confessions, Detective Michael Malchik, one of the arresting officers, had suggested to him that he might have killed the girls because he didn't want to go to jail. "They kept asking me this all day. It was mostly after the tape. I was with them for another twelve hours," he said. Michael insisted he never said he was trying to avoid jail time but that they talked about that motive only hypothetically.

"The problem with that," I said, "is that some of the things that you say aren't true are things that you actually said on the tape. In a lot of places you say, 'I raped them and got scared and tried to kill them.'"

Michael was surprised. "I haven't seen them in so long that I can't tell you what I said. The last time I heard the tape was eight years ago. So I don't remember, and I don't understand it. I was trying to understand why I did it back then. . . . I know that before those taped statements, they fed me some of that stuff. Why did I kill? I think if you listen to the tapes, it sounds more like that."

I told him that he had said it himself without any prompting.

"I don't know. Maybe that's what I thought back then. I don't believe it to be true, but you know, maybe that's what I said. They didn't believe me whatever I said. I don't know why I did it. That's why I said this other stuff." He was still trying to convince himself that the tapes were doctored in some way.

I read him one section: "I took her in the back and I raped her. She didn't really struggle or anything. I didn't know what to do because I had got in trouble before, and I killed her and I strangled her."

"Oh. . . . Well, if I said it, I'm not going to dispute it now. That's what I said. It's not true but . . ." Everything was a "yes, but." Yes he said it, *but* it wasn't true. I had questions about contradictions from statements of girlfriends as well as contradictions on the tapes. He had confessed that he and Tammy Williams had been making out, and then she wanted to stop. He said he got angry, lost control, raped, and murdered her. Why did he say that if it wasn't true?

"Because before when [Malchik and I] were discussing it, it made it sound better that they were doing something. In a way I was sort of blaming it on the victims. . . . That came four hours before the tape was ever turned on. . . . He just had to play me until I fuckin' said it. All right?" I could hear the fury in his voice, but we had a lot more to cover.

The bigger question for Michael to answer was why he killed Leslie Shelley. This murder couldn't be attributed to his mental illness. As Dr. Borden had explained, for all the others the murders had been the sexual climax of the rape. However, after he had achieved that when killing April Brunais, his sexual sadism should have been satisfied. He killed Leslie after he had killed April and even apologized to her before he killed her. This issue could not be avoided. I began gently. "I think there's only one of the murders which is really an issue, and that is Leslie Shelley. That's the hardest to explain. . . . On the tape you said you didn't rape her."

"Yeah, well there's some things about that that you don't know. I can't tell you. Well, actually, I can. Satti knows. She was sodomized."

"Why didn't you mention that before?"

"Because I had a problem with that. I had a problem with her being so small so I said all I did was kill her. It made me feel better and then afterwards, I didn't want it to come out because I didn't want the parents to know, and I didn't think Satti knew until I found out during our conferences. He asked me point blank at one of the conferences," Michael said. "See, I felt bad about that because she was the only one I sodomized. All the others were vaginal rapes. She was so small, and I just . . . I'll tell you some other time. I don't want to talk about it on the phone. She always bothered me. I don't know if it was because she was so small or the other." He seemed embarrassed to say "sodomized" again.

"You somehow think that sodomizing her is worse than vaginally raping her?" I was trying not to sound too incredulous, but controlling my reactions was getting more difficult.

"Yeah. I tried to rape her vaginally."

"But you're talking as if sodomy is worse than killing. How could that be worse than killing?" I asked.

"Huh? I don't know. I guess that's just the way I feel. I tried to do it vaginally and I couldn't penetrate her, and I raped her anally."

He had confounded me again, but now I was also angry. "In the grand scheme of things, compared to killing, this is nothing."

The phone cut off. I thought he had hung up on me until it rang again. "I thought you hung up on me. I was afraid it was because of what I said," I admitted.

"I won't get another fifteen minutes, just another eight minutes," he said curtly.

"Rape, whether vaginal or anal, is rape," I argued.

"It don't make any sense," he admitted, regressing into his farm-boy dialect. "I don't particularly want the parents to know. They think that she wasn't raped, and I'd prefer to keep it that way." He heaved a big sigh, apparently hoping that the conversation would end.

"You keep saying how important it is for you to prove your mental illness, but you pleaded guilty in Windham County to two murders. Why wasn't it important then?"

"Fred and Peter [his attorneys] wanted me to plead guilty. They were telling me back then I didn't have a defense anyway." It wasn't until after the trial that he became determined to prove that he wasn't faking a mental illness.

"They made me out to be such a big liar," he began. He said if he had pleaded guilty, he wouldn't have felt the need to prove he was mentally ill. "I thought the truth was going to come out at the trial, but it was just a big circus. All right? I gotta go."

We'd been corresponding and talking for more than six months at the time, but he had never been so mad, and I wasn't sure if he would ever call back again. When he made his weekly call to Ann a few days later, he told her he was "tired of talking to Martha." He knew Ann better than I did; he had trusted her for a decade. Perhaps he wanted to see if she would counsel him to stop contacting me, but she didn't. In fact, she told me what he had said.

He did, however, write me a long letter a few days later. He said he owed Malchik an apology because, "If I did in fact say that I killed the girls so that I wouldn't go back to prison—if that's on tape, then I can't deny it. I don't remember saying it that way. All this time I thought that Malchik had made it up and was lying, and now I find out that it was I who was lying to myself. I am sorry that I misled you and I'm sorry that I falsely accused Malchik."

He said he truly did not believe that he killed to avoid detection. But he admitted, "If I could make myself believe that I wouldn't kill again, then I can make myself believe anything. I know that I want to believe that the mental illness did the killing, not me. But maybe I'm just using that as an excuse. Maybe I'm hiding behind it because I'm afraid to face what I might truly be. Maybe I am the monster that Satti says I am. How am I supposed to know when I can't believe myself?" He told me to send Ann and Father John copies of the confessions and apologized for taking up my time.

The next time he called, he confounded me again. "Well, it hasn't been easy. These interviews seem to be getting harder and harder, and you ain't asked me no tough questions, neither." I thought he had hung up on me because I had pressed him too hard.

"So what should I have asked you?"

"I don't know," he said, whining like a little boy. "But you really haven't confronted me on anything. You ain't challenging me, accusing me of lying. . . . I think that's why the confessions bothered me so much. It's because I try to be open and honest, and then I find that I've been saying stuff that ain't what happened."

"In the last two weeks, I have called into question almost everything you have told me. I *have* been asking hard questions."

"I don't know. It just seems like you aren't calling me a liar."

Perhaps I wasn't yelling and screaming, but I had pressed him on a lot of tough subjects and shown him where there were contradictions in his story.

The next day, April 20, he wrote to me trying to explain his position. "The real issue boils down to just two simple facts. One, I raped and murdered eight women. Two, I am responsible for those actions and the consequences of those actions on the families of my victims." He said he often got so caught up in proving his mental illness that he forgot his responsibilities. He said he got so excited when I read the transcripts, interviewed his doctors, and acknowledged the lies and distortions in his case because he wanted the truth to be known that he was not evil but merely sick. "I don't want to be hated and despised—I don't want people cheering at my execution. I get concerned with how others perceive me. It is self-centeredness. But I have to fight the urge to protect how others perceive me because in my case it carries a dreadful cost. And in the end, which is more important: how others perceive you or how you perceive yourself?"

If he continued to try to prove his mental illness, he would run the risk of hurting the victims' families. "If I allowed [them to be hurt], it would affect how I perceive myself, for in my mind it would take me one step closer to being exactly the person Satti portrays me as being. Right now I have nothing left except who I am, and I can't let anyone take that away from me—even if it costs me in how I am perceived by others. I have to do what I believe is the right thing to do—even if it is misinterpreted, misunderstood, and/or unappreciated by others— to do anything less would be to betray who 'Michael Ross' really is (to betray myself). Ultimately, I guess that's what this whole thing is about—

being true to one's self and beliefs." In other words, trying to change how others perceived him wasn't worth the chance of doing more harm. "And ultimately how I perceive myself is far more important than how others perceive me. Am I making any sense?"

It remained hard for me to understand why anyone wouldn't want to fight for his life or fight to prove he was mentally ill. Perhaps there comes a point for all death row inmates when they give up because letting go of hope actually sets them free.

12

CORNELL
1980–1981

It took many telephone conversations and letters to unravel what had happened to Michael in college and for me to have the courage to ask him about the individual murders. Over the course of three years, I was able to piece it all together.

By his senior year, Michael was a day student and a night predator. Neither of these two personalities thought about the other. In Michael's mind, the day student was Michael Ross and the night predator was the monster. "As time went on, it was less me doing the stalking and more the monster within. I believe he was slowly beginning to gain control. In the beginning, when I was in charge, I worried about being recognized, but as he took control, that was no longer a concern. I know that this sounds crazy, but because I was becoming two people with two separate identities, it didn't matter if the 'stalker' was recognized because he wasn't me. On some level I believed that it wasn't me doing the stalking."

As the denial became greater, the monster became more real to Michael. "[The monster] didn't have much power at first, and only controlled for brief periods of time. That's why I was so confused after the first attacks. I didn't understand what had happened. He grew out of my fantasies. He drew power out of the fantasies as they became more and more violent. When the fantasies weren't enough to satiate his appetites, he drew off the stalking. The stalking made the fantasies more powerful and, in turn, fed him. But the big step was when the women were frightened during the stalking. Their fear fed him more than any fantasy could. I remember how delicious it felt, how it satisfied him to feel their fear when they realized that they were being followed." Soon he needed more, and he grabbed a woman. But the act of grabbing shocked Michael back to reality, and "he [the monster] lost his momentary control over me. I became frightened and confused, not understanding what I had done. Before that, it had been just a harmless game, a harmless way to feed a part of me that hungered. God, I was so stupid. I can see how the little bastard did it. And I let him because I didn't see the danger; I didn't see the potential harm."

Michael said that if he had faced the monster then, "I could have beaten him. But I pretended nothing was wrong. I did what I always did and pretended that if I ignored the problem, it would go away. It always comes back to my being a coward and not doing what I deep down inside knew had to be done." Michael saw himself as an inherently good person. He could not have stalked or attacked a woman or even had the dark thoughts that accompanied the stalking. The only way to explain what was happening to him was to bifurcate his personality into Michael and the monster.

Whether consciously or unconsciously, Michael was trying to relieve the conflicts within his mind through sadistic behavior. He went out to stalk to "relieve" the frustration he was feeling with his relationship to Betsy. His compartmentalization of the monster enabled him to go on living day-to-day. If he melded the two, either the monster would be completely unleashed or he would have to kill himself because he could not accept who he had become.

Dr. Berlin, who had prescribed Depo Lupron and Depo-Provera for

Michael, suggested that the monster was a metaphor. "He's not presenting it as the devil made me do it. . . . If somehow God could have allowed him to cut off the part of his brain that drove him to do this, then it could really allow his behavior to be a reflection of what his conscience and his intellect wanted, rather than the things that are pushing him that he can't control." In effect, Michael was describing his violent fantasies and actions as a cancer of the mind.

I wanted to ask Michael to describe one of these sexual fantasies, but at that point I did not have the courage.

During his senior year at Cornell, Michael became a teaching assistant for Professor George Conneman's course Farm Business Management; he worked late at night, sometimes past midnight. The new title provided him with a different twist to his fantasies; in his dream world, he was the teacher of a huge group of female students who wanted to have sex with him in hopes of a higher grade.

On the evening of May 7, 1981, Michael was attempting to grade papers but found it almost impossible to concentrate. He and Betsy had been fighting again, and he'd become increasingly aware of a growing sense of anxiety about their relationship. Now finally finished with his work, he was in his red Chevy Chevette on his way home to Betsy but was distracted by the attractive young woman walking alone. As Michael drove out of the parking lot near Rice Hall, he stopped to let her pass on the crosswalk. She was not a Cornell student, but a coed from another school visiting her boyfriend. He could think of nothing other than following her. As he headed home, he should have turned right but instead drove directly across the street and parked the car. Removing his glasses, he got out of the car and began to follow the unsuspecting woman until she got near the greenhouses about a hundred yards away. His heart pounding with the excitement and thrill of the chase, he grabbed her from behind and wrapped a shoelace around her neck. But the shoelace snapped, and he quickly shoved his hand over her mouth and dragged her through some bushes, then he threw her onto the ground. According to the woman's report to the police, he said, "Scream and I'll kill you." He forced her along a deserted path and then told her to lie down on her stomach. She says that is when "the rope" was removed from around her neck and that her wrists were tied behind her. "I had her take off her jeans, perform oral sex on me [as she knelt at his feet], and then I raped her." She reported to police that he exposed himself to her and said, "Now do this for me, like a good girl, and you won't be dead tomorrow. Suck." She said he pulled out before ejaculating and then raped her, reporting that the rape lasted less than thirty-five seconds.

Michael's version was similar but without the dialogue and time frame. He concurred that "the whole thing couldn't have lasted more than a couple of minutes." Afterward he ran back to his car and went home; the victim went for help and called the police.

After he had cleaned himself up, he "crawled into bed next to Betsy, who was already asleep." While Betsy had been peacefully asleep and safe in her bed, Michael had acted out the rage that he felt when fighting with her—on another woman who, to Michael, was not a real person. His objectification of his victims haunted him. He'd feel shame about what he'd done, but he "couldn't feel the proper remorse for my victims." When he talked to me about the women he killed, he continually lamented that they didn't seem real to him, that he couldn't feel any empathy toward them. He felt terrible shame for the grief he caused their families but felt nothing for them.

When he woke up the next morning, Michael was disgusted and ashamed, and he considered suicide. "From time to time, reality would force its way through my denial and I had to face what I had done. Most of the time, my denial was strong, but on occasion, reality would emerge and I would feel enormous guilt and suicidal urges." A few days after the rape, he went to the road bridge overlooking the gorge near Beebe Lake and considered ending it all. "I don't remember thinking of going to the bridge, just sort of finding myself there, looking into the gorge, and fighting an urge to jump." But it never went beyond an urge. Although he hated himself and what he had done, he could not bring himself to end his life—or to turn himself in. Instead, his denial became more effective and he "forgot" about what he had done.

Dr. Borden said, "The force of the sexual aggression fusion at that point broke the first taboo . . . rape." Up until that time, he had been a law-abiding citizen. "There was a conscience, primitive conscience based on parental harsh controls, but nevertheless, something holding him back, something keeping that rage, fused rage in check." Now it had disappeared.

D zung Ngoc Tu came to Cornell in the fall of 1980 to earn a graduate degree in agricultural economics. Vivacious and outgoing, the twenty-five-year-old was known for her spirit and her intellect. She spent her free time working as a Big Sister to local disadvantaged girls. She was pretty and petite, just four feet ten inches and ninety-five pounds. Born in Vietnam, she moved to Bethesda, Maryland, in the late 1960s. Tu took education very seriously; she graduated from Vassar College with honors in 1978 and came to Cornell after spending a year at the London School of Economics.

It was after midnight on the night of May 12, 1981, the last day of classes and only a few weeks before graduation. Tu had been working late in the Agriculture library and was going home that warm night when Michael Ross spotted her walking toward Beebe Lake after he had finished grading papers.

Until that night, Tu and Ross had never met, although she also worked as a teaching assistant in an office down the hall from where Michael worked. He followed her down a hill to the footbridge, a dimly lit and secluded area near the Pancake House. His pace quickened as he came up behind her and grabbed her, putting his hand over her mouth and dragging her out of sight behind a nearby building. His fingers squeezing tightly around the back of her neck, he forced her to take off her skirt. Making her kneel at his feet, he shoved his penis in her mouth, thrusting it hard to degrade her but pulling out to avoid an orgasm; then he pushed her onto the ground and made her take off her underwear, and then he raped her. He told Dr. Borden that he made the women remove their own underpants as an act of control. When the sexual attack was over, he instructed her to put her skirt back on. Then he had her roll over onto her stomach. Straddling her tiny back, he strangled her, squeezing the life out of her with his calloused hands. It was over in minutes. He pushed her body into Beebe Lake, only a few yards away, and ran to his car even though he wasn't sure if she was dead or unconscious. He went straight home to the apartment and found that Betsy had already gone to bed. Still not sated, he woke her up, insisting that they have sex.

A few days later, after a thunderstorm, Tu's body was found in the gorge below, about sixty yards downstream from the Triphammer Bridge on Thurston Avenue. Police first classified the death as an accident or suicide, but friends and classmates insisted that she had not been depressed or upset. Because the body had been in the water for several days, the cause of death was first listed as either a fractured skull or drowning, and a later autopsy report was sealed by police, who began to suspect foul play. Tu's boyfriend immediately hired an attorney. There weren't any witnesses, and due to the lack of physical evidence, no one suspected Michael Ross. Even if semen could have been collected after all that time in the water, this was long before the days of DNA testing.

Michael claims that the whole episode was surreal, as though he were watching a flickering old black-and-white movie, full of jump cuts and all spliced together with tape. He was there, and yet he was not a complete participant because of the dissociative state in which he "watched" himself rape and kill. These descriptions led Dr. Merikangas to later suggest that he suffered from depersonalization disorder, a dissociative pathology in which the sufferer feels disconnected from his own experience.

Yet even though he didn't feel like a participant in the action, he told me he felt what the monster felt, an orgasmic exhilaration from the brutal acts. It was not the oral sex or the rape per se that aroused him. It was the ritual of degrading the woman that gave him exquisite pleasure. His foreplay was the act of total domination. The ultimate climax was the murder. As Dr. Borden explained, "The sexual part, the sexual rape was pleasurable, gave him a sense of sexual release, but what really gave him a sense of his heart beating, adrenaline pumping, the sense of real power was when he was killing. And that in reality, the killing was much more powerful than the sexual part of it, and that's what was surprising to him."

In one sense, Michael had symbolically punished Betsy for the misery in his life. The oral sex represented her attack in Washington, her degradation. She was asking him to make choices he did not want to make, to take a job he didn't really want. He wanted to move home to Brooklyn, but she wanted none of that. He feared that he would lose her, so he wanted to kill her. Michael did not understand it at the time, but Dr. Borden suggested that when he strangled Tu, he was killing

Betsy and his mother and any other woman who would hurt or abandon him. When I first brought up the possibility, Michael was quiet. Even the thought of it shamed him. "I honestly don't know, but it's probably true."

The night after the murder, Michael went back to the bridge near the Pancake House. Although he was afraid to die, he felt he deserved to die. The only way he could stop himself from hurting anyone again was to jump. He couldn't face going to the police; admitting what he had done would have been too painful and humiliating. For more than an hour, he stood on the bridge staring into the blackness of the gorge. He convinced himself—as he had before and would do again—that he really wasn't a bad person and that he would never hurt anyone again. Up until college, Michael had lived a life in which everything was controlled. His mother ruled the roost. He had no social life because he either went to school or worked, and he took Ritalin to help him stay organized and less hyperactive. Everything had been about control. Those days were over.

The threat of losing Betsy had triggered a rage deep inside him. "He's going to lose her," said Dr. Borden. "He can't lose anybody. If he loses somebody, no matter what the reasons are, it triggers rage . . . and that rage becomes homicidal rage. It's primitive. It's not just rage in the ordinary sense. This is a very primitive homicidal, murderous rage." Dr. Borden explained that the rage had not gotten to this point with the first rape, but the closer he got to graduation, the more the relationship deteriorated, the worse the rage. He was about to be separated from Betsy, even lose her, and the rage inside him grew with every day. Dr. Cegalis said that Michael was "unable to contain the sexual aggressive impulses" that drove him to rape and murder. He said Michael's reactions were a kind of automatic "inexorable acting out of those impulses." Both doctors said that Michael was unable to control his impulses to rape and kill.

Michael graduated at the beginning of June 1981. He couldn't tell me what day of the week it was or who spoke at the graduation ceremony or even which members of his family attended. Those were insignificant details compared with the guilt and horror that were consuming his mind, but even what he described as all-consuming guilt was not enough to stop him. In the next three years, seven more innocent women would die before he was caught. He said the murders were more important than the raping. As Dr. Borden explained, "he really got off on the killing. That's what gave him a sense of absolute control. That's what gave him his release." Up until then he had been struggling not to act out on his inner torment. Even the fantasies were a subconscious attempt to keep his rage under control, but by graduation, he could no longer hold it in. Ironically, he needed a woman to keep him under control. "His mother was a rudder, a very strong rudder," said Dr. Borden. He resents it, but he needs it. When he is about to lose her, he's "like a barge full of nitroglycerin adrift without a rudder."

"This is a rare bird," explained Dr. Borden. "We are dealing with a homicidal maniac."

13

SOMERS, CONNECTICUT
WINTER 1997

Many of Michael's descriptions of the murders were devoid of the kind of detail that would help explain his obsession. There was no emotion or rage in his descriptions. I finally mustered the courage to ask him to try to describe his violent sexual fantasies. What made him get in the car and go out looking for prey? After he started stalking, raping, and murdering, his fantasies were primarily memories of his crimes, horrific scenes forged together. For the first several years, he could not or would not describe any of this on the phone or in person, but just before Christmas 1997, he sent me six chilling handwritten pages. They may or may not represent what was going on in his head at the time he raped and murdered or afterward, but at least they represent the sexual fantasies and urges that he had after he was incarcerated.

The fantasy is not easy to read. Even though I had known Michael for more than two years and had gotten past the serial killer label, it revolted me. But not revealing the monster would distort the story. After reading it, one can understand why he wanted to keep "the monster" separate from "Michael," why he had to keep him chained up deep inside his psyche. In his discussions with me, he had described the murders with clinical detachment and very little detail. That was the only way he allowed himself to remember them. The fantasy is filled with the rage that put him on death row. This is a glimpse of the torturous and abhorrent images that went through his mind as he committed his crimes.

I am outside. It is a beautiful day. It is mid-afternoon and the sun is out. It is not too warm—the air is very comfortable.

I see her. She is still 100 yards away, walking along the road. We are in some sort of a park. The area is wooded; the road is more of a trail than a street. We are alone. There are no houses, no people, no civilization in sight.

I am getting closer to her. She's small, a dirty-blond, young. She hasn't seen me yet. She has no idea of the danger she is in. I feel a sense of contempt because of this. I have locked on to her; she is my target, yet she is oblivious to this. This seems to anger me and I feel her arrogance. She thinks that she is strong, independent, and can handle herself. She is so foolish. She is not even aware that I am there, that she's going to die. She has no idea of the danger yet. My contempt for her ignorance continues to grow as I draw nearer.

I'm 100 feet from her now. She senses my presence for the first time, a strange ominous feeling that she can't explain. She looks over her shoulder and sees me. I see fear briefly flicker in her eyes. Then she makes her fatal mistake. She dismisses the fear. If she listened to her instinct, she would run and would probably survive. But she considers herself a rational, intelligent woman and dismisses the feeling as paranoia.

I know what she is thinking and it angers me further, feeding my ever-growing contempt for her. She has dismissed me. She has turned her back to me because I am of no consequence to her. She felt the fear for a second, but she rationalized it away. It's broad daylight, and I look harmless to her; I am of no consequence.

I'm getting much closer now. She looks over her shoulder again. Fear flickers again in her eyes, stronger this time. She tells herself that it is nothing, that she is being foolish—she can't see me as a possible threat. But she is feeling increasingly nervous and she doesn't understand why.

"You stupid, arrogant bitch," I'm thinking. With every step my anger and contempt for her grows. She is so stupid to not see the danger. Why doesn't she see that I'm going to kill her? Why has she dismissed me as no danger? I want to hurt her now. I want to show her that I'm not some impotent fool to be so lightly dismissed.

I'm within a few feet of her now and she looks at me once again. She doesn't know why, but she is afraid now. I can see it in her eyes. I can see her trying to fight it. She's still trying to rationalize the fear away. She's still trying to tell herself that she is being foolish. Her instincts are trying to warn her of the danger. But she's too arrogant to heed her instincts. She's too intelligent to allow herself to be ruled by fear. But the fear is there. She's just trying to deny it, to control it like she controls everything else in her life.

But she has no control. I want to show her that she has absolutely no control. I am full of anger, contempt, and rage. She is nothing but a foolish, petty, ignorant bitch. She must be taught to see the truth. I want to hurt her, but not too quickly. I want her to see and experience my control. I want her to regret her arrogance and acknowledge me. She's going to die. I know this, but I want her to understand why first.

I'm only a couple of feet away now and she's very nervous. I smile at her. That's all it takes to disarm her fear. A little smile and she feels relieved, and I am all the more enraged because of her stupidity. I do not understand how she could dismiss me so. She's dead and she doesn't even know it.

I reach out and grab her around the neck. My thumbs crisscross the back of her neck. My fingers sink into her soft neck. I feel her windpipe as I squeeze my fingers tighter.

Her eyes grow wide. My God they are so huge. It's like I can see into her soul. They are like huge saucers. Finally the danger is sinking in. Finally she acknowledges the fear. Finally she respects my power.

She tries to scream. A deep primal scream from a place she never knew existed but no sound comes forth, no sound can escape my grip.

I am dragging her toward a wooded area now. She stumbles along aside [sic] me. She can't breathe and she is in panic. She can't even think as I drag her along.

I see a small opening in the trees, a grassy area where the sun shines through the trees. And I throw her roughly to the ground. She gasps for air. She is lightheaded, dizzy, disoriented. She is confused. She doesn't understand. Her mind is racing, full of disjointed thoughts. Fear fills her body.

I stand over her, looking down at her, waiting impatiently for her to come to her senses. Strangely I know that she still doesn't understand. She looks at me and whimpers, begs me not to hurt her. I ask her if she wants to live. She does and she will do anything that I ask.

I tell her to take off her pants. She is afraid and hesitates as she realizes that I am going to rape her. I lean down and angrily grab her by the neck. She quickly complies to my demand. Strangely she feels a little better and tries to tell herself that it won't be that bad. I don't know how, but my contempt for her continues to grow. I pull her to her knees and unzip my pants, pulling out my penis. I see the disgust in her face as she realizes what I want. She tries to turn away and I slap her. She sees the rage, the anger and the hatred on my face and she complies taking my penis into her mouth. I grab her by the back of her head and force myself deep into her mouth. She struggles and gags but this just pleases me more, and I continue to drive myself into her mouth again and again.

I am growing more and more excited. Her disgust and revulsion feeds me. I'm afraid that I'm going to have an orgasm too soon. I'm not ready for it to end yet, so I pull myself out of her mouth.

I push her to the ground and vaginally rape her. She just lies there allowing me to penetrate her. She thinks that it will be over soon and that I will let her go. I hate her ignorance. I hate her lack of total incapacitating fear. I want to hurt her more. I roll her over and enter her anally. I drive myself into her hard and deep doing everything possible to hurt her. Her cries of pain feed me. Her feelings of humiliation and helplessness please me to no end. The more she is degraded, the more pleasure I feel.

Still it is not enough. She must know her complete and utter defeat. She is allowing me to degrade her because she thinks she will live. She must know the truth that she has allowed all this for nothing.

I reach up and wrap my hands around the soft flesh of her neck and begin to squeeze. I am very excited now, fighting off the urge to complete my orgasm. I want it to last. I want to enjoy every last possible second. She begins to struggle now. I drive my penis deeper, harder into her and I squeeze my fingers harder around her neck. She finally understands. She finally knows that she is going to die. It is the ultimate degradation. She is mine completely, undeniable, and irrevocably. My victory is complete.

My orgasm begins. The feeling is indescribable, the power undeniable. I want it to last forever. Time stops; nothing matters. It has a narcotic quality. There is no feeling more powerful more pleasurable in the world. I try to hang on to it.

I slowly come back to the reality of my cell. I close my eyes and try to sleep, trying to savor the feelings while they last. I want to sleep now, before I start to think about the fantasy that I have just lived. If I can sleep now I won't feel the disgust until later. The disgust and self-hatred will come. It always does, but for right now I am content.

At the end of the pages, Michael wrote, "I have just re-read what I have written. It seems empty, hollow. I am unable to convey the power of the feelings and emotions. I may try again, but not for a while yet."

He never did try again—or at least he never told me that he did, and I certainly never requested that he try. I realized that I had asked him to temporarily unleash the monster. He couldn't describe it without experiencing his nightmare.

As Dr. Borden had explained to me, he felt emasculated by his mother and other women, and the violence was his way of lashing back. The fantasy illuminates the integral link between the stalking, raping, and murdering. It also shows his need for control and his need to assert his manhood.

I still find it hard to believe that the man I knew could have such noxious thoughts. More than anything else, reading those pages made me understand the difference between Michael and the monster. I was now convinced that he experienced two separate realities, because I didn't know the man who had written those six pages.

14

RALEIGH, NORTH CAROLINA
JUNE 1981–JANUARY 1982

The day after graduation from Cornell, Michael headed for his new job in Louisburg, North Carolina. He started work at Cargill as a production management trainee the following Monday in the egg-processing plant. On the weekend, he looked for a place to live and rented a small trailer about ten minutes outside of town on the road to Raleigh. The move did nothing to calm his obsessions. He was in an unknown environment, feeling cut off from his family and fiancée. If anything, his frustration fueled his urges. "I began stalking the day I got to Louisburg—even before moving into my trailer—and soon I began to make regular trips to Raleigh on stalking excursions."

Michael's job was similar to his job on the family farm in Connecticut; he oversaw the management of chicken farms. The eggs that came into the processing plant were from contract farmers who cared for the birds and collected the eggs, but Cargill owned the birds. The eggs were sent to the plant in Louisburg to be washed, graded, packed, and sold to customers. Each of the farms had about fifty thousand birds, and Michael was responsible for overseeing ten farms.

Lonely, he bought Betsy a round-trip ticket to come visit him one weekend in August 1981. Because she was able to finish Cornell in three years, she was a senior and starting to think about her upcoming job search. The weekend went badly. Michael felt emasculated by her career ambitions and still clung to the hope that Betsy's priorities might shift in his favor. "We had a big-time fight. . . . I thought that if she was to be my wife, my career came first, and she would go wherever I was assigned."

Unprompted, Michael interrupted his telling of the story to tell me, "Don't say it, Martha. I know what you're thinking. I know that it's sexist."

Betsy's attitude made Michael feel worthless. He didn't want to admit to her that he knew she could make more money than he. "We fought, and we both felt terrible at the airport when she left." Nothing had been settled, and he cried as she boarded the plane. "I knew that I was losing her, and I didn't know how to deal with it," Michael admitted. Dr. Borden told me he could not deal with rejection and separation. He testified that Michael "couldn't be alone. . . . He would get restless and have to go out and he would drive. In his car driving, he got into fantasies. . . . He was a James Bond character and he was driving along and there was a kind of cat and mouse with the enemy." Betsy's visit had upset him, so he went out stalking after he dropped her off at the airport.

"Martha, I know this is going to make you angry," Michael cautioned when he told me about this attack. I had two toddlers at the time. By the time he was telling me this story, I could predict Michael's reaction to things I said, and he could predict mine as well. He knew that I would tell him his attitude toward Betsy was sexist and that I'd be horrified at his trying to kill a woman in front of her child. His awareness of my inner thoughts made me uncomfortable, but I had to come to grips with the fact that he was getting to know me as well as some of my friends knew me. Whether I liked it or not, he could also predict my reactions.

On his way home from the airport in Rolesville on August 25, 1981, Michael attacked another woman. He was prowling around when he spotted Carol (not her real name) leaving the local post office, pushing her seven-month-old baby in a stroller. As she did almost every day, she walked the quarter mile back to her house, unaware that she was being followed. When she got home, she noticed a man watching her from across the street but assumed it was just a new neighbor.

Her porch needed sweeping, so she went inside to get a broom. Then she picked up her baby and went around to the backyard, but before she got there a man, whom she identified as Michael Ross more than three years later, came up behind her and wrapped a belt around her neck. In the struggle, they knocked over the baby stroller and the baby started screaming. Angry, Michael started punching Carol and threw her on the ground.

She said he told her, "If you don't do what I want, I'll smash the baby's head against the house," which was made of brick. Carol pleaded with him to leave the baby alone and tried to cooperate. She said he made her lie on the ground and pulled her skirt up over her head, then went to get the baby and said, "If you look up, I'll kill the baby." He dragged her into a field using the belt around her neck and carried the baby.

Desperate, she cried, "If you believe in Jesus, you wouldn't do this."

"I don't want to hear that shit," he snarled.

She doesn't remember much about what happened next, because she was repeatedly punched until she was nearly unconscious. She was nude but couldn't remember if he took off her clothes or if he made her do it. All she knew was that he made her perform oral sex on him and kept saying, "Do it hard." She made no mention of a rape in her statement.

Michael admitted that the baby kept trying to crawl to her mother, but Michael kept ordering Carol to "Get the baby away." He ejaculated into her mouth and told her to swallow it. She remembered that he made her lie on her stomach and then strangled her from behind with the belt. Two hours later, she came to and crawled to a neighbor's house for help.

Michael's version was much less graphic than the victim's report, perhaps because his denial allowed him to forget a lot of things or because he just couldn't admit the brutality of what he did. In his version, there was vaginal rape instead of oral sex. "I raped and strangled her and left the mother for dead, with the baby at her side. The baby was trying to suckle—what I thought to be—her mother's dead breast." Michael was never prosecuted for this crime, in part because the woman didn't want to go through a trial or participate in his murder trial, but after his arrest, she did identify him from a photo.

It is impossible to be sure how many times Michael stalked women or how many he raped. He couldn't even estimate the number of times he stalked—although he claimed to remember all the rapes. He insisted that there were no other murders than the eight to which he confessed.

A few weeks after Betsy's visit, Michael was required to attend a monthlong management seminar, mostly at the corporate office in Minneapolis but including a week in Illinois visiting various Cargill companies. The first night in Illinois, his coworkers planted themselves in the motel, eager to drink beer and watch a football game. But Michael was restless. He told everyone that he was going to find a local bar. "But I was on the prowl," he admitted to me.

It didn't take long before he saw a fifteen-year-old girl walking along the road. About seven o'clock, Priscilla (not her real name) says she decided to walk three blocks to a nearby motel to buy a pack of cigarettes. On her way to the motel, she became suspicious when a car passed her three or four times. While she was inside the motel, she noticed that the same car was parked outside, and the driver was staring at her through the window. She left the motel and went home along the same well-lit path. Michael said he "parked the car on a side road and grabbed her near a wooded area and dragged her into the woods."

Priscilla gave the police much more detail about what had happened than Michael gave me. Her statement reveals what Michael's ritualized killings might actually have been like—as opposed to what he could or could not remember. She saw Michael coming toward her, trying to hide behind telephone poles as he wove back and forth. As he passed her, he grabbed her from behind and put both arms around her throat and told her not to say anything. "I'm not going to hurt you; just give me your money." She screamed, but he put his hand over her mouth, put a knife to her throat, and pulled her into the woods. Initially, he threw her on the ground, but then he stood her up. Thinking that he wanted the money, she gave him the two dollars she had in her pocket, but instead of taking it and leaving, he walked her deeper into the woods—all the time seeming nervous. Finally he threw her down to the ground again and stuffed his handkerchief into her mouth as she lay on her stomach. He took her coat off and made her put it on backward; then he took his belt off and made it into a loop, putting it around her neck to keep control of her. She says he began to rub her ankles, an odd detail that no one else reported and he didn't remember. After a while, he rolled her over onto her back and sat on her, keeping the belt tight around her neck.

She began to worry that he was about to hurt her or rape her, but then she heard police searching in the woods, responding to a neighbor who reported her initial screams. Scared, Michael jumped up and ran. "I could have raped her but just kept her quiet while I tried to make sense of what was going on. When I saw the police car, I ran off, but I don't think I would have hurt her even if the police didn't come." He claimed that was all he could remember—or at least allowed himself to remember.

When the police were driving Priscilla home, she spotted his rental car parked along the road. The police waited for him and arrested him when he returned on foot to pick it up. The attack lasted less than fifteen minutes, but it traumatized Priscilla so much that she quit high school and went into seclusion. That was the last report of her in the police record.

This was the first time that Michael had been caught and arrested. He was not only scared of what would happen to him legally, but also ashamed when he had to call his parents to get them to bail him out of jail. He was also terrified that someone would connect him to the murder and rapes at Cornell. On the advice of a lawyer, he pleaded guilty and was sentenced to two years' probation for unlawful restraint. After resigning from Cargill, he returned to Connecticut to try to put his life together, again convincing himself that he could stop. He was in so much denial that he actually thought that Betsy would never find out about the arrest. He never told her, but he later discovered that his mother made sure she knew. He believed Pat wanted his relationship to fall apart because her own marriage was a failure. Or maybe, as Betsy had tried to tell him over and over again, Pat was jealous of Betsy and wanted her out of Michael's life because of the control she had over him.

His parents were in the midst of the divorce, and he lived with his mother and worked for his father. All day he listened to his father rant about his mother, and all night his mother bad-mouthed his father. He was miserable, but he had no other option at the time. Michael and his mother were on bad terms because earlier that year she had tried to trick him into signing over his 10 percent of the farm to her in order to gain leverage in her divorce. She had flown down to North Carolina "to visit" for twenty-four hours and told Michael that she was offering to take his shares because the farm was losing money, and she didn't want him to be left with debt now that he was about to get married. He considered going along with her request until he went home and his grandfather told him that the business was not in danger and was still profitable. Pat was angry because Michael didn't sign over the shares, and Dan was upset because Pat had told him that Michael had given her his 10 percent. The future of the farm added even more pressure and uncertainty to Michael's precarious mental state. He later told psychiatrists that his mother's threatening the farm was unforgivable.

He told Dr. Zonana during the 1985 psychiatric evaluation, done at the request of Michael's lawyers, that what upset him most was that his mother was going out with other men when he lived with her. He admitted that Dan was also seeing other women, but somehow in his mind there was a difference. Pat would not come home for a couple of days, and he immediately judged her and assumed she was "sleeping around." He couldn't explain why he thought it was wrong if his mother was having sexual relationships with other men, but that he wasn't upset with his father's dating. He never asked either of them about their relationships with other people. "It don't make sense. I was for equal rights and all that, but it just seemed wrong to me."

Michael and Betsy's relationship became even more strained when Betsy came to visit him in Brooklyn between Christmas and New Year's 1981–1982. Betsy knew about the arrest but said nothing. Instead she told him that she wanted to postpone their June wedding indefinitely. That was more than he could take. Everything that had kept him together was now gone. Even if he didn't want to admit it, he knew that he and Betsy would never marry, and the rage inside him grew until once again he could no longer hold it in.

15

CONNECTICUT
JANUARY 1982–JUNE 1984

Seventeen-year-old Tammy Williams was a high-school dropout, a "street kid," according to the missing person report that was filed after her disappearance. Originally from the area, she had lived with her mother, Norma Deems, in Honolulu, Hawaii, but moved back to live with her father and stepmother in Brooklyn when she was thirteen. According to the police report, "her father did not take any steps to control her and let her do as she pleased; if she did not attend school, he didn't force her; at times she remained away from home for long periods of time, but would notify her parents of her well-being." She didn't have a criminal record other than an arrest for disturbing the peace when she was fighting with another girl. She stayed out of trouble but did what she wanted.

During the holidays in the fall of 1981, Tammy had been hired by King's Department Store in Danville to work part-time in the camera department. Apparently she had finally found something that she enjoyed; she "showed promise," according to her supervisor. To her friends, she seemed happy that she had found a job that she liked.

Tammy spent the night on a friend's couch and then stopped to see her boyfriend, Andy Willett, at his house on Dyer Street in Danielson, Connecticut, at about 9:00 A.M. on January 5, 1982. He was twenty years old, and they had been dating for a year. According to Willett, they chatted for about an hour, and then Tammy left to walk to her apartment on Prince Hill Road. Several people saw her on the way home, including two friends who talked to her when she dropped in at the Brooklyn Bowling Alley. They told police that "she was in a good mood" and told them she had to work that evening and left.

Sometime around 11:00 A.M., as Tammy was walking along Route 6 in Brooklyn, Michael Ross spotted her. He was driving to the satellite farm to prepare it for a batch of baby chicks that were to arrive soon. When he saw Tammy—whom he said he didn't know even though they lived about a mile apart—Ross pulled off the road behind her. A school bus driver who knew her reported that she saw Tammy walking west on Route 6 and that a white male was following her. Michael also recognized the school bus driver and later worried that she would identify him. Another witness said she saw a white male running through the fields toward Tammy. A third witness driving by a little later reported to police that he had seen Tammy "tussling with a white male, with dark hair, wearing a hip-length coat, dark in color." The man had his arm around Tammy's neck, "as if they were playfully wrestling." But there was nothing playful in the grasp, and Tammy's five feet two inches and 100 pounds were no match for Michael's six feet one inch and 165 pounds.

Michael's report of what happened next is sketchy. "I grabbed her from behind and dragged her into the woods. I brought her to my car, bound her hands and drove her about a mile away to a deserted area of South Street where I could pull my car off the road and not be seen." Once he was sure he was out of sight, he took her out of the car and dragged her even deeper into the woods, making sure that no passersby could see them. Then he began what had become his ritual. He forced her to undress, made her perform oral sex on him while on her knees, and raped her. Then he turned her over on her stomach and straddled her as he strangled her.

He stuffed Tammy's body into the trunk of his car and drove around looking for a place to dispose of the corpse. Although Michael's descriptions of all the killings sound like those of an observer, suggesting a dissociative state, once the killing was over, he became aware of what he had done and always panicked that he would be caught. He thought that moving and then hiding or burying the bodies would protect him from being caught because no one would know if they were alive or dead.

Finally he settled on an area east of Church Street in Brooklyn and buried her body in a swampy area under mud, grass, and sticks, according to his confession and confirmed in what he told me. He claimed he didn't remember much more about the incident.

Before noon, Charles Sherrill of Danielson spotted Tammy's purse lying by the side of the road as he was driving by and turned it in to the police. For the next several days, firemen, policemen, dogs, and two helicopters searched all over Brooklyn but failed to turn up a trace of Tammy Williams. At times there were hundreds of volunteers looking for her. With no motive or suspect, the search was called off, and the case went cold. Although foul play was suspected, no one knew her fate until Michael led investigators to her grave site on June 29, 1984, the day after he was arrested and confessed to her killing.

Michael had been scared and stayed away from the area for a week or two. After the search had been called off, however, he couldn't resist the urge to return to the burial site. As he had with Charlie Brown, he periodically stopped by to stare at the slight mound of the grave, which searchers had walked right by. "I could pull my car off the road where it couldn't be seen by people driving by," he wrote to me. "I would feel comfortable enough to stay for a while—an hour or so usually or longer. I didn't do anything weird like masturbate. I just sat there on the stone wall where I could see the mound. I never actually went right up to her, but I had to get close enough to actually see where she was. I don't know why I went back. It was stupid. It doesn't make sense. I just had this need to go to her, to be with her, and I would feel terrible the whole time. I wouldn't relive the event. I would do that at home when I would masturbate to a fantasy reenactment of what I did. I just sat there and felt bad."

Once he was off probation, Michael needed a job, and his mother used her "connections" to get him an interview with Croton Egg Farms in Croton, Ohio. A week before he was to start his new job, he drove unannounced to Cornell to visit Betsy. He was waiting for her at her apartment when she came home with another man, a fraternity brother of Michael's. "It was awkward," Michael remembered. "He left at her request. I thought something was odd, but she told me I was being foolish, and he was just a friend. I reluctantly believed her because I *wanted* to believe her." Betsy remained irritated the whole weekend that he hadn't called in advance. "We had a rather tense weekend together, and I was upset when I left."

He still held on to the hope that they would work things out and get married. "I don't know. It was crazy. I was in denial that it was over between us. Thinking back on it, it seems ridiculous that I would go there unannounced." Even years later, he was embarrassed by his naïveté.

Monday morning, Michael started the drive back to Connecticut but was still upset about the other man. Instead of calming down during the long drive, his anxiety increased. He saw a girl hitchhiking along the road in front of a high school.

According to local newspaper reports about her death, Paula Perrera was a good student and loved to read. Her high-school friends described her as "spunky" and said that "everybody loved her." The family had moved from New Jersey when she was in elementary school. Paula lived with her single mother and siblings in a trailer at the Valley View Mobile Home Park in Middletown, New York. All her friends knew that her dysfunctional family life was strained, so she spent as much time as possible at her friends' homes. Her friends said that when she visited their happy, two-parent homes, she would say, "I never knew people had lives like this." She never complained, but apparently the stress of an unhappy home became too much for her; she tried to commit suicide by swallowing pills in October 1981 and was nicknamed "Tylenol" by teasing classmates.

Paula liked to ride her bike along Route 211 or hitchhike into town or to one of her friends' houses. Her friends begged her not to hitchhike, but she kept telling them that only nice people picked her up. On March 1, 1982, she left school early because she didn't feel well. Her intention was to go to her boyfriend's house a few miles from school—but she never made it.

Of all the murders, Michael said he was "fuzziest" about this one, perhaps because it was so far from where he lived that he didn't see reports of it in the newspapers. Reading the news stories may have helped him remember what had happened during the other murders. At the time of his arrest, Michael admitted to all the Connecticut murders but denied for twenty years that he had killed anyone else.

He said that once he had "denied there were more bodies," he was embarrassed to admit that he had lied. However, once he made the decision to forgo another trial and accept death, he felt he should make a full confession.

"I was in denial for a long time about this murder. I remember that I saw her hitchhiking," he told me. "I drove past her, turned around, and then picked her up. She gave me directions, which I followed until I got to pull off in a deserted area. I dragged her out of the car, forced her to undress, perform oral sex on me, raped her and strangled her and got back in the car and drove home."

About a week later, on his way to his new job, he drove past the site where he had killed Paula—although he didn't know her name and wouldn't until nearly two decades later when he officially confessed to the crime to New York police. "I did not go back to the actual site like I did with the others. I wanted to but was afraid of being seen in the area." He kept driving to his new job at Croton Egg Farms as an assistant complex manager in charge of forty workers and 1.2 million egg layers. Donald Harvey, a truck driver at Croton, told police that Michael was "belligerent and a know-it-all at work." He also kept odd hours, sometimes coming and going late at night. Harvey said, "Ross had no friends."

It was during his time in Ohio that Betsy told him that she didn't wear the engagement ring anymore because if she did, no one would ask her to dance at parties. He knew his relationship with her was over, but he still couldn't admit it to himself. His obsessive, sadistic behaviors became more frequent. He began driving around almost every night, looking for women. On April 26, 1982, Michael spotted a woman leaving a Laundromat in Johnstown, Ohio, at about 10:30 P.M. and followed her home. Sharon (not her real name) was a police officer with the Columbus police department. She was driving her car and said she "thought she saw a small red car following her" but was not positive. She arrived home at about eleven thirty to an empty house because her husband was working.

Instead of trying to grab her when she got out of her car or to break into her house, Michael went through an elaborate charade of knocking on her front door and pretending that he had car trouble. He even told her his real name when he asked to use her phone, pretending to call someone but actually dialing his own apartment. He told her that there was no answer and asked to borrow a flashlight to "look under the hood." According to Michael, she was in the kitchen cutting up vegetables when he came back. She says he asked for a phone book and to use the phone again. When she returned with the phone book, he had put a glove on his right hand. He grabbed her around the neck and threw her to the floor, dazing her when her head hit. The police report says that he "pinned her arms back and had his leg over her as they wrestled on the floor." He punched her in the face over and over, perhaps as many as ten times. She said that "the first two punches hurt considerably and then it went numb." He was choking her with one hand and punching her with another. She felt herself about to pass out but pulled one arm free and reached up and yanked his hair as hard as she could, and with that he let her go. Sharon got up, but he lunged at her, and they fell on a stone fireplace with Michael on top of her, knocking the wind out of her. Surprisingly, he got up and ran, and she ran after him. When she reached the road, they stared at each other for a moment before she ran back to the house to get her gun, but by that time he had driven off in his car.

Michael's version was much different. He said he grabbed her, but after a brief struggle, he somehow lost the urge to rape and kill her. I wondered if this was an attack in which he had been in control the entire time, which was something he would never admit. It would contradict his sadistic compulsion. But if that was the case, it would explain his ability to stop and run. Alternatively, he may have stopped because she was one of the few women who fought him so vigorously. Either she ruined his fantasy of the woman who submits in fear, or he was afraid that she would be able to fight him off. It's a mystery to which Michael either didn't know the answer or refused to give it. "She claims to have fought me off, but *I* stopped. I became confused and not sure about what was happening and just wanted her to be quiet and stop struggling."

A few days later, police came to Michael's office and said a woman had been attacked by someone using his name and asked if he had any idea who would do such a thing. Michael gave them a list of people who had been recently fired. A few days after that the police showed up at his apartment and asked him to step out onto the front porch. The woman was in the police car and looked to see if she could identify him. When the police left, he assumed she had not recognized him, but he was arrested at work the next morning. After his sister Donna bailed him out, he returned to Connecticut to await trial.

The Ross family didn't talk about things, so Michael just went back to work and quietly waited for his day in court. This time Michael got an apartment on South Street in Brooklyn. As a condition of his release on bail, he had to go into therapy, so he began to work with Dr. Raymond W. DuCharme, PhD, head of the Learning Clinic in town. His relationship with Betsy was all but over, but when she came down to visit, she went to see Dr. DuCharme as well. "I'm not sure what the purpose was. Our relationship was over, but maybe I couldn't admit it to myself then." However, Dr. DuCharme's report reveals that in March 1982, Betsy had seen a counselor "in a state near suicide." Michael not only was unable to admit that the relationship was over, but also was unable to see what it was doing to Betsy.

According to Dr. DuCharme's report, "Michael's purpose as he perceived his reason for calling me was to understand and unroll the motivation of his behavior, associated with the assault on a young woman in Illinois and the assault on the woman related to his pending case in Ohio." His conclusion, after working with Michael for several months, was that Michael "did not appear mentally ill." Dr. DuCharme attributed the attacks to Michael's poor coping skills and the pressures of work, the disintegration of his relationship with his fiancée, and his parents' pending divorce. He noted Michael's anger toward his mother for trying to manipulate him to give her his stock and control the family business. He also noted that Michael could not accept his mother's relationship with other men. DuCharme suggested counseling, community service, college courses, and physical exercise. "In my judgment, if Michael had been involved in counseling after the first incident, there would have been a substantially lessened probability of a second incident," he concluded. "Michael's prognosis of benefiting from counseling is within a positive range of expected outcome."

Michael was very critical of the treatment. "I went to DuCharme because my family had a relationship with him, but he was a learning specialist. The first time I went to see him, he said something like, 'I can't deal with anything violent or sexual.'" Maybe Dr. DuCharme was warning Michael that he had no expertise in that area, but to Michael it meant that violent sexual fantasies were so revolting that even a psychologist could not talk about them because he was "the scum of the earth." Michael continually tried to blame Dr. DuCharme for not stopping him from more killing. However, after he was arrested, Michael told another psychiatrist that he enjoyed his sessions with Dr. DuCharme at first and that he attributed the break in his killing spree to his work with him. He felt the one-on-one therapy sessions were helping him but soured on the treatment when Dr. DuCharme wanted him to use biofeedback machines to relieve his stress.

Biofeedback became very popular in the 1960s to treat conditions like migraines, stress, high blood pressure, and even paralysis. The machines monitor heart rate or temperature or brain waves. Patients learn relaxation exercises that help to control things that trigger their conditions. The procedure became less popular by the 1990s because there was no empirical evidence that some types of feedback were effective, but biofeedback is still successfully used today. Michael later told Dr. Cegalis, a defense psychologist, that he gave up his treatment with Dr. DuCharme because he felt his doctor was "more interested in biofeedback and in his machines than in hearing about and treating his personal difficulties."

I tried to interview Dr. DuCharme in 1996 and again in 2012 to let him respond to Michael's criticisms. Michael even wrote him in 1996, giving permission for him to talk to me. However, when his office finally responded to my requests via telephone and e-mail, I was told he could not speak to me "in regards to Michael Ross because of confidentiality." No other doctor refused to speak with me. My assumption was that Du-Charme did not want to have to defend his treatment of Michael or his misdiagnosis.

Betsy graduated from Cornell in late May 1982 and specifically asked Michael *not* to come to the graduation. They had once planned to get married the weekend after her graduation. Instead, she was traveling cross-country with another man on a motorcycle. It infuriated Michael. What also infuriated him, according to a family member's statement to police, was that his mother refused to go with him to Ohio for the trial and suggested that Dan go instead. It was one of the few indications that Michael was still dependent on his mother. But his anger toward her was growing. He wrote her a ten-page "nasty" letter. "It was all the things I wanted to tell her. I really told her off, but at the end I said 'that's how I feel now, but maybe I'll feel differently in a couple of years.'" Just before he was to return to Ohio for the trial, he killed his fourth victim.

Debra Smith Taylor was living with her parents in June 1982. Her marriage of a year and a half had been stormy. Her husband, James, was possessive and suspicious that she was seeing other men, so when they were together, they were often quarreling—and often drinking. She was very petite at four feet eleven inches. According to what James told police, she had a serious operation in April and in June weighed less than eighty-six pounds.

On June 15, 1982, Debbie told her mother that she was going out for a drive, not mentioning that James would be with her, because she knew her mother might object. According to what James told the police, they drove around all day, drinking beer and talking. At one point they went into Rhode Island, took a walk on the beach, and then returned to Connecticut to continue to bar-hop. They ran out of gas in a remote area of Danielson, Connecticut. A trooper picked them up and took them to a gas station, but he couldn't take them back to the car because he had been summoned on a police matter.

Debbie began quarrelling with her husband. Angry and drunk, James hit her, threw the gas can into a ditch, and then began hitchhiking in the opposite direction. James later told police that he didn't think she would hitchhike, "but that if she was offered a ride and a drink, she would accept, especially if she had been drinking."

Debbie kept walking but never made it to her car because Michael Ross stopped, agreeing to give her a ride to Jewett City. He had been out on the prowl, unable to control his urges to go "on a hunt." He picked up Debbie and took her to a remote cornfield in Canterbury. "In my statement to the police, I said we started to make out but she stopped and I got angry—that is not true." He explained that after his arrest, he had taken Malchik's suggestion that there must be a reason for his killing. Somehow in his mind, if Debbie had rebuffed his advances, raping and killing her was more justified. He told me later that when he stopped and told her to get out of the car, she was very cooperative and did whatever she was told. He drove to an area he knew well, near the satellite farm where chicks were raised, far from anywhere that a passing motorist would notice them. He ordered her to take off her clothes, and perform oral sex on him, and then he raped her. It was the same rundown he gave of all the murders. "Her only concern was that she get home in time to wake up her younger brother for school. She never made it because I strangled her instead. I put the body in the car and drove to a more remote location on the farm and put the body in a shallow streambed under some brush." Again, he visited this location several times after the murder. He had hidden the body far enough off the main road that he felt secure in visiting the site and staying as long as he could while he stared at her remains.

Debra was reported missing two days later. James Taylor, her husband, immediately became a suspect because of their troubled marriage. Debra's brother, James Smith, told police he was sure that his brother-in-law had killed his sister. Debra's friends also suspected James. Although he insisted he was innocent, he didn't help his case with comments he made around town. When asked if his wife had been found, he said, "No, it will take a bulldozer to find her." Finally James offered to take a polygraph test. According to police reports, the tests confirmed that he was telling the truth about not knowing what happened to his wife.

Eventually hunters found Debra's remains on October 30, 1982. The location of the remains brought suspicion on some of the employees of Eggs, Inc. and should have made authorities wonder if Michael, who now had a record as a sex offender, was involved. The site was very close to an area known as Gluck's fields where Eggs, Inc. dumped two loads of chicken manure every day. A neighbor told police that the only people who frequented the area on a regular basis were from the Ross farm. On November 3, officers interviewed Dan Ross about whether he ever was in the area and saw anything suspicious. Dan responded that two of his employees went up every day to dump the chicken manure, so the officers interviewed the two workers, who both said they often saw people in the area, but usually they were either hunters or people who didn't arouse any suspicion by their behavior. Neighbors said that the only other people whom they noticed were kids having keg parties or hippies. Michael was worried that the police or his family would "put two and two together and suspect me." But no one did—or at least admitted to it. No one connected the dots, Michael believed, because he wasn't in town when the body was found; he was serving time in Ohio for the attack against Sharon.

The more he told me about his crimes, the more I saw patterns. Eventually I had to question him about the similarities.

"Did you have a ritual way of killing your victims?"

"I don't know. It was sort of automatic. I wasn't thinking 'do this or do that.'"

"Why did you flip them on their stomach and straddle them?"

"Maybe to get a better grip on them and make the killing go faster. I told you I didn't think about it. It just happened."

"But you could have straddled them from the front after you raped them."

"Then they could fight me," he said.

"So you were thinking about that?"

"Not that I remember."

"Do you think it was because you didn't want to see their faces as you killed them?"

He hesitated. "I really don't remember, and what difference does it make now? I killed them. Okay?" By this time I could tell he was angry at me for pressing him. "I guess that may have been part of it, but I don't really know. I don't remember thinking about it. It don't matter now. Okay? Can we drop it?"

"After one more question. Do you think you were symbolically kill-ing Betsy when you killed the girls?

After a few minutes of silence, I asked, "Well, do I get an answer or not?"

"Not. I don't know. Okay?"

It was odd, because when he described his stalking and the oral sex, he admitted that he was acting out Betsy's nightmare. I could only guess that he had experienced the urge to strangle her and was ashamed of admitting it when he was talking to me. He later admitted to me that he had felt violent urges to hurt Betsy, but that he had actually hurt her only once or twice when he had been drinking.

Betsy showed up in Brooklyn for Michael's birthday on July 26, but not to celebrate with him. She only wanted to return the engage-ment ring, making their breakup official. "I think she thought she was being kind by doing it in person, but seeing her only made me feel worse," he told me. A few days later, he was sentenced to six months in prison for the Ohio attack, but he was released for good behavior after four months and returned to Brooklyn in time for Christmas. He lived with his father briefly until he found an apartment.

Perhaps jail had sobered him—at least for a while. But on May 23, 1983, after taking a date home, he raped another woman in Moosup. Margaret (not her real name) said she pulled out "a buck knife" that she carried and threatened him with it when he grabbed her. She told police that he spread out his arms and pushed his chest up against the knife, daring her to stick it into his chest, but that she couldn't do it. "I just started bawling my eyes out," she said. "I looked up and he just smiled at me and grabbed me by the throat and started strangling me." Michael never told police about the knife. When he tried to explain why he didn't kill her, he said, "I don't know why I let her go. After I raped her, I felt confused and not sure what was going on. She got up and ran off, and I didn't try to stop her."

Margaret did not want to testify at Ross's trial because she didn't believe in the death penalty, but after his execution, she said that she felt responsible for the four women who died after she had had a chance to thrust the knife in his chest. When interviewed in 2005, she said she wished he had killed her like the other women because she's had to live with the nightmare ever since.

The fact that he raped her but didn't kill her was used against Michael at his trials. The prosecutor's theory was that the rape proved that he didn't always feel the compulsion to kill his victims and that he didn't have to kill Margaret because it was dark and she wouldn't be able to identify him. Michael later told me, "I don't know why I didn't kill her any more than I know why I killed the others."

In the fall of 1983, Michael began to date a woman named Diane (not her real name) who soon moved in with him in Jewett City. When Dan invited him to Thanksgiving dinner, Michael asked if he could bring Diane, but his father said there wasn't enough room. That launched Michael into another rage. "I had to tell Diane that we weren't going to my dad's. That really upset me," he said, trying to explain what led to his fifth murder. He didn't seem to understand that I couldn't comprehend his rage over a dinner invitation.

Robin Stavinsky, nineteen, had been trying to pull her life together. A natural athlete and former state discus champion, Robin had moved out after a fight with her parents during her senior year in high school. At first she stayed with a friend and later with her older sister, Debbie. Robin had been with Ron and Joan Stavinsky, her father and stepmother, for ten years. She had come to them when she was starting the fifth grade, after being taken away from her mother and put into foster care. Ron and Joan had also taken Robin's half sister, Debbie, who was thirteen—even though Debbie was not Ron's daughter. They didn't want to split the girls up because they had always been together. The Stavinskys also had two small children from Joan's previous marriage, David, four, and Jennifer, one.

For Joan, it wasn't easy to instantly become the mother of two teenage girls. She was an at-home mother and alone with them most of the time because Ron worked for a drilling company and was out of town at least half of the year. It was a challenge because she didn't have any experience with teenagers. "Robin came from a place that was not happy," explained her younger sister, Jennifer Carcia. "Foster care in the sixties and seventies—the stories she'd tell me about it were awful, so she knew how to self-preserve. She had seen a lot, but what she had lived through made her stronger."

Robin was always full of energy. Her family said she could clean their Columbia home from top to bottom in a couple of hours and then take a five-mile run and not seem tired at all. "She was so strong," said Jennifer, that some of her friends "nicknamed her the hulk woman" because of her muscles, "but she had a feminine side to her." In seventh grade, a coach got her interested in track and field—discus and shot put—and from then on, she was always in training. She was also a rebellious teenager who was spiteful and a little defiant. When she channeled her energy positively, things went well, but "like the little girl with the curl, she also had her difficult side," a family member reported.

Although Robin did well in school, getting mostly Bs and some As, she didn't know whether she wanted to go to college, so after graduation she got a job working for a dry cleaner and moved in with her boyfriend Dave in New London. She also got a job answering phones for a phone-sex business. All she did was transfer the calls to the women who actually took the calls, but later the media tried to intimate that the job had something to do with her death.

Her job was in Norwich, about twelve miles from New London. Without a car, Robin had to hitchhike back and forth. On November 16, 1983, she was on her way home from work, walking along Route 32, a busy commercial area, when Michael Ross spotted her. He parked his car and caught up with her as she walked along. They chatted for a while. She told him she was furious with her boyfriend and was going to walk to New London and stay with a girlfriend. Michael realized that she was physically fit and might be able to resist him, so he waited for her to be off guard and then began to strangle her right away. She passed out and was "half dead" when he pulled her out of sight. "I almost didn't rape her, but then she started to come to. She tried to fight back when I raped her but she was too weak. The rape took only a few minutes, and then I strangled her. It was over very quickly." He told the police that she did something to upset him. "But this was never true for any of them. I assaulted them without provocation. It was just an excuse because Malchik said they must have done something to anger me, and I picked up on that as an excuse." The area was too well traveled to risk trying to put the corpse in the car, so he hid her remains under some brush and leaves. "They found the body a week later so I never returned to the scene—though I did drive by on a few occasions before her body was found. There was no place to pull off the road so I didn't stop. I was afraid someone would see me," he remembered. He also said that the medical examiner incorrectly estimated that she had been dead for two days, when it had actually been at least a week.

A few days after the murder, her family heard from her friends that she was missing and hadn't gone home to New London or appeared at work. It was her pattern to sometimes disappear for a while, staying with a friend because she didn't want to be found. Having reconciled with her father, she occasionally dropped by his home, but they didn't worry until she didn't show up for Thanksgiving dinner.

Late in the afternoon, Joan heard that a body had been found in Norwich, but she didn't think it was Robin. At the urging of others, she finally called the police and gave a description of her daughter, including scars and birthmarks. She later learned that the detective she was talking to was standing right next to the body as she described Robin and that he knew instantly that the body had been identified. That evening, Detective Michael Stergio arrived at the Stavinsky house and hinted that he suspected that the remains that were found were Robin's, but the police could not be sure until they had her dental records.

Yet despite that news, Joan and Ron still didn't think that the police had found Robin; they hadn't processed what the officers had told them. About three o'clock in the morning, Joan sat up in bed and said, "Ron, she's gone. It's Robin."

Robin's death was one of the two that specifically haunted Michael. Every Thanksgiving he would fall into a deep depression and stay in bed because he incorrectly thought that Joan Stavinsky had gone to identify Robin's body on Thanksgiving afternoon.

Michael was seeing Dr. DuCharme twice a week at the time of Robin's murder, but he never spoke about the murders during his sessions. DuCharme had persuaded him to apply for a job as an insurance salesman for Prudential, but Michael felt that abandoning his dream of being a farmer was compromising his manhood. He was a failure. "I started drinking and had the classic signs of alcoholism. I drank alone. The first thing I did when I got home was make two or three drinks, Scotch." The more he worked at Prudential, the more he felt oppressed and even ashamed—and the more he drank. He wasn't performing well on the job, even though he lied and told his father that he was one of the top salesmen. "I had to be a success for my father even if it was all a lie." Michael only wanted to take over the family farm, but years later, Dan Ross would say, "What did he think I was going to do? Roll over and play dead? I was years away from retirement."

By May 1984, Michael said he kicked Diane out of his apartment because of their constant bickering. "I don't know why I ever started dating her. We had nothing in common. It was all physical." He got angry with her because she didn't have a job and was satisfied to collect unemployment. "I come from a family with the Puritan work ethic. You don't go on unemployment. You work."

He began stalking almost every night. He had killed Leslie Shelley and April Brunais in April; committing four murders in less than a year made it impossible for him to convince himself that he could control his urges. The denial he had lived with since college was no longer feasible. He knew he was a killer, but he couldn't bring himself to go to the police and turn himself in. But he wanted to stop, and he began to believe that the only way he could manage that was suicide. He now rehearsed his death by driving a hundred miles per hour down Route 169 in Lisbon, but he couldn't muster the courage to drive into the bridge abutment and actually kill himself. "I was a coward. I was too afraid to be a man," he said shamefully.

Years later, I could see that he wanted to admit his guilt and weakness, but I think it was also one of the many times that he also wanted to be comforted, to hear me say, "It's okay, Michael. I understand."

After talking to Dr. Berlin and Dr. Borden many times, I didn't doubt that his mental illness and his sexual sadism were responsible for his murderous behavior, but I also didn't think he was without culpability. I continually brought this up with Michael for more than a decade, but he could never adequately articulate why he didn't turn himself in or kill himself to prevent another murder. The reason was some mixture of denial, shame, not wanting to go to jail, and the irrational hope that he could stop himself from killing again.

On some level, he must have made the decision to let himself get caught. He grabbed Wendy Baribeault in broad daylight on a busy stretch of road in Lisbon on a warm June day. If he didn't have the courage to stop himself, maybe someone else would. Someone would see him, and he would be caught. He says he didn't actually "plan" to go out and get caught, but "why else would I grab a girl in broad daylight on a busy stretch of highway?"

Wendy, seventeen, was five feet two inches and 103 pounds. She was also an athlete and liked to take long walks, despite her mother's warning that she shouldn't walk alone on Route 12. She had finished her exams at Norwich High School and decided to take a walk to get some exercise. Dressed in blue shorts, a white T-shirt with black sleeves, blue socks, and red sneakers, she left a note on the kitchen table to tell her mother where she was going at about four o'clock in the afternoon of June 13 and headed toward Chucky's Convenience Store. Roger Baribeault, Wendy's father, who was working in the backyard, saw her leave but thought nothing of it. She never reached Chucky's, because Michael was also on that stretch of road after a coworker with whom he was supposed to go out canvassing had called in sick.

Michael was driving around aimlessly until he saw Wendy walking in the opposite direction. He turned his Toyota around so recklessly that some observers thought he had a tire blowout. Screeching to a halt, he parked his car and walked quickly to catch up with her. "I got out and went after her. I think in the confession I said something about asking her to the company picnic or that she said something to make me mad, but she didn't. I just made that up to have an excuse for why I did it." Describing the event with the same detachment as he did every crime, he said that he came up to her from behind and "grabbed her and dragged her into the woods. I forced her to undress, forced her to perform oral sex on me, raped her and strangled her." The coroner's report said that Wendy had been strangled manually, but in his confession to the state police, Michael said he had killed her with a belt. When they told him that was inconsistent with the evidence, he admitted that he couldn't really remember how he had killed her. "It was all a blur. I covered her body up with some stones I took off a stone wall and left." I don't think Michael was obfuscating about what happened. He really couldn't separate one murder from another with the exception of the date, location, and distinguishing features of the landscape. He couldn't have even described the women unless he had seen a picture of them in the paper.

Multiple witnesses had seen his reckless driving and confrontation with Wendy. John Nelson, owner of Nelson's Garage on Route 12 in Lisbon, told the police that he saw a man about eighteen years old with long hair walking about fifty feet behind a girl. He said he saw the man "grab the girl by the arm." When he looked out a short time later, the car was gone. Cheryl Ciliano was driving her car on Route 12 while on her way to cash an insurance check. She said she saw a clean cut–looking man walking about eight feet behind the girl, and the girl "had a distressed look on her face." She reported that the man was trying to catch up with the girl and that she had "the impression that it was a boyfriend/girlfriend dispute." She described Michael more accurately as being close to six feet tall with a skinny build. George MacDonald drove by on a motorcycle and later told police that he had gotten a good look at the car, first thinking it was a Datsun, but when he couldn't find a similar model, he went to a Toyota dealership, looked at a brochure, and was certain the car was a blue Toyota Celica. He even drove around and saw the car parked near Michael's apartment.

When Wendy didn't come home that afternoon, her parents became concerned because it wasn't like her to stay out. By five o'clock, her mother, Sharon Baribeault, went out looking for her. They searched for her all evening, and at about ten thirty finally called the state police in Montville. The police interviewed her friends and found that Wendy had not seemed upset and that there were no problems at home. So the police took some of Wendy's clothes and started looking for her with blood-hounds. Her body was found on June 15.

Michael stayed away from the crime scene. "I didn't visit the body because police were in the area searching for her. It would have been too risky." On some level he wanted to get caught, and yet he was afraid. I believe Michael wanted more than anything to be able to over-come the monster himself, but by the eighth murder, he knew that he would never stop on his own.

But the killing spree was finally over.

16

CONNECTICUT
JUNE 1984

Michael Malchik was a handsome state trooper and a member of the Connecticut major crimes unit. In 1983, Tammy Williams was still missing, and Malchik had been assigned to the case to see if he could come up with any new angles. Coincidentally, he sat next to the detective assigned to the Debra Smith Taylor case at the station, and as the two of them began to compare notes, he started to see similarities between the crimes. The women were the same size and were seen roughly six miles apart, so he surmised that one person might be responsible for what were classified as a disappearance and murder.

While he was working on this theory, Wendy Baribeault disappeared. Four days later, her body was found in Lisbon, about eighteen miles from Danielson, and Malchik was assigned as chief investigator. A dozen witnesses had given a description of the man they saw in the vicinity of the crime. A few saw him abruptly turn his car around, almost as if he had lost control of the vehicle. For the first time, the police had a description of a car and a description of the perpetrator. Malchik looked at the list of 3,600 Toyota owners and selected names of those who lived closest to the crime scene for questioning. Michael Ross's door happened to be the first one Malchik knocked on because of its proximity to the crime scene. Malchik knew nothing about Michael's past convictions but did have a reason to go to Michael's apartment first; George MacDonald had already reported that he'd found the car.

No one was home the first two times Malchik knocked on Michael's door, but on the third try, Malchik arrived very early in the morning, catching Michael before he left for work on June 28, 1984. Michael was still in his bathrobe when he answered Malchik's knock. The detective identified himself and explained that he was investigating the homicide of Wendy Baribeault. Seeming relaxed and unfazed by the visit, Michael said that he had been expecting the police because he had read in the papers that the police were looking for a small blue car like his. Despite feeling a sense of relief and an impulse to confess to Malchik, at the same time Michael was petrified of being arrested. He told me later he felt as if Malchik could see his heart pounding under the bathrobe.

At first Malchik thought he had the wrong man. Michael was wearing glasses when he answered the door, and that didn't match the composite sketches of the man who had been seen following Wendy. While stalking, Michael always removed his glasses so he wouldn't be recognized—a kind of magical thinking that he had held on to since the stalking began. Yet every time Malchik indicated that he might be ready to leave, Michael would drop a crumb to make the investigator think that he should ask more questions. Michael couldn't bring himself to confess, so he dropped hints instead. Still, Malchik wasn't entirely suspicious. "I can't say I was that smart. I thought that one person had killed everybody, and yet this looked like a mild-mannered guy. He had me as fooled as anybody else."

Malchik was ultimately tipped off by Michael's memory of June 13, the day Wendy had disappeared. He could remember in great detail what he had for breakfast, what color socks he had on, when he arrived at work, and to whom he talked, but his memory was spotty at best starting about 3:00 or 4:00 P.M., just about the time that Wendy was last seen alive. After that time, he remembered only that he went home. "He also placed himself in a direct line from where the girl was last seen, and I thought that was odd," Malchik remembered.

As Malchik stood at his door, Michael was in excruciating turmoil. He wanted to be stopped from killing again, but he didn't want to be caught. He wanted Malchik to figure it out and arrest him, but the thought of being charged with murder was unthinkable. Michael finally revealed that he had been arrested twice for sex offenses, so Malchik decided to bring him down to the temporary command post at the Lisbon Town Hall for questioning.

Michael claimed that after the questioning began, he asked to call his father to get him a lawyer, but he was not allowed to do so until all the confessions had been signed. Malchik denied this assertion. If Michael had actually asked for a lawyer, the interrogation should have stopped. If he had not been free to go, Malchik should have read him his Miranda rights and allowed him to make a phone call. If Michael had been telling the truth about his requests and Malchik's refusal, the confessions would not have been admissible as evidence, because his Fifth and Sixth Amendment rights had been violated.

A talented and experienced law enforcement officer, Malchik slowly calmed Michael down and gained his confidence at the command post. They talked about Michael's family and the farm. They talked about college and Michael's former fiancée. The conversation went on for about four hours, varying between small talk and pointed questions about what Michael had done on June 13. It was by all accounts exquisite police work.

Malchik was able to make Michael feel as if he were on his side. Perhaps this was because Malchik had yet to make up his own mind about Michael. "Sitting across from him, I'm asking [myself], Is this someone who has killed a number of women or just some guy? He doesn't have a tail, fire or horns. He looks just as much like the average guy as anyone," Malchik remembered.

Then Michael asked Malchik what he thought about Christopher Wilder, a serial killer who had recently been in the headlines after being killed in a shoot-out. Michael wanted to know if Malchik thought Wilder was sick, and Malchik responded that he didn't really know. Michael also wanted to know if psychiatrists would examine an accused murderer, and Malchik answered in the affirmative. Hypothetically, Michael asked, if a suspected killer went into psychiatric therapy, would that person not be charged? Malchik was quick to assert that "would not be possible."

Michael then asked if the detective thought he had killed Wendy Baribeault. Malchik responded that he did think that he had killed her and that he would probably kill again, but that he probably really didn't want to kill again. He told Michael that the most important thing was that he not hurt anyone else. That was just what Michael Ross wanted to hear.

Within hours, Michael had confessed not only to Wendy Baribeault's murder, but also to five others: Tammy Williams, Debra Smith Taylor, Robin Stavinsky, April Brunais, and Leslie Shelley. However, he didn't initially mention Debbie Taylor until the officers mentioned where her remains had been found, because part of his denial was actually forgetting he had killed her. He not only convinced himself after each killing that he would never commit another murder, but after a while he also forgot about some of them. In his mind, they became all one big murderous fantasy. His inability to remember this murder was consistent with Dr. Cegalis's test results that revealed memory impairment. But when he was told the location of her remains, he did not hesitate to confess.

Malchik had to control himself because he didn't want to let on that he was both viscerally disgusted with Michael Ross and excited that he had caught a serial killer. Malchik also knew that he had to obtain evidence of the crimes. He had to find the bodies for corroboration that Michael wasn't just confessing to crimes he hadn't committed. Malchik taped the confessions and then had Michael sign confessions that had been composed by Malchik and the other officer, Detective Frank Griffin, summarizing what they said Michael had told them.

By the time of his first trial, Michael felt betrayed. He thought that Malchik was his ally and that they were going to "solve" the case—in his mind that meant that Malchik would help him understand why he had committed the crimes. He had no idea why he had done such horrendous things, and he naively hoped that by cooperating with the police, he would find answers. "We were a team," Michael said bitterly, almost crying. "They kept hounding me. Malchik said, 'Well, maybe you did it because of this,' and then he said, 'This is why you did it.' He put a lot of stuff down. I thought we were trying to figure it out. I was a real idiot. I trusted him completely. I talked to him all day long, and I thought he was my friend and I was trying to help him. He said, 'Did you do it because you didn't want to go back to jail?' And I said, 'I don't know. Maybe.' 'Could you have done it because of this or because of that?' He took this stuff down and then everything got twisted. Things that I said were completely taken out of context. I never said that I had killed the girls to escape jail or identification. That was *his* theory," Michael insisted.

The next day, Michael took Malchik to most of the crime scenes and to the places where he'd hidden the bodies that hadn't yet been recovered—Tammy Williams, April Brunais, and Leslie Shelley. Malchik had found his killer.

17

BRIDGEPORT, CONNECTICUT
1987

It took almost three years for Michael Ross's first trial to commence. In that time, Michael had been examined and reexamined by all five expert psychiatric witnesses on both sides in preparation for their evaluations and testimony. The first phase of the trial dealt with guilt. Michael did not deny that he had committed the crimes, so the defense psychiatric witnesses had to convince the jury that Michael's sexual sadism made it impossible for him to control his compulsive need to rape and kill. If they succeeded, Michael would be found not guilty because of mental disease or defect. Even if the jury were not convinced, the psychiatrists would have a second chance during the penalty phase to convince jurors that Michael's sexual sadism was real. If jurors found there was mitigation because of the mental illness, he would not be eligible for the death penalty. The prosecution had to convince them that his mental illness was a ruse and that he killed to cover up his rapes. During the penalty phase, they also had to prove aggravation—that his crimes were cruel and heinous.

The defense psychiatrists were Michael's most frequent visitors at the jail, and even though the purpose of their visits was evaluation rather than therapy, Michael found the sessions helpful. His father and sisters had come at first, but after a while, only his father visited. He made sure that his mother was not on his visitor's list and was adamant that he have no contact with her. "She sent a card once in a while, pretending to be the dutiful mother, but I just threw them away, sometimes without even opening them."

Before the trial began, the defense raised the issue of where Leslie Shelley and April Brunais had been murdered. In 1986, there was a closed hearing held in response to a defense motion to dismiss those charges because the murders had been committed in the Arcadia woods of Rhode Island, not Connecticut. This was extremely important because Rhode Island did not have a death penalty and because the Leslie Shelley murder was the one that Michael had told psychiatrist Howard Zonana "would hang me" during his psychological evaluation in 1985. Did he kill Leslie because of his sexual sadism or did he kill her to cover up his rape and murder of her friend April Brunais? Even the doctors could not answer that question. If committing a rape and murder satisfied his sexual sadism, it would explain the first rape/ murder but not necessarily the second. After killing April, he would have been relieved and no longer overcome with sexual rage, but then he would have been faced with the fact that he was placing a dead girl, naked from the waist down, in the front seat of his car and having a live one tied up in the trunk. Also significant was the fact that in his original confession, Michael said he didn't rape Leslie Shelley. Was her murder committed just to silence her?

The closed hearing in Judge Seymour Hendel's chambers was Michael's "proof" that there was a "faked crime scene" concocted by Malchik. Michael claimed that at the time of his arrest, he told Malchik that the murders had taken place in Rhode Island, but that fact had never ended up in any report or confession. Michael said he didn't bring it up again because Malchik had convinced him that he did not want to face another trial in another state. Why Malchik ignored the crime scene was unclear. He said he didn't have time during the initial investigation because it was more important to locate all the bodies. The danger was that Michael would change his mind and not cooperate. Without the bodies, the state didn't have a case. That made sense as the reason why he didn't go immediately, but it didn't make sense that in the two years between the arrest and the suppression hearing, Malchik had never attempted to find the actual murder scene.

The question at the hearing was whether the state police had ignored Michael's directions to the crime scene because they didn't want the double murder to be tried in Rhode Island or whether Michael had made the Rhode Island location up after the fact. The prosecution team suggested that when Michael found out that a double murder was almost by definition especially cruel and heinous and would result in a death sentence, he concocted the story about the Rhode Island crime scene as a ruse.

At the suppression hearing, prosecutor Bob Satti produced a report written by Malchik only weeks before the hearing—two years after Michael's arrest—containing what Malchik said were Michael's directions to the crime scene. Malchik said they were inadvertently left out of the written and taped statements taken two years earlier, but Michael insisted he never gave them. Those directions, Satti contended, would place the crime scene within Connecticut, not a mile or so down the road in Rhode Island.

The defense produced strips of cloth, found in a secluded area in the woods, just over the border into Rhode Island, that purportedly matched a slipcover from Michael's apartment and a ligature found around the neck of one of the girls. The defense lawyers were also able to show that on the taped statement Michael had offered to take officers to the crime scene three times, despite Malchik's memory to the contrary.

Near the conclusion of the hearing, Judge Hendel lambasted the prosecutor and the police on the court record. Hendel screamed at the prosecutor and threw a map at the investigator. Convinced that he had been lied to, he roared, "Gentleman, there is no question in my mind this happened in Rhode Island. There is absolutely not one scintilla of doubt it happened in Rhode Island. I disbelieve the testimony of both officers, Malchik and Officer Griffin [Malchik's partner]." He accused the two officers of lying for no reason other than keeping Rhode Island officials out of the case. He said he was glad that it was a closed hearing and a sealed record. However he warned that the whole matter "bothers me greatly" and that "at some point this record will become open when this case is over. Let the chips fall where they may."

Three years later, however, when Judge Hendel unsealed the record, he said, "With the benefit of hindsight, I realized that the officers made a judgment call at the time based on information which was available to them, that it wasn't important to go to the site of the killings, since they were looking to secure corroboration of the defendant's confession and they felt that by going to the place where the bodies were, they would get that corroboration." He had reflected on the matter, he said, and changed his views on their testimony. "I do believe that they testified truthfully during the hearing." Malchik said that Hendel changed his mind because he believed Michael was a liar; Michael pointed to the hearing to prove that Malchik and Satti were liars and that the system was stacked against him. In a just system, he contended, those two murders would not have been tried in Connecticut, and Satti and Malchik would have been exposed for corruption.

When I first started reporting on the case, in 1995, Michael was obsessed with the idea of exposing this cover-up. After reading the hearing transcript, I could understand his frustration with the system. It seemed that the judge believed that Malchik had lied about the directions that Michael had given him in order to "prove" that the murders happened in Connecticut. I wondered why the judge had changed his mind. It could have been because Michael was telling every journalist who would listen about the "faked crime scene." I decided to try to follow both sets of directions. I found that Michael's directions, which had been given when he sat in a jail cell, took me to the exact place where the defense said the murders took place, but Malchik's directions made absolutely no sense. They did not lead to a secluded area where someone could have raped and murdered two girls. Just to be sure, I repeated the experiment, this time with someone else driving and me reading the two sets of directions. We came up with identical results.

The 1987 trial lasted almost six months. None of Michael's family sat through the proceedings, but his father and sisters did testify during the penalty phase, primarily in the hope that describing Michael's childhood would influence the jury to spare his life. Ed and Lera Shelley were among the victims' families who faithfully attended every day, along with the Baribeaults and the Roodes. Lera could not sit in the courtroom because witnesses are not allowed to hear other witnesses' testimony; instead she sat in the hallway conducting her own vigil while Ed sat inside the crowded courtroom.

With Bob Satti at the helm, the courtroom was filled with theatrics and emotion. During his closing argument, Satti even got down on his knees and reenacted one of the murders. The state's case was clear and simple—Michael Ross was a rapist who murdered to cover up his crimes. Each of the crimes was carefully documented using testimony from grieving family members and the investigating officers, as well as Michael's confessions and the gruesome pictures of crime scenes and autopsies.

What was missing was any psychiatric testimony from the prosecution to prove that Michael was not mentally ill. Satti had deliberately kept Dr. Miller's letter, admitting that he thought Michael was mentally ill, from the defense until the guilt phase was almost over. When Dr. Miller took the stand, Satti deliberately didn't ask him any questions about Michael Ross's mental illness because he didn't want the jury to know that his witness agreed with the defense's contention that Michael's illness was real and a mitigating factor that would preclude death. He asked him only general questions about sexual sadism, nothing about Michael's pathology. This prevented the defense from questioning Miller about his evaluation of Michael in cross-examination because cross is limited to the topics discussed in direct examination.

In contrast, defense had to prove that Michael's mental illness was real. Because of his mental illness, his lawyers argued, he should either be found not guilty by reason of mental disease or defect or be convicted of manslaughter because he suffered from extreme emotional distress. Dr. Cegalis and Dr. Borden were the chief witnesses for the defense. In trying to sum up his several days of testimony, Dr. Borden told the jury that Michael had a borderline personality disorder, which the DSM-IV defines as "a pervasive pattern of instability of interpersonal relationships, self-image, and affects, and marked impulsivity that begins by early adulthood and is present in a variety of contexts." He said that the borderline personality "feels like a helpless, weak little child" who has a lot of rage inside. What people with this disorder hate in themselves, they find in someone else. "If they hate their weakness, they will attack, as in Michael Ross's case, what appears weak." He also said that Michael was a sexual sadist, that he had a sadistic personality disorder (then a new diagnosis in the DSM-III but no longer recognized as a diagnosis), which was the "ultimate extreme of sadism. . . . It's a homicidal maniac" who has "an intense drive to death, to kill, that is . . . a primitive, brutal death drive." In effect, he was telling the jury that Michael's sexual sadism was so extreme that it went well beyond the DSM guidelines. He not only got pleasure from sadistic behavior, but also did not achieve sexual release until he had murdered his victims.

It's important to understand that not only was the jury hearing about new pathologies at the time, but also that the term *serial killer* was new to many people in 1987. After all, it didn't enter the lexicon until the mid-1980s. Perhaps that's one reason why the Bridgeport jury didn't believe the psychiatric testimony. Or perhaps it was because Michael Ross looked too "normal." He smiled and joked with his attorneys. "I wasn't foaming at the mouth," Michael explained to me.

Whatever their reason, it took the jury less than eighty-seven minutes to decide that Michael Ross was guilty and less than a day to decide that his penalty should be death. Judge G. Sarsfield Ford set an execution date of thirty days after his sentencing—July 4, 1987, the same day that Ed and Lera Shelley had buried their daughter three years earlier.

During the trial, Michael wrote to Ann Cole, one of the few people he considered a friend. His letters explain how he perceived his first trial—and himself. He was scared and confused and full of self-loathing. He was lonely, but, perhaps most important, even during his first trial he was ready to give up and accept execution.

After sitting through eight days of psychiatric testimony, Michael was distraught from listening to psychiatrists tell the world what he both hoped for and feared the most—that he was mentally ill. Although he wanted to know why he had committed the murders, he did not want anyone to say he was a sexual sadist—at least not at that point—because of his cultural belief that mental illness was a weakness and an excuse for bad behavior. How could he now use it as an excuse? On the other hand, if he wasn't suffering from a psychiatric disorder, he was nothing more than a cold-blooded killer. While the court was recessed over the Memorial Day holiday, he spent his time writing to Ann to thank her for her support because his family wouldn't attend the trial. "They would be too ashamed to come to court. They once told me that if they did come to court, it would be a slap in the face of the victims' families. I always thought it ironic that they had more concern for the victims' families than for me."

He poured out his feelings to her. "I have to keep up my damn facade. I'm beginning to hate that outward face. I'm a lie, a phony. The person who I thought I was doesn't exist. I've lived with the lie so long that I don't really know who or what I am. I'm also afraid of who I really am." It was clear that listening to Dr. Borden was excruciatingly painful, and he wrote that he didn't "like the glimpses [Dr.] Borden has given me, but how can I deny them? He has no reason to lie but I have every reason not to want to believe him." He was of two minds. He wanted to prove that he was not responsible for what he had done because of his illness, but he didn't *want* to be a sexual sadist, because that disorder disgusted him.

Dr. Walter Borden had painted a picture of a very sick man who was the extreme of sadism—a lustful murderer. Michael wrote Ann, "I am evil pure and simple. You can't deny that. I am evil in its purest form, lustful and murderous. How can I accept that? I am everything that I hate and despise. The more I see, the more I hate." Michael wrote that he was like "a rabid dog that should be taken out behind the barn and shot. The jury should sentence me to death not for what I've done, but rather out of mercy—to put me out of my misery, to stop the suffering." He was full of self-loathing. "I'm facing this hateful murderous monster that is me, and I hate me. Everything of redeeming value, everything that I thought was good about myself is falsehood."

As articulate and aware as he was, Michael did not grasp his own pathology in 1987, and neither did the court or the jury. During the penalty phase of the trial, the jury had to decide whether he would receive several hundred years in jail or death. Dr. Berlin was the chief witness during that part of the trial, but family members, neighbors, and even prison guards were also called to testify. If they had believed that he was mentally ill, as Dr. Berlin testified, a death sentence could not have been given. But once again the jury was not swayed by the psychiatric testimony and sentenced Michael to death in less than a day of deliberation. "It took them longer to come back with a decision than the guilt phase," said Michael. "But I think they just hung out in there for a while because they didn't want anyone to think they hadn't considered the evidence."

Fred DeCaprio, one of the defense lawyers at the first trial, has worked for decades as a public defender. When I met him in 1996, he was working in a cramped, dumpy office. Small of stature, balding, with scruffs of hair ringing his pate, DeCaprio spoke softly, sometimes almost inaudibly, but became emotional when I asked him if Michael had gotten a fair trial. "No, not at all," he said. I asked why not. "Oh God, there were a lot of factors. I think that the jury we—I want to say were stuck with—the jury we selected was not a very good jury for us. That may be the luck of the draw or a by-product of the location of the trial. But it wasn't a very good jury for us, to be able to understand or at least emphasize [with] some things we were trying to tell them. I thought that the trial judge was tremendously offended, wounded by the crimes," he said, adding that he thought that the nature of the crimes had tilted Judge Ford against Michael. "It was very subtle. He was very smart. So there are a lot of times that there is nothing on the record. It's done with inflection, gesture. It's devastating . . . I thought we had a pretty compelling case, but we never got heard."

In all his years of practice, DeCaprio said he had never had a judge take such an active role in trying to influence the outcome of a trial. DeCaprio mentioned the way Ford treated the psychiatric expert. "It was outrageous. . . . Dr. Berlin's a nice man and an excellent witness. It was tragic. I was appalled . . . because this guy didn't deserve it. He was just trying to do his job." After the trial, Dr. Berlin filed a complaint with the state commission on judicial conduct about the way he was treated by Judge Ford. He was later told that there was no evidence of misconduct, and no action was taken to censure the judge.

Others, including Karen Clarke, a reporter who covered the trial for the New London *Day*, later confirmed DeCaprio's characterization of the trial judge. She said he took a demeaning tone with the defense attorneys, pronouncing their names incorrectly, for instance. Another reporter who covered the trial, but did not want to be identified, concurred with Clark's observations, as had Ann when I first met her.

DeCaprio felt that the jury was not open to the psychiatric testimony. "It was absurd. They didn't take time. . . . How can you make that kind of decision with the amount of evidence they had before them in less than ninety minutes?"

18

DEATH ROW, SOMERS, CONNECTICUT
JULY 1987

Michael was tired yet happy when the first trial was finally over. "It was strange, and I doubt if anyone can truly understand, but my lawyers were more upset about my being sentenced to death than I was. What devastated me was the guilty verdict itself. It still bothers me that no one seems to understand this—even you don't understand it, do you, Martha? Everyone focused on saving my life. Yet I didn't give a damn about my life. I would have been ecstatic with a verdict of 'insane but fry the bastard anyway.' Freedom didn't interest me. Life didn't interest me. All that was really important to me was to prove that I wasn't the cold-blooded animal that everyone portrayed me to be. That is all I ever cared about."

After sentencing, Michael was brought back to the Bridgeport Correctional Center and placed in an isolated holding cell. He was stripped and given a pair of flip-flops, a T-shirt, a pair of pants several sizes too big with no belt—so he had to hold the waist of the pants to keep them from falling to his ankles—and no underwear. A few hours later, a lieutenant and correctional officer escorted him to Somers, where he arrived just after 11:00 P.M. Two or three guards with shotguns, as well as two K-9 officers and their dogs, surrounded the van. Two officers, a captain and one of the K-9 officers, escorted him into the prison, which was locked down, meaning all inmates were locked in their cells. "Their faces were pressed up to the windows, jostling each other to get a better look, but I ignored them."

This was all new. Michael was the first person to be on death row since the last execution in 1960. He was taken to G-basement where he was processed, fingerprinted, photographed, and given his prison uniform. Then he was put in the deathwatch cell, F-36, at the end of the row, isolated by a door at the end of what was to be death row. This is the cell that condemned men are now put into just prior to execution. The cell's furnishings consisted of a bunk, a sink, and a toilet, unlike other cells on death row that also have shelves and desks. About five feet from the cell was a small wooden desk at which a guard was posted 24/7 whose sole responsibility was to watch Michael and log anything he did into a logbook. "I was pretty wound up. I hadn't slept at all the night before and I wouldn't sleep for another twelve hours."

That was Friday night. On Monday, he returned to G-basement, where his property was searched, and he was allowed to bring it to his cell. To get there he had to walk past the inmates on the tiers adjacent to the death cell; the cells were later to be used for death row inmates but at the time held men who had been put in segregation. Because he was such a high-profile inmate, the inmates peppered him with bars of soap and rolls of toilet paper as he walked by. "The guards, for the most [part,] always kept a couple of steps away from me so that they wouldn't get hit." While in G-basement, he also had a meeting with the deputy warden, during which he was told the rules. Michael brought up several issues. He asked for a desk and a shelf, which were granted and installed within a week.

Michael knew there would be an automatic stay of execution until the state Supreme Court had reviewed his sentence, a mandatory appeal in all death penalty cases. But every time he left his cell "there were the ever present catcalls from both inmates and guards. Most common was the buzzing sound," like the electric chair. Yet the hardest to deal with was his complete lack of privacy. No one has much privacy in prison, and Michael had learned to deal with it in his three years in county jail, but now a guard was posted directly in front of his cell, monitoring every movement every minute of every single day.

When he first got to death row, Michael was consumed by anger. He felt that he didn't get a fair trial and that Malchik and Satti were "twisting the evidence" to secure a death sentence, that the judge was against him, and that the jury ignored the evidence. It was a very personal feeling of injustice, not a critique of the entire justice system. He began to do legal research to keep busy. Eventually he was allowed to get books from the law library, but he also got lawyers to donate their outdated books for a death row library and even got the *Law Tribune* to provide a free subscription. He read articles that charged that the death penalty was meted out in a capricious manner. If one compares capital prosecutions state by state, prosecutor by prosecutor, or case by case, it is impossible to see any logic in prosecutors' decisions as to whether a death sentence is sought. After about a year, he realized that his case was not unique and that abuses occur in many capital cases. Seeing this, he started writing anti–death penalty articles. But instead of making Michael feel less persecuted, these activities made him feel hopeless. He had decided that the entire system was broken and corrupt.

Michael slowly spiraled into a deep depression. Prozac helped, but his violent sexual fantasies became much worse. One of the cruel ironies of prison—with its lack of physical and mental activity—is that it's the perfect place for mental illness to grow stronger. "On the outside, at least I had work and daily activities to keep my mind busy and drive away the thoughts. When there is nothing to do but sit in an empty cell, the thoughts of raping and murdering became a much larger part of my life. The hardest time for me was in the evening when it was time to relax and go to sleep. I couldn't relax without the sexual imagery invading my mind and without feeling an immense compulsion to masturbate. If I fought the urge, I could never get to sleep, so daily masturbation just before bed became the norm. Once I gave in and satisfied the urges, I had no problem sleeping."

Even during the day, he felt the need to masturbate. Usually he masturbated when he woke up and before his usual afternoon nap. He said that his illness had cycles and seemed to ebb and flow. "There were periods when he [the monster] came on with a vengeance and I would masturbate several more times a day. During these periods I would masturbate myself raw—literally open raw spots on my penis. At these times, masturbation would often be painful as I rubbed the open sores."

Before the first trial began, Dr. Berlin told Michael about his clinic at Johns Hopkins and the success he'd had treating patients suffering from sexual sadism with Depo-Provera. Some refer to the controversial treatment as chemical castration, but Dr. Berlin objected to that term's negative connotations and considered it misleading. "I prefer talking about medications that suppress sexual appetite," he explained. "With an appetite suppressant, it would be easier for you to diet, but not impossible to eat." Dr. Berlin pointed out that many of his patients with appropriate sex partners are able to continue functioning sexually without the temptation to act out in harmful ways. When the sex drive is diminished, a sexual sadist can control his behavior. Even if he has the thoughts about the abnormal behavior, it no longer overpowers him.

At the Johns Hopkins clinic, sex offenders are carefully screened and evaluated, then given the medication in concert with extensive psychotherapy. In a study of 626 males who were treated at the clinic, only 9.7 percent repeated their crimes. According to Dr. Berlin, other studies have shown that recidivism of sex offenders without this treatment is as high as 65 percent. The effectiveness of hormone-suppressing drugs drove California, Florida, Georgia, and a growing number of other states to enact or consider mandatory chemical castration for sex offenders: no hormone treatment, no parole. However, Dr. Berlin cautions that this is a misguided public policy. Not all sex offenders are suitable for the chemical therapy—only those with paraphiliac disorders, such as certain pedophiles or sexual sadists. Research has shown that for treatment to work, the offender must acknowledge that his conduct is out of control and must want treatment. Treatment also must include psychotherapy during parole, because it helps teach clients how to control their former behaviors.

Depo-Provera, the most commonly used drug in this type of treatment, is marketed as a female contraceptive because it blocks ovulation. When one is sexually aroused, the brain secretes endorphins, opiate-like substances that are biochemical stimulants of pleasure. Dr. Berlin speculated that in men, Depo-Provera blocks opiate receptors, thereby preventing the endorphins from having their normal, pleasure-producing effect, but no studies have been done to prove or disprove that theory. It's interesting that hormone therapy may be more effective than surgical castration, because testosterone is produced in the adrenal glands, not only the testes. Moreover, unlike physical castration, the effect of the drugs is not permanent.

A normal adult male has a blood testosterone level of 400 to 800 nanograms per deciliter. With Depo-Provera, those levels go below 200. Dr. Robert Prentky, who researched the connections between sex and aggression, says that elevated testosterone levels have been linked to aggressive behavior but not necessarily criminal behavior. "Corporate

CEOs and professional hockey players have been shown to have abnormally high levels of testosterone," Berlin explained. High levels of testosterone can produce constructive aggression. There is also a correlation between high levels of testosterone and paraphiliac disorders, such as sexual sadism. No study has been able to predict criminal behavior based on testosterone levels nor explain how and why some commit sexual violence but not others.

After Michael was placed on death row, Dr. Berlin again suggested that he try Depo-Provera because of the success that he had with this treatment at his Johns Hopkins clinic. By this point, Michael was still reluctant but also desperate. "To be perfectly honest, I didn't believe in Depo-Provera before I got my shots," he admitted. At first, the mental health department refused to approve Dr. Berlin's treatment, saying that it was not a medication it prescribed, nor was it FDA approved for the treatment of sex offenders. Dr. Berlin wrote a letter to the Mental Health Unit offering to prescribe the medication and go to see Michael every couple of months to monitor his progress, but he was still refused treatment. Then in 1989, Bryn Freedman from WTNH Channel 8 did an extensive investigative report on the case. One of the issues she looked into was the refusal by the Department of Correction to offer the treatment. She interviewed Dr. Berlin, and the policy was soon reversed.

On October 16, 1989, Michael's blood test revealed a testosterone level of 434 nanograms per deciliter, near the low end of the normal range and inexplicably significantly below his pretrial level of 645, which is also within the normal range. There was no medical reason for the drop in testosterone levels or any explanation as to why Michael appeared to be so sensitive to even levels within the normal range. His first shot was 500 mg on November 15. During the first few months, he didn't notice any effects, so the dosage was increased twice until it got to 700 mg per week. Michael said that shortly thereafter "I noticed a decrease in my need for masturbation and less desire to engage in sexual fantasizing." He said the changes were gradual. But at some point after receiving 700 mg per week, his incessant urges to masturbate began to subside. As his need to masturbate declined, so did the violent sexual fantasies in his head. By the time his testosterone levels dropped below 50, he masturbated only once a day. Below 35, he could abstain for a couple of weeks, and at 20 or less, he reported that he had "essentially no sexual urges at all and [did] not masturbate at all."

"It cleared my mind and allowed me to be quiet," he explained. "Before the Depo-Provera, I had to always be actively doing something mentally or the obsessive sexual fantasies would pop up. What Depo-Provera did was greatly lessen the control that the monster had over me. It didn't take so much effort to force the fantasies out of my mind. I could fight the compulsive urge, yet still be able to get to sleep. I was in control. He [the monster] was still in my mind, but banished to the back." Michael's whole world changed. He said for the first time in years he could watch a movie without later fantasizing about raping and murdering one of the female actresses. "I could just lie there and do nothing but let my mind wander without drifting into some sexual murder fantasy. I developed extensive nonsexual fantasy worlds where I could escape for hours on end and not have guilt to deal with afterwards."

Michael understood that most people would have difficulty understanding the change he had undergone. So he came up with an analogy that he often repeated to me and wrote in articles printed in several publications, "I often describe it as living with an obnoxious roommate. What the Depo-Provera did was move the roommate to his own apartment down the hall. You still had to deal with him, but it was much easier without him always being in your face. Yet he was never ever totally gone. He was always there—just over the horizon waiting for his opportunity." He explained that he was never totally free of the problem because "he just sits there waiting for you to let down your guard and let him back in the front of your mind."

In 1990 and 1991, Michael began to have complications of high blood pressure and liver dysfunction and was permanently taken off Depo-Provera on October 1, 1992. Depo drugs are injected into muscle, and the medicine is slowly absorbed over time. Depo-Provera injections are given every week because of the relatively rapid release of the drug into the bloodstream. Dr. Berlin, who had been allowed to prescribe the medication in exchange for promising to monitor it for the DOC, recommended an alternate, Depo Lupron. Because it is released more slowly into the bloodstream, it has to be injected only once a month and has fewer side effects. However, the DOC rejected his recommendation. Without the medication, Michael's violent sexual fantasies returned, and he became so depressed that he even attempted suicide by putting a plastic bag over his head. "I considered trying to castrate myself with a razor blade. And though I prepared myself on several occasions—got the razor out and sterilized it with a match and tied off the scrotum with a string to slow bleeding—I could never actually cut myself." Scared that he would completely revert to "what I was before my medication," he went on a hunger strike for twenty days.

His sexual urges began to return, and he became concerned when he had urges to hurt one of the nurses. "That really scared me and bothered me because she was one of the nurses who always looked out for me. It bothered me tremendously that I wanted to rape her and hurt her," he admitted. There was shame in his voice, but also a distance, a sense that he was telling someone else's story.

Finally in February 1994, eighteen months after Depo-Provera had been discontinued, the DOC relented, and Michael was given his first

Depo Lupron shot. With that, he says, his mind was returned to him. "So Depo-Provera was pretty wonderful stuff. . . . Depo Lupron was even more effective than Depo-Provera. It freed my mind; it gave me control. It allowed me to be 'Michael' again. But there was a price. Now instead of being plagued by sexual fantasies and compulsive urges, I had the freedom to consider the effects of my past actions on others." Without the medication, his total focus was on his own sexual pleasure. But once he had been freed of the noxious fantasies, he "found it increasingly difficult to not focus on what I had done. I guess that for the first time, it had really sunk in." He mused that most of the men on death row "seem to have no conscience, and I often find myself envious of them for that." He added sarcastically, "I'm the only guilty person here on death row. It's really amazing how many innocent people have been sentenced to death."

It was difficult for Michael to comprehend why he didn't feel empathy toward his murder victims. He spent the anniversaries of their deaths praying for them, trying to honor them in some way, but in many ways they were never real people to him. He couldn't properly explain this to other people. To Michael the women were not human beings, just names. "I have a lot of self-loathing of how I could commit a rape/murder as I did, but no individual sorrow for the victims themselves. They remain faceless and almost anonymous to me." He said he regretted what he did and wished he could bring them back, even substitute his own life for theirs, but "their deaths don't haunt me the way that I feel they should."

I came to believe that he could not *allow* the women to be real to him. When he killed them, they were objects. He did not know them as people and had to keep them as only names and ages to be able to cope with his brutal crimes. Otherwise the pain of his shame would have been too great. He could not, however, depersonalize the family members. They sat in the courtroom. They answered questions on the nightly news. Their tears accentuated their pain. He could not neatly tuck their pain away into some cubicle of his psyche.

He wrote that his greatest fear was not being executed but that he would receive a life sentence and that "someday down the line some bean counter will decide that my monthly Depo Lupron shot is too expensive and stop my medication." He said that a positive aspect of his execution was knowing that he would never have to live with the monster again. "My death, through execution, is not to me an unreasonable insurance policy to see that it never happens."

CONNECTICUT
1996–1998

In April 1996, the *Connecticut Law Tribune* published my story "Why a Killer Offers to Die," which tried to explain Michael's determination to spare his victims' families more anguish and his frustration with the criminal justice system. Then in July 1996, I left the paper. I needed a rest—I'd spent more than nine months investigating the Ross case. I wanted to cleanse my thoughts of rape and murder and executions. I wanted to forget everything I knew about him.

However, Michael was not about to go away. He still called me almost every week. After the article came out, I was one of the few people whom he could trust—and among the half handful who would take his calls. But I was well aware of his loneliness and didn't have the heart to ask him to stop calling. We didn't talk so much about his case, but about everything from the weather to world events. Once he realized that I would answer him truthfully on almost any topic, he began to trust me as completely as he was capable of trusting anyone, not only with his story, but also with his deepest thoughts and feelings, whether I wanted to hear them or not. At first he needed me to get his story out and may to some degree have been using me, but after I had written "Why a Killer Offers to Die," he needed me as a friend, and for the most part, the manipulation stopped.

He was not unlike a demanding child. Sometimes he got pushy, starting our conversation with a request or order for me—something he wanted me to do or somebody he wanted me to call for him or even a request for other men on death row. The instruction or request might be his excuse for calling. At first he was embarrassed to call merely to chat, because the calls were expensive. MCI and the Department of Correction had quite a racket. The cost of accepting the call was five dollars no matter how long you chatted, and each subsequent minute was a dollar for the collect, automated call. He wanted my full attention when we talked—even though I was paying for the call and often had to multitask because I was in the middle of something when the phone rang. It drove him crazy if he could hear me typing. "Are you on your computer?" he would ask. "Yes, I'm trying to finish ordering something for Hannah and James for Christmas. Got a problem with that?" It wasn't difficult to get him to back off.

Like most young children, mine always became neediest when I was on the phone, whining or tugging on my pant leg for attention or getting into fights in their playroom next to my office. That also annoyed him. "Tell Hannah we're busy," Michael would say. I'd tell him that I would be the one to decide if my kids needed my attention.

Although at first it made me uncomfortable when he asked about my children, they eventually became part of our conversation. Sometimes he would send them birthday cards or a book at Christmas—meaning that he would call Ann or someone else to make the purchase, and he would get the state to reimburse them through his inmate account. My favorite present that they received from him was the children's book *The Story of Ferdinand*, about the bull who would rather smell the flowers than fight, but who gets sent to the bullring because he's stung by a bee and his reaction is so violent that it is misinterpreted as aggression.

Michael made most of the money he had from articles he wrote about the death penalty and forgiveness. The publications sent him payments that ranged from twenty-five dollars to a few hundred. Most were for Catholic publications, but he was even published in the *Utne Reader*. He had a lot more cash at his disposal than when he was sweeping the tier for a few cents a week, so he would get Ann or me to do his shopping for him. Later the state confiscated any money he earned from writing, so Michael had his earnings and donations from supporters sent to Ann, who served as his banker. For the most part, the money went for postage to send his newsletter, *Walking with Michael*, which he began in place of keeping up with the large volume of individual letters he received. He hand-printed it and sent it to more than two hundred people every month or two.

The twins were less than two years old when I began corresponding with Michael. I had adopted them as infants just about the time that Michael adopted me. By the time they were old enough to understand that Michael was in jail, he had become a household item. At age five, the inevitable question came up. "Why is Michael in prison?" "He did some bad things," I would say. That was enough for a while, but eventually they wanted to know more, and I had to tell them that he had killed people. They weren't fearful or opposed to me talking to him. They wanted to know what was going to happen to him, and I had to tell them I didn't know but that he would always be in prison. Perhaps because they had grown up in my household, they were adamant that they didn't want him to be killed.

We sent Michael "Christmas packages." Prisoners could receive books only if sent directly from the publisher or bookseller, and at Christmas the DOC allowed families to buy boxes of approved assorted treats from a company that specializes in gifts for inmates. The packages included coffee, hot chocolate, cookies, crackers, cheese, and even sweatpants. He didn't ask me when I was writing the article, but maybe a year later. "I want to ask you a favor. No pressure," he would say sheepishly. "Want to send me a Christmas package?" I was happy to send them, although I thought they were overpriced—especially considering that most people who would be getting them came from families who didn't have a whole lot of extra cash—about fifty to more than one hundred dollars. Sometimes he would ask me to send a package to his one friend on death row, Bob Breton, because "he has nobody. It would mean a lot."

I soon found out that Michael also had a series of girlfriends. I had not been aware that most high-profile murderers, especially serial killers, receive letters from women once they are sentenced to die. One psychiatrist told me that some women like the idea of a dangerous man with whom they can fall in love but who can't ever touch them or have sex with them. Many of them have had abusive relationships with other men. Other women see themselves as angels of forgiveness whose duty it is to comfort misunderstood souls. One woman sent half-naked sexually suggestive pictures to him. Another told him she was a witch. One time Michael spent his entire savings from writing articles on wedding bands—but was in effect jilted at the altar. I had no patience for the drama. It's unfathomable for me to understand the attraction—but then again, I never thought I'd have a serial-killer friend.

In some ways, I considered Michael my community service. He was going to pay for his crimes by spending the rest of his life in prison—whether the state shortened that life or not—and if calling me helped him get through the day or week, then so be it. When he was only calling once a week for fifteen minutes, he didn't take up much time or get in the way of the rest of my life. At first he called my house only at specific times, but eventually he began calling me at my summer cottage or on holidays—basically whenever he could get to a phone and knew I would be home. By that time, neither I nor anyone in my family minded—or at least no one complained.

Underlying all of the discussions were questions—not just the questions he had about my life and about the outside world, but also questions I had to ask about his growing up, his college years, and about his inner world. Those conversations and letters were how I slowly began to piece together how the Michael I knew had gotten to death row and also how I got to really know him.

"Do you ever fantasize about what life could have been?" I asked.

There was a deep sigh on the other end of the phone. "Of course. Remember Rachel, my first girlfriend in college—not the one I was engaged to—the one I got pregnant? I let her down. I was scared and didn't offer to be there for her, so she had an abortion. We were good together and I often fantasize about what would have happened if she had the baby. In my fantasy it was a girl, Ashley. I picture us on a picnic, all of us sitting on a blanket playing with her. It would have been nice—one happy family."

"You'd get up at night and change diapers and all that?"

"I cleaned up chicken coops. Diapers are nothing. Of course I would. I would have been a good dad." I wondered whether he was deluding himself to think that he would have been capable of caring for a child, but I didn't want to destroy the small comfort he got from that fantasy. Before I had the chance to react, he attempted to change the subject.

"But it don't make sense wasting time talking about what could have been."

"Doesn't that take you away from your current predicament for a few minutes?"

"Yeah, sometimes I lie on my bed with my headphones on, listening to classical music, and I just close my eyes and I am gone for a while. I leave this place." When he was extradited to New York to stand trial for one of the two murders he committed in New York, he was able to pick up the Cornell radio station. "That was the best." He told me about a concert he had heard that began with chimes from some tower on campus. "I was back in college before this all happened. I wish it were that easy to go back." Another time he wrote about drifting back to college as he listened to *A Prairie Home Companion* being broadcast from Cornell. "Two hours of leaving this place. It was heaven."

Michael kept a journal from May 1997 until October 1998; the entries were daily reflections of how he felt, sometimes in the form of prayers. I had been trying to get him to do it, but it was Father John who actually got him started by giving him a notebook. He used the journals as a tool for the spiritual growth he was undergoing as they worked together. When Michael found that he had been baptized a Roman Catholic, he began catechism with Father John, made his first communion, and was confirmed.

At first, writing down his thoughts was cathartic. He could get things off his chest, let go of fears and emotions. It was also another way for him to communicate with God, a type of prayer. After he filled each notebook, he mailed it to me. When he sent me the first full notebook, I hesitated to read it; to do so felt voyeuristic. After a few weeks, however, I slowly did begin reading. In his first entry, Michael said that Father John had just visited him, and he had done his first formal confession and received absolution. "I wish I could say it changed my life—that a huge weight has been lifted off my shoulders—but it hasn't. I know that God has forgiven me, but I can't seem to let go of my past." The page-long passage implied that intellectually he could accept that God forgave him, but emotionally he didn't feel it. He wanted to feel "cured." He had his first communion and confirmation three months later, on August 28, 1997, but he wrote nothing about them. I wondered if the reason was that they were also a letdown, that nothing magical had happened.

He talked about wanting to reunite with family members and about his occasional contact with his father. In one entry, he says he "chickened out" of calling his dad because they no longer had anything in common. While on death row, Michael had transformed from a conservative like his father to, as he described it, "a bleeding-heart liberal." He said that every time he talked to his father, he could sense "that I disappoint him. And often he makes me feel hurt and angry." Michael was proud when two of his essays were included in a book of essays on capital punishment and sent his father a copy of the book. But his father was critical. "You are suspect. . . . You have to remember who you are and where you are and that the public doesn't want you to have anything." He was stung by the comment not just because his father did not show pride in his accomplishment, but also because of the harsh truth it represented. He shrugged it off, though, lamenting that he didn't know his father better, but thought it might be best to leave things as they were "and try not to hurt each other."

Some entries made me realize the importance of things we take for granted, like human touch. "In prison you can't touch anyone. . . . That's why when Christoph Arnold [an elder in the Bruderhof Community] gave me a hug during our first visit, it felt so strange that I broke down and cried. I've wanted to ask Father John for a hug at the last couple of visits, but I felt awkward and didn't say anything." At Osborn in the visiting area, he could see others getting hugged by their families, "but not me. The best that I could hope for was a brief handshake. Closeness to others is an important part of living. I don't know why it has taken me thirty-seven years to figure that out."

In a few of the diary entries, he wrote about his feelings about me and some of the others who called or visited. He thanked God for his friends—especially Father John and Ann. I found some of those entries the hardest to read because I could see the repercussions of some of our phone conversations and the impact I could have on him. It made me want to have a seven-second delay before I spoke. In May 1997 he wrote, "'Be careful what you wish for.' Martha told me that when I talked to her on Tuesday night." Presumably I had said something about accepting a death sentence. "I was a bit taken aback by those words. Martha is a close friend, one of the very few who really know and understand me. Yet those words sounded like maybe she thought that I'm playing some sort of game. I get accused of that all the time here. I don't need my friends accusing me also. I know that's not what she meant but for a second that's what it felt like." He wrote the line "Be careful what you wish for" over and over, and then, "I know what I am doing and I know that, in the end, I will be executed. This is not a game, for I *will* die. And while I can't deny that a part of me looks forward to that day, the greater part of me dreads it." Besides the fear of dying, he knew that with his death, all hope of proving his mental illness would die with him.

He was also concerned about how he would be remembered. "I will forever be known as the biggest piece of shit that ever walked in Connecticut—a deliberate, cold-blooded, murdering, raping son of a bitch." That bothered him more than dying. He had to believe he was not evil, that in his core he was a good person. "I want to prove to the world that I'm Michael Ross and distinct from that 'monster within.' I don't want people cheering my death—visions of that bother me greatly. I want to prove that I'm not a monster; that I am a good person, that I couldn't help it; that I was sick." He wished for a miracle. He wished for a way for people to be able to see into his mind and understand the truth, but he also wanted another way out. "The truth is I wish I didn't have to do this. I wish there were another option, in which no one (including myself) would get hurt."

On May 30, 1997, he wrote, "If God loves me why does he allow me to suffer so?" He quoted Archbishop Fulton Sheen that life is a struggle: "Unless there is a cross in our lives, there will never be the empty tomb. . . ." The message was clear: You have to have pain and sacrifice to find joy and salvation. He said his problem was that he could never trust anyone but himself and that he had to let go of himself to trust in God. "I must sacrifice my very being to make room for God. It's sort of a suicide—but we know my track record on suicide." He suggested that just as he couldn't jump off the bridge at Cornell, he would be unable to do what was necessary to give himself fully to God.

Almost a year later, on March 12, 1998, he wrote, "I don't know why I have been chosen to travel down this path. But I *do* know that this is the path that I have been guided to, directed towards my whole life. Please, my Lord, please don't let this be for nothing. You have the power to make goodness out of this evil mess. Please do not fail in this. . . . Your Will Be Done." He ended many entries with a prayer asking God to help him through his doubts, often concluding with "May Your will be done, not my will." I wondered if he really meant those words. Because no matter what God wanted for Michael, Michael had already made up his mind. He was determined to be executed. How did he know what God wanted? In truth, I think that Michael made up his mind and then decided that it was God's will because he knew—or thought he knew—that what he was doing was right, so it must be God's will.

Sometime after I read Michael's journals, we began discussing theology. It could be about what he had read in Henri Nouwen or anything that occurred to either of us. The longer I knew him, the bolder I got in what I was willing to discuss with him.

"Did I ever tell you that I don't believe in the doctrine of atonement?" I asked.

"You don't think Christ died to save us?"

"I don't believe that God sent his son here to die. I don't want to believe in a God who demanded human sacrifice to save the sins of the world. I also don't believe that one person dying saves another—unless they push the other aside and take a bullet for him."

"How can you not believe in that?" Michael asked.

"I believe that Jesus had it right. Love God and love your neighbor. That would make it a better world and it's all that really matters."

Michael was silent for a moment. I knew I was treading on areas that would upset him, but I also wanted to know what he believed. "So you think that I'm not going to heaven?"

"Michael, I never said anything like that. I said I don't think that someone dying two thousand years ago saves you. What saves you is you. You are sorry for what you did. You want forgiveness. That's what matters. Dying did nothing and *will* do nothing," I said, hoping that he understood that I was referring not just to Jesus's death, but also to his own death.

"So you don't believe there is a heaven?"

"I was trying to figure out what you believe in."

"You started it."

"Okay, I started it. Do I believe in heaven? I want to. I wish I had no doubts."

Again there was a silence. "I have to [believe]," he said softly. "I have to." I knew that if there was ever a time when he was telling me the truth, this was it. I knew that this was a difficult subject for him because he always felt he wasn't making enough spiritual progress. I let it go.

There were also passages in the journals that worried me. For the first years that I knew him, Michael had adamantly denied that he was suicidal and insisted that what he was doing was *not* state-assisted suicide. I had lingering doubts. He had not convinced me when we first discussed it in 1996, and when I read through the journals, I saw hints of a death wish. "There are days when I pray to God just before I go to sleep to 'please, take me in my sleep.' I see no purpose in my life. . . . Get this over with. . . . Let me go quietly." He said if he had the courage, he'd kill himself, but that he was a coward. "At my funeral they should put a sign above me: 'Here lies a coward—too afraid to be a man—may he *not* rest in peace.'" He wrote that "there are days when I wake up and say, 'Damn it, God. Why I am still here?'" It would have been easier for Michael to die in his sleep—to let God take his life and ease his pain. Instead, he was asking the state to do it.

I brought up state-assisted suicide again during a phone conversation, asking him to convince me that he wasn't suicidal. He didn't answer me on the phone when I challenged him. But a few days later, I received his answer in the mail. It was a very long letter, and at the end, he finally answered me. "Now for the issue of 'state assisted suicide.' Publically I have always maintained that I am *NOT* suicidal and that I do not wish to die. However, the truth is probably not quite that clear-cut. And while I feel uncomfortable admitting it publically, I have to admit to you that part of (perhaps much of) my initial desire to drop my appeals was due to a suicidal ideation. . . . Suicide was nothing new to me (as you know), so here I will discuss only suicide in the form of dropping my appeals." He wrote that Depo-Provera was a miracle that allowed him to feel human again. "But . . . even with God, there is no such thing as a free lunch. And that price is guilt—a painful, gnawing guilt that never really goes away. . . . You know, I've often been asked, 'How can you look at yourself in the mirror?' For many years I literally could not look at myself in a mirror without feelings of deep loathing. Did you know that I can shave without a mirror? And that one of the reasons I began to cut my hair short is so I wouldn't have to look in a mirror to comb it?" He made it clear that it was unbearable to be judged every day by the worst thing he'd ever done. "It's a living hell. It's *my* life."

He said he wanted to leave the world for a noble cause, sparing the families more pain. He admitted that was, in part, selfish. He said not to think of him as a total fraud because he was committed to sparing them more anguish. "But it is true, that in the beginning, it was more 'State-assisted suicide' than altruistic feelings for the families of my victims. I'm sorry. I wish I were a better man."

The letter confirmed my suspicion but added other questions. Was this the writing of someone in emotional pain or of a narcissist who thought only about himself? Or both? And if his mental illness included suicidal ideation, how could his decision to offer to die be reasonable or even sane?

I reread Michael's letter from April 20, 1996. He wrote that he didn't care how others perceived him and that the only important thing was how he viewed himself. He insisted that he had to be true to himself. After rereading it several times one afternoon in 1997, I went out for my two-mile afternoon walk on the winding roads near my house in Connecticut. It was early fall and the air was crisp, the leaves just starting to turn. It was obvious that the opinions of others were incredibly important to Michael Ross. I stopped walking, feeling stupid that I hadn't seen it before, and sat down on a stone wall to think.

Michael Ross desperately wanted to be liked, to be loved, and to be known as he knew himself, as the core person he called Michael. He had never had many friends growing up. His only real friends in college had been his two girlfriends. When he was arrested, he wanted Michael Malchik to like him, so he tried to help him solve the case, somehow thinking that Malchik would be grateful and see him as a friend—not some evil serial killer. Michael confessed to Malchik for three reasons: He wanted the killing to be over, he wanted to give something to Malchik so that Malchik would be his friend, and he thought Malchik could help him understand why he had committed all those unimaginable crimes. He didn't have a clue why, and Michael desperately wanted an explanation for his horrendous behavior. He thought that Malchik wanted to help him understand—not to make sure that he got the death penalty. It was no wonder he felt betrayed.

Seeing Michael from this perspective, I could understand why it was so important for him to prove that he suffered from mental illness and why he called it his monster. Paradoxically, it seemed to explain why he wanted to take responsibility for his crimes and offer to die. He wanted the families to forgive him instead of hate him for all of eternity. He desperately wanted to change the way he was judged by the world. He could not bear the thought of being known for the worst things he had ever done, so he wanted to do something that he deemed selfless to overshadow those deeds. He was willing to give up his life to prove that he was sorry and make amends with the hope that maybe someday he would be forgiven.

He didn't care about death. He cared about labels—of being known as a serial killer instead of the "good Michael" that he saw as his core identity. He also feared eternal loneliness. In escaping execution, he was afraid he might lose what few friends he had because the death penalty issue would be moot. They would move on to the next death row crusade; he would be alone.

I got up and started walking again, trying to put all this in perspective.

I finally understood an important aspect of why he was willing to die. He would exchange the label of serial killer for "repentant martyr," a modern-day Sydney Carton, the unscrupulous lawyer from *A Tale of Two Cities*, going to his death to save another from the guillotine. I could almost imagine the execution scene and his last words, "It is a far, far better thing that I do, than I have ever done . . ." Fade to black.

I kept my thoughts to myself but, after a week or two, got up my courage and decided to see if he agreed with me. "Michael, I want to tell you a conclusion I've come to," I began.

He sighed. "Oh, I can tell this is going to be good," he said sarcastically. "Should I be worried?" He was laughing, but of course, deflecting anxiety by joking was his form of self-defense.

"No, it's not bad," I assured him. "I've decided that the reason you're determined to accept death is because you can't stand the fact that you will be remembered as a serial killer. You want your last act to be what you consider to be a noble one. You can separate Michael from the monster, and you want everyone else to be able to do that as well. You hope that someday, somehow, the families will forgive you. You hate your life but can't find a way to kill yourself, so you are making the state do it for you."

He didn't argue with me at all. He thought about it and said that I was right about both things. "Is it so bad to not want to be remembered for your worst deed? Is it so bad to want to be forgiven? Is it so bad to want to rid myself of the guilt? The families want me dead. What they don't understand is that death will bring me peace."

Most of us cherish life. We want to hold on to it, live every moment to the fullest. The idea that waking up every day could be the worst thing that happens to you is hard to comprehend, but that was Michael's so-called life. He was a man who never had a childhood, went to college with no interpersonal skills, felt no love from his family, felt emasculated by his mother and his only serious girlfriend, became obsessed with sex and death, killed eight women and raped more, and went to jail in 1984 at the age of twenty-five.

He knew that in this life he would never get what he wanted most—to be forgiven.

20

NEW LONDON, CONNECTICUT
1998–2000

Judge Thomas Miano rejected the stipulation that Satti and Michael had crafted, saying that it did not meet the requirements for due process. Now Michael needed an attorney, because there would be a full-blown penalty trial. Public defender Barry Butler took the case, and the whole period was deeply distressing for Michael. He even tried to take his own life, saving his antidepressant sleeping pills with the intention to overdose, when he learned that he would have to sit through the horror of another trial. However, guards found him lying on the floor and rushed him to the hospital.

After the suicide attempt, the defense team asked Dr. James Merikangas, an award-winning neurologist and psychiatrist who at the time was at Yale–New Haven Hospital, to evaluate Michael, because his work concentrated on the evaluation and treatment of disorders that include both a neurological and psychological dysfunction. Dr. Merikangas concluded that Michael had brain abnormalities. The MRI of his brain "revealed a mild prominence of the ventricles and mild generalized volume loss, particularly in the parietal lobes. There were also areas of white matter hypersensitivity, predominantly in a subcortical and periventricular distribution. These findings are diagnostic of brain damage, perhaps on a congenital or developmental basis." A single-photon emission computerized tomography (SPECT) scan showed an abnormally low blood flow to parts of his brain. Dr. Merikangas said that "the compulsive behaviors that affected Mr. Ross are a consequence of physical biological abnormalities."

When I met with Dr. Merikangas, he cautioned, however, that neither he nor anyone else could explain how or if Michael's particular brain abnormalities led to his murderous behavior. However, he said, the scans did show that his brain was different from a normal brain. "There was something wrong with his brain. I can't say what was wrong, but there was something wrong. . . . There was an impulse disorder, but impulse disorders are caused by several things. Some are caused by brain damage, some are caused by epilepsy, and some are caused by mental illness." This diagnosis had been suggested by Dr. Cegalis in his 1984 evaluation for the defense. In his conclusions, Dr. Cegalis said that Michael might have a central nervous system lesion on the right side that "can contribute to the crimes alleged by compromising his ability to control his own actions."

In discussing cases like Michael's, Dr. Merikangas pointed out that many times people are convicted because of what they do after the crime—and certainly Michael's hiding the bodies fits that pattern. He explained that when coming out of the fugue-like state, people "wake up and they say, 'What did I do?' And so they hide the body and [the authorities] take hiding the body as evidence that there was intent . . . but there was no intent when they killed them." Dr. Merikangas said the prosecution or the Department of Correction had not allowed him full access to Michael, so he couldn't do a complete examination when he assessed him at Yale. He was not allowed to do many routine tests and there was no confidentiality because guards were posted nearby.

However, he said it was clear that Michael suffered from "dissociative episodes" in which he went into "some kind of fugue state." He said that he agreed with Dr. Borden's conclusions in his 1985 report that negative events in Michael's life would launch him and lead to a rape and murder. "That's my opinion. I think he went into an automatic dissociative state. . . . But once it began, he was just an automaton. However, dissociative states are not generally believed by juries." He compared dissociation with what happens to some people when they take the drug Ambien. They can walk around, drive cars, and appear to be awake, yet actually be unaware of their actions. Michael was not unaware of his actions, but, according to Dr. Merikangas, he didn't consciously make a decision to commit the rapes or murders.

After reading Dr. Merikangas's reports, Michael thought that finally somebody could explain why he had killed. He had something wrong with his brain, and he couldn't wait for the jury to hear this evidence. Never being totally comfortable with the reality of sexual sadism, Michael was relieved that there was also something physical that you could see on a brain scan.

Sixteen years after he was arrested and thirteen years after his first conviction, his second penalty phase trial began. I had just moved to California the summer before, but I would fly back and forth to attend the trial. The major difference in my relationship with Michael was that I couldn't visit as often, and his calls came at six on Saturday or Sunday mornings.

From the first day, it was clear that the only similarities between Michael's first trial and the second were the defendant and the crimes. Satti could not prosecute the trial because of his negotiations with Michael during the stipulation. Too much had been said in those meetings that would prejudice the case. Kevin Kane's prosecution of the penalty phase was nothing like Bob Satti's. There were no theatrics or reenactments of the crimes. This is not to say that Kane didn't push hard for death and try to take every opportunity to put in information that supported his position. Lera Shelley later characterized the second trial as being "more spiritual" than the first trial. It was certainly less strident.

To secure a death sentence, Kevin Kane had to prove to the jurors that Michael Ross had committed the murders, rapes, and kidnappings in an especially cruel or heinous manner that constituted aggravation. According to the law, the aggravation had to be beyond the pain or suffering from the killing itself. It had to be intentionally cruel, heinous, or in a depraved manner in each of the murders. Kane also had to convince the jury that Michael had murdered the women to cover up his crimes of rape. He also needed to convince them that Michael didn't have a mental illness but was merely faking one, because mental illness was a mitigating factor that would rule out the death penalty. Kane relied on the victims' family members and state troopers to prove the bulk of his case. Missing were any expert psychiatric witnesses. If Kane hired another psychiatrist to examine Michael, he would have to share any exculpatory information with the defense. Since every psychiatrist who had ever examined Michael agreed that he was a sexual sadist, the chances of getting a totally different diagnosis were slim to none, so Kane didn't take the chance. He would simply try to refute the defense testimony under cross-examination.

The defense had to convince the jury that Michael suffered from mental illness. If they could do that, they also had to convince the jury that his mental illness rose to the level of mitigation. Juries have a difficult time believing expert psychiatric witnesses when there are multiple victims. It's up to them to decide whether an expert witness is credible; they can ignore any or all of the scientific evidence. Evidence that should prove that a defendant is mentally ill—such as the number of victims—is sometimes ignored by the jury because of the magnitude of the crimes. They feel the defendant should pay for his many crimes even if the psychiatric evidence suggests that mental illness should mitigate the penalty. This was why Michael Ross felt the system would never be fair to him. This also is why juries have such a hard time when a defendant claims to be mentally ill in death penalty cases.

Going into the trial, Barry Butler and Karen Goodrow gave the impression that they believed they could convince the jury that Michael should not die. They had a battery of experts who would testify not only that he suffered from mental illness, but also that he had physical brain abnormalities that could help explain his behavior. However, in the end, Dr. Berlin and Dr. Merikangas—the two witnesses who Michael thought were crucial to his case—were never called to testify for technical reasons that involved preserving an issue for appeal. It was a decision by the defense lawyers that frustrated and angered Michael.

On April 6, 2000, at 4:00 P.M. EST, the jury informed Judge Miano that they had reached a verdict after nine days or 208 hours of deliberation. This jury took its time, methodically going through the testimony of forty-three witnesses and 180 pieces of evidence. As of that morning, the deliberations had set a record, lasting longer than any other capital trial in Connecticut, and even ranked among the longest in the nation. Precisely because the jury took so long, I began thinking that Michael would get life or at least a hung jury.

Families of the victims, reporters, and Michael's few friends held a vigil in the hallway of the courthouse, sitting on the hard, uncomfortable benches that line the wall. When the announcement was made summoning everyone back into court, most were taken off guard. It was so late in the day that almost everyone was about to go home. The Shelleys and Roodes, neighbors at home and in the courtroom, had been waiting sixteen years for this day. But as the days dragged on, they, too, had begun to lose hope that this jury would return a verdict of death. They were well aware that the first jury had taken only four hours to make that decision. "This is worse," Lera Shelley told reporters.

The family members seemed apprehensive as the jury filed in. Ellen Roode, sitting in Lera Shelley's usual seat directly behind Michael, crossed her fingers and held them to her lips as she waited. Lera, across the aisle from Roode, clutched Ed's arm as the clerk asked for the verdict. I looked around and could not help but notice that none of Michael's support group was there. He was awaiting his fate with only his legal team and me.

Juror number ten, the foreman, stood with both hands on the rail of the jury box and announced each decision. Every time they voted yes for aggravation, the prosecution had proven its case. Every time they voted no for mitigation, the defense had failed to prove its case. On each count, the foreman read the decisions: aggravation, yes; mitigation, no. Between each count, he turned to look at Michael, making eye contact. Did he want to see Michael's reaction or was he trying to make sure that Michael saw his certainty?

Even though Michael was on trial for the rape and murder of only four of his victims, there were six death sentences in all, because death was imposed for both the kidnapping and the murder of April Brunais and of Leslie Shelley. In the end, either the jury had not believed that Michael Ross was mentally ill, or they ignored the law because they thought Michael Ross should pay for his crimes. It's also possible that they believed he suffered from sexual sadism but did not believe that his mental illness had limited his ability to control his actions.

Each of the twelve jurors was individually polled on aggravation and mitigation for all six counts. As each juror answered, Mrs. Shelley wiped away her tears. Across the rail, Michael tried to comfort Barry by squeezing his shoulder. At one point, he gave Barry a gentle punch in the arm, but Barry did not change his sullen expression. Michael had shut down his emotions, but he was devastated.

As we filed out of the courtroom, Ed Shelley spoke. "When twenty-four people convict a man, I think that's justice," he said. "Some might say it's revenge, but I say it's justice."

For the five years I had known him, Michael was not under a sentence of death even though he was housed on death row. I wondered how he would react, what he would say when he finally called me. Mostly I wondered what I could possibly say to him that would have any meaning. What do you say to someone who just got six death sentences? I knew that avoiding the ultimate issue of the verdict and sticking to the details was the best way to subdue Michael. He was much calmer when he ignored the larger picture.

When he got back to the prison, he called me right away, sobbing. "I thought I had a chance. It took so long. I figured there was a hold-out. I was afraid there might be a mistrial if the jury was deadlocked. But they didn't believe the evidence. They didn't believe my mental illness; no jury will ever believe me." He complained about some of the defense decisions and harped on the fact that Dr. Berlin and Dr. Meri-kangas had not testified. It was clear that despite saying that he didn't care if he was put to death, he still had held out the hope that the jury would sentence him to life in prison. What he wanted to avoid was the actual trial, but if the state of Connecticut insisted that a trial was necessary, he had hoped that the jury would believe his mental illness and spare his life.

It was likely that Leslie Shelley's murder had been the deciding factor; Michael had said that that crime was "going to hang me." If there ever was a time when he was going to tell me the truth about Leslie Shelley, this was it. "What's the truth about Leslie? What you said in the tape and in your confession or what you have been saying since 1994?" I needed to know whether he'd raped her anally, as he claimed after 1994, or whether he'd killed her without sex to hide his crime.

He was sobbing so hard he could hardly talk. "The tape. What's on the tape. I never tried to rape her." I didn't know what to feel. I was relieved that I knew the truth, but also disappointed, even hurt to know that he had lied to me. I didn't tell him, because I knew the tears were real. He had let himself believe that this jury had accepted the psychiatric evidence and would not recommend death. I didn't have to tell him how I felt because I was fairly certain that he knew.

I had watched the Shelleys in court for five years, but purposefully had not tried to interview them until the legal proceedings had come to a close—albeit temporarily. Instead of approaching them in the hallway, I wrote them a letter—as I did all of the families—explaining that I wanted to talk to them about their daughters, promising not to hound them if they decided not to speak with me.

Just before sentencing day, I received a letter from Lera Shelley. She wrote about how she and Ed had developed a good relationship with Barry and the other attorneys and didn't blame them for representing "M. Ross." She said that they hoped I would keep an open mind but wrote, "I am not sure about meeting with you. I did not even plan on talking to you, but I will give you our phone number. I am trusting you, and I hope that you will not give our phone number or address to anyone."

Sentencing day was May 12, the anniversary of Michael's first murder.

He felt he deserved to be sentenced to death on that date—especially because it was the only murder for which he had never been prosecuted. He would never serve time in New York because he already was under a death sentence in Connecticut, so the prosecutor in Ithaca declined to pursue the case.

The media trucks were everywhere, and the courthouse halls were filled with reporters. Five of the jurors and three of the alternates had also come to hear Judge Miano mete out justice. Everyone had to wait in the hallway for the sheriff to unlock the door. Just before the crowd filed into court for the sentencing, Mrs. Shelley came up to me in the hallway.

"Are you Martha Elliott?"

"Yes," I said, hoping that she wasn't about to scream at me or tell me that my writing to them had been hurtful.

"How did you get my address?"

I explained to her how I had gotten it, and she realized that there was nothing unethical about how I had figured it out.

"You can call me," she said. "You have my number."

Judge Miano gave each victim's family a chance to speak. Ed and Lera Shelley didn't speak. All during the trial, it seemed as if Ed was champing at the bit to express himself, to say what he had been feeling for sixteen long years. Later he explained, "I sat there and I thought about saying something, but what can you say? I felt that enough had been said. . . . I had burned myself out, really. I kicked that around for the first five or six, maybe ten years, I would have had plenty to say, but after a while you have to realize that life goes on. You just can't dwell in the past. I think the jury spoke volumes when they gave the verdict, and I couldn't have said anything any better." Lera echoed Ed's sentiment. "I had something memorized, but then I thought, no, I won't."

Finally, Michael was given the chance to speak. It was his chance to apologize. "I am sorry I was not strong enough to fight the illness in my mind. I am sorry I did not have the courage to take my own life at Cornell before I allowed my illness to take the lives of others." He also repeated his wish to exchange his life for the victims, sobbing as he spoke.

Judge Miano spent twenty minutes going through the evidence to reiterate that the jurors had made the right decision. He made it clear that he did not believe that Michael Ross was mentally ill, but rather had raped and then murdered to cover his crimes. He set the execution date but explained that the State Supreme Court would stay the execution until it had upheld the jury's decision.

21

THE SHELLEYS' HOME
JUNE 6, 2000

It was a torrentially rainy day when I drove to the Shelleys' modest home in Griswold, Connecticut. I was more than an hour late, and my anxiety levels were escalating. The rain was causing accidents everywhere, and traffic on the interstate was at a standstill. The Shelleys knew I had been talking to Michael for years, and I didn't know how they would react to my questions. Very few family members actually agreed to talk to me, so in my mind the Shelleys represented all the families who suffered the excruciating pain of losing a child at the hands of Michael Ross.

Jumping mud puddles, I ran to the Shelleys' front door and rang the bell. Within seconds, a cacophony of barking sounds greeted me as the five family dogs scrambled to be first to the door. Inside, I could hear Ed and Lera Shelley trying to get their brood of dogs and endless cats under control. Even before Ed opened the front door, it was obvious that the house was in need of a lot of repairs, but he made no bones about the state of his property. He must have seen my eyes dart around, because he brought it up as soon as I stepped inside. "My house has been falling apart for sixteen years," he admitted. "I didn't do squat. I really didn't. I've got so much stuff to do because of the time spent in court and time spent with Jennifer [the Shelleys' youngest daughter] doing whatever she wanted to do. Dad was there, and it was time that I had set aside. . . . So now my house is falling apart. I've got to put siding on. I've got to paint it."

The Shelley family had been consumed with the fate of Michael Ross since the day he was arrested. They attended almost every hearing and never missed a day of either trial. Nothing else mattered; for Ed and Lera, holding their vigil in many different courtrooms was far more important than painting or fixing the holes in the bathroom wall or even satisfying a supervisor at work.

Sitting around the kitchen table, animals crowding, and smoke swirling as both Shelleys chain-smoked, we began a conversation that went on for years and continues to this day. No one had to say that their daughter's murder had wreaked havoc on this family. It is evident in every word they spoke and everything around them. Their hurt and anger permeates the house—and only one person was responsible.

It was easy to like Ed and Lera. They were decent people, straightforward with no pretensions. Ed spent a good part of his career working for the U.S. Postal Service, but at the time of my first visit, he had retired and was working at a golf course. Lera worked as a nurse's aide at the state mental hospital in Norwich. They both had a sense of humor and were willing to laugh at themselves.

Lera could not speak of her daughter without tearing up; Ed got teary at times, but he also had a visceral hatred of Michael Ross. He got right to the point early in the conversation, looked me straight in the eye and said, "When he took Leslie out of the car, he apologized to her and told her he was sorry, and then he murdered her. And the fear that kid went through knowing what was happening to her friend outside the car is unimaginable." He paused and sighed. "That's the thing that really gets me. What was she thinking? What was she saying?" It was easy to see why he became obsessed with Michael Ross's fate. To know that his child died in agony and fear must have been almost unbearable. As a parent, I could only imagine their excruciating sorrow, and I understood their crusade. Ed was adamant that Michael should be executed. Period. Lera, a Roman Catholic, said she never thought about it much before her daughter was murdered. "In some cases, I do believe in the death penalty," she said thoughtfully. "But I believe that God is the only one that can decide when and how Ross will die. If Ross had gotten life without the possibility of parole, we would have lived with it," she said. "If this had happened to one of your daughters, how would you feel?"

I had asked myself that question ever since I first started talking to Michael Ross. I took a deep breath because I wanted to be honest with them but not offend them. "How would I feel? I know I would have wanted to strangle him with my bare hands. But I hope that I wouldn't because I believe that all killing is wrong," I answered. "I've thought about it a lot. How would I feel if someone were drunk and had an accident and killed somebody? We would never have the death penalty for him, but the person who drinks and gets behind the wheel is doing something they could control, and the person who is mentally ill doesn't have control. Isn't the mentally ill person less culpable?" I asked.

"Yes, but how do we know for sure that Michael Ross or anyone is really mentally ill?" Ed asked.

"That's part of the problem," I admitted. But I didn't want to do the talking. "Tell me about Leslie." They both smiled. Leslie's life was a topic they both liked to think about. Ed's most vivid image of Leslie was as a little girl, covered with chocolate ice cream. "I can always remember her as that little runt with a dirty face, big smile, long hair, happy face, sitting on the porch."

I looked at a picture of Leslie. "She looked a lot like you," I told Lera.

"She was Lera's daughter," Ed said. "They were very close." I looked over at Lera, the tears streaming down her face as she looked at the picture of her daughter. He said Leslie had hoped to someday go to nursing school and become an RN, following in her mother's footsteps. "Les often waited up for her mother on weekends so that they could play cards or watch a horror movie. She liked watching shows that were scary but wouldn't watch them alone."

Leslie also liked to spend time with her dad, sometimes playing softball. She wasn't much of an athlete, but she loved to play softball. It didn't matter that she wasn't very good at it. "The only hit the kid got the whole year was a home run. I mean, there were errors all over the place, kids throwing the ball the wrong way. And she couldn't run. She was as slow as a turtle," Ed said chuckling. "But everybody's yelling, 'Keep going, keep going' and she got her home run. She was just ear to ear with a grin," he remembered.

Leslie Shelley was devoted to the things she loved, like her pets—dogs, cats, ferrets—who were equally devoted to her. Casper, her pet Chihuahua, wouldn't let anyone but Leslie go near him. "He was Leslie's dog, and that was it," remembered Lera. Casper would follow her to the Roodes' house and sit on the front steps until Leslie came out and went home. He slept with her at night, and if someone walked past her bed, they'd be lucky not to be bitten by Casper. "He was so protective of her," Lera recalled. "You couldn't even go into her room because he was guarding her."

Both Ed and Lera agreed that Leslie was headstrong. Ed tells the story of when she was six or seven and they were driving home in the car. "You know how kids can get going in the car. I said, 'Leslie, if you don't knock it off, right now, you are going to walk home.' Well we were just pulling into the project and she says, 'You wouldn't put me out.' I stopped the car and that little devil got out. I had to drag her back into the car." So it's no wonder that if she was determined to go to the movies that Easter afternoon, she would find some way to do it.

The year before, the pair had been missing for about four hours. April had decided to run away from home, and Leslie dutifully accompanied her, even though running away was not the way that Leslie usually handled her own problems. She was more likely to call her married sister, Robin, who was nine years older. On average, she called Robin a few times a week for advice or just to talk. For whatever reason, when they decided to run away, Leslie decided against consulting her sister and packed up enough clothes for a lifetime. Before leaving, Leslie instead told her younger sister, Jennifer, that they would be staying at their friend Sandy's house. A seven-year-old, Jennifer was not a good confidante and reported all she knew to her parents. So Ed, Lera, and Raymond Roode, April's stepfather, drove over to Sandy's to retrieve their daughters. Leslie came downstairs when Ed called and then confessed that April was hiding in an upstairs closet. It was over in less than four hours.

Because of the earlier runaway attempt, April's and Leslie's parents first assumed that they were up to the same shenanigans. Nevertheless, they were concerned and began searching for the pair in familiar places. "We drove down the railroad tracks," says Ed. "We went to see my son. We went to a friend's house. We checked all around, and then it started— rumors, sightings." One of the girls' friends insisted that they had called from Florida. Someone else said they had seen them in court the next day. Someone else claimed that April had been spotted at the soup kitchen.

Ellen Roode and Lera rode down to the soup kitchen, where a number of Lera's patients from Norwich Hospital worked, and showed them pictures of the girls, but no one remembered seeing either of them. "So then we went over to the Wauregan Hotel," said Lera, because someone reported seeing a girl resembling April. "At that time, it was drugs, alcohol—you name it—were in there. So I got a room number and I went up, and this woman answered the door. I showed her a picture of April, and she said that the girl that was staying there could pass for April's twin but that it wasn't April."

They contacted the missing-children's bureau in Rhode Island, and called Ed's nephew, a police officer in Florida, to try to get the word out. Ed, a postal worker, sent a letter to the *Postal Record*, a monthly newsletter that goes to all postal workers, asking them to run a picture of Leslie. The picture was published on June 28, the day Leslie's and April's bodies were found.

For the two months the girls were missing, the Shelleys never let themselves believe that Leslie wasn't coming home. "You have to understand that people are in shock," explains Ed. "She was gone about two weeks, and I was at Nelson's, which is an auction house . . . and I bought a beautiful French provincial bedroom set for her, and I had the bureau and the night table, the bed all set up. That would be Leslie's room when she finally came home." He said it took two or three years after their remains were found before he finally put an ad in the paper and sold the furniture.

"The thing that got me the hardest," Ed said sullenly, "was the day they recovered the bodies." He had taken his youngest daughter, Jennifer, to Plainfield to watch the horse races from the road. Afterward, they went to meet his daughter Robin and her four-year-old daughter for some ice cream. "We were driving down the road, and the news flash came on the radio that they had recovered two young girls' remains in Preston. My little eight-year-old girl looks at me and says, 'Daddy, that's April and Leslie.' I just sat there and I knew. I knew. I went in and I got her some ice cream and then when I saw my oldest daughter come in, I had no doubt. So I had Robin take Jennifer with her."

Lera heard the news while she was at work at Norwich Hospital. The state police came to the hospital to ask her for Leslie's dental records.

When Ed got home, he saw a detective leaving the Roodes' house and heading over to talk to him. "I said, 'It's my daughter Leslie, isn't it?' And he said, 'Well, we're not sure.' And I said, 'Like hell you're not sure. We gave you exactly what the girl was wearing. You mean you can't tell me what she was wearing?'" The officer told Ed they had to wait for the autopsy report.

The next morning Ross was arraigned for the murders of Robin Stavinsky, April Brunais, Leslie Shelley, and Wendy Baribeault. "They didn't want us at the arraignment," Ed says. "They told us about five minutes before the arraignment was going to start. I guess they came walking down Water Street with about twenty state troopers surrounding him. They had sharpshooters on top of the Shannon Building, on top of the courthouse, on the parking garage to protect him. You know, I don't think that would have protected him, not the way I was. I would have taken my shotgun and blown him away."

After the police and media had left the place where they found the bodies, Ed and Lera needed to go to the spot. "It was eerie," Ed remembered, gesturing to Lera. "She'll tell you. When we went over there, the road curves around and there is a swamp there. I got out of the car with her, and we went walking over to the swampy area. And I told her, 'This isn't the spot.' I walked across the road and the hairs just jumped on my arms. I mean the back of my neck just crawled, and I knew right then and there, where it was." They took pictures of the area and left. Although Lera had promised Ed that she wouldn't go back, she was compelled to go again. One day while Ed was working, she drove over and went down the embankment to the spot where Leslie was found. She sat down and just put her head down, her hands covering her face, and began crying uncontrollably. "That was the last place Leslie had been. It was hard."

People's reactions to the murders both helped and hurt the family. The night Leslie's body was found, Ed called a friend in the middle of the night. "He says, 'What the hell do you want at two o'clock in the morning?' I said, 'They found my daughter's body.' He said, 'Come on down.' I stopped to get some cigarettes, and some guy picked up the paper and said, 'These girls asked for it.' And if I had turned around and told him it was my daughter, I think I probably would have poked him right out on the spot, because I did have a temper, but I just ignored him and walked away." Ed felt that people are always too willing to blame the victims. "Wendy Baribeault went out for a walk. She was in her shorts. So they say she was asking for it. People are so asinine when they think that kids—girls, boys, or whatever—go out and are asking to get killed or get raped; it's stupid. People just don't understand. But some care. People care. It's just that they don't know how to show it. Just a pat on the back. Or 'I'm sorry' suffices. . . . You can survive it. It's tough. But you have to survive. You have to go on."

Lera joked. "With all the people at Norwich Hospital, I had five hundred pats on the back. I had enough. They can keep their pats to themselves." She chuckled for the first time since we had begun to talk.

Even Ed's own mother showed no sensitivity. "She was a wench," said Ed. "She says to me, 'Well, it's better than being in white slavery.' And I said, 'But then at least she'd be alive. I could get her back, but this is eternal.'" He shook his head as he considered the comment.

Because the girls' bodies had been so badly decomposed, both families had decided to cremate the remains. "There was no reason to spend thousands of dollars on a casket," Ed explained. "There wasn't much there."

The Shelleys also wanted to get the funeral over as soon as possible because they knew it would be a painful ritual. The funeral was not a bonding experience for the two families; in fact, it was the beginning of a rift between them that would result in the next-door neighbors barely speaking. Ed said that Ray and Ellen Roode wanted to have a big funeral with Channel 3, Channel 8, and Channel 30 allowed to come to the grave site, but Ed and Lera wanted no media attention. "My thought at the time was, Let's get it over with and make it as easy as possible on everybody," Ed explained. "I didn't want to go through shaking people's hands and having them tell me how sorry they were." The Shelleys told the Roodes that they didn't have to bury April when they buried Leslie. They could do what whatever they wanted to do.

Reverend Lou Harper of the First Congregational Church in Griswold, where Leslie and April attended the youth group, conducted a brief service by the mausoleum near the gate to the tree-lined cemetery on Route 38 in Griswold. The girls' urns had been placed side by side—friends forever. After the service, Ed picked up Leslie's urn and Ray picked up April's. "Ray did his thing with April's remains, and I got up and I was really nervous. I said something." Although the formal services were short and without fanfare, Ed and Lera have carefully tended to the grave site, planting flowers every year. One Easter, Lera even hung Easter eggs on a tree that Ed had planted.

Eventually, the conversation circled back to Michael Ross. Lera and Ed were convinced that Michael had no remorse for what he did. They also didn't buy his mental illness. "Do you think he is mentally ill?" I asked.

Lera answered immediately with a resounding "No!"

Ed extrapolated. "I look at it this way. Evil? Yes. I think he could control himself when he was in homes selling insurance." He pointed to one case in Moosup, Connecticut, where Michael forced a girl to perform oral sex but let her go. "Well, like the girl said, 'I can run faster than him with my pants up than he can with his pants down,' and that's exactly how she got away. It wasn't that he let her go. He admitted to having stalked women. So there wasn't a question of, Is there a mental illness?—because he could control himself when he was stalking. He wanted what he wanted regardless of what damage or harm it caused."

Michael never could explain why he had let the Moosup woman go or why he had stalked many women but did not rape or murder all of them. "Raping and murdering isn't a logical thing. I didn't just go out and think I'll rape this one and murder that one. I don't know why any of this happened."

Ed was certain that the sexual sadism was all faked. "All it had to take was one person to put the idea of sexual sadism in his mind. It wouldn't take him long to digest a book on what sexual sadism consists of—voices in his head. Things like that. And if it could keep me from the death penalty, you could shoot me with Depo-Provera all day long. . . ." Ed explained, "I honestly feel that if a person is truly mentally ill and I didn't feel that he could control his actions, it would have a bearing on my feelings towards him." Not wanting to leave any doubt about how he felt about Michael Ross, he added, "But knowing that Ross could control himself when he felt like controlling himself, that was the deciding factor in my feeling toward wanting the death penalty."

"Do you think he's mentally ill?" Lera asked, turning the tables on me. "Because you talk to him a lot."

I thought for a moment. "I think that anybody who kills anybody is sick," I began slowly. "I don't think a normal person can kill another— except defending oneself or in a fit of rage—and even that shows that there is something wrong if he can't control his anger. So I start with that point of view. I don't see how anybody could do what he did and not be mentally ill."

"I don't think Ross has remorse, though. I really don't think he does." Lera was adamant.

"You really don't? So you didn't buy the apology he gave in his statement at the sentencing?"

"No, I'll tell you like I told Barry. . . . I could have predicted every time Ross took off his glasses and wiped his eyes, tears, looked down at the floor when someone was on the stand that was testifying when he didn't like what they were saying. If someone was on the stand that he liked, he looked right at them, smiled," she observed. "No, I don't think he is sorry. I think the only thing he's sorry about is that he got caught and he's in jail. I don't think he's remorseful."

She was right on one level. He didn't like to see the pain and destruction he had caused. The question was whether he felt remorse about it or just sorry for himself or a combination of both. Only Michael Ross could know what he felt, and I wasn't even sure he was capable of separating the two emotions. Even the psychiatrists disagreed about whether he felt remorse or empathy. I tried to explain. "I think the thing that drives him crazier than anything is that he will always be known as Michael Ross, the serial killer. In fact, I think that is where the stipulation came from. He was trying to do something that would take the onus off what he had done."

Ed felt that the fact that Michael had changed his story about how Leslie died was telling. "He was his own worst enemy saying that he had raped Leslie anally."

"You should know. That part is just not true," I told them. "I made him admit it to me. He didn't rape Leslie."

"We knew that. We knew that," Ed said. "That's when he hung himself, when he killed Leslie. That's when the jury lost all credibility in his statements."

Lera got up and came back with a scrapbook. "I kept every newspaper article since they found the girls—ten scrapbooks full." She put the first one on the table and opened it. It began with pictures of Leslie.

Tears filled Lera's eyes as she turned the pages. "If you read it, you'll see the difference between the first trial and the second."

We flipped through the pages of several of the books as I scribbled down notes. "Would you mind if sometime I made copies of some of the scrapbooks?" I asked.

Lera hesitated. "You can have them," she said. "I'm done clipping newspapers. I've got to move on. I just want to take out the pictures of Leslie."

"Are you sure?" I asked. "These must be very important to you."

"Yes, I'm sure," she said. "I need to move on."

It was almost 7:00 P.M., and we had come to a place where we didn't have more to say or ask without some time and reflection. I was hoping that I could look for the location where the girls' bodies had been found, but I didn't want to ask directly, not wanting to seem too morbid. "How far was it from here where the girls' bodies were found?" I asked Ed.

He offered. "You got a minute? Let's take a ride."

"Are you sure?"

"Yes," he said confidently. Then turning to Lera, he said, "Put that out," pointing toward a scented candle.

"No, I'm staying here," she said adamantly. The day had already been too much for her.

It was still raining steadily as we got into his car and headed toward Route 38. The constant beat of the windshield wipers clicking back and forth added suspense and tension. Finally we arrived at the culvert where Michael had dropped the two girls' bodies—on a lonely stretch of road in what seemed like the middle of nowhere. "I'd never have found this on my own," I admitted.

"That's what I thought," he chuckled. "No use in you getting yourself lost out here."

"Right over there," he said as we got out of the car. It had been sixteen years. Some areas had become overgrown, some had been cleared, but it was not difficult to see the spot where the bodies had been thrown into an irrigation ditch on the side of the road.

I just stood there staring for a minute, trying not to visualize the gruesome crime scene photos of the girls' partially decomposed bodies. He said that some of the other family members had not realized what happens to a body after being exposed to the elements for more than two months. "I've been out hunting enough to know that they would be in no condition for anyone to see. That's why we decided to have them cremated."

"Do you come by here much?"

"No, you can't. You have to move on. You have to move on," Ed said and then paused. "Okay, now let's get macabre." I looked at him, wondering what could be more macabre than what we were doing. Reading my puzzled expression, he said, "I'll show you where the girls are buried, only a few hundred feet from each other—Love Ya Always Like a Sister." As we drove into the small cemetery, Ed pointed to a large gravestone partway down one of the first rows, "That's where Debra Smith Taylor is buried, right over there."

"That seems so improbable that three of the victims would all be buried in the same cemetery," I said.

"Not if you start to look at how small an area it is. You know, that's why I wanted to start a civil suit against Ross's father. He should have known. His son had already been convicted of two attacks, and then women start being murdered. He should have known. We went to a lawyer at the time of the first trial, but you know what he said? 'Got thirty thousand dollars?' And of course, I don't have anywhere near that.

So the suit didn't go anywhere. I was hoping that he'd sue me for defamation in court, and then I could have countered with a wrongful death suit."

We drove near the back of the cemetery and stopped by the two girls' graves. I got out despite the rain because I wanted to see the headstones. A large rose-colored stone that says SHELLEY marks Leslie's grave. There is also a plaque on the ground that says LESLIE ANN. The grave is decorated with little brass angels, two lying down on the top of the headstone and two sitting by the front of the stone. Flowers are planted around the stone. At first they planted a tree, but the roots got too big. "I had a heck of a time getting that tree out."

A mystery surrounds Leslie's grave: A few times a year someone leaves flowers. Ed and Lera have tried to figure out who the mystery person is, to no avail. "It's strange. I have no idea who's been doing it. It's almost eerie," Lera had explained.

Ed showed me April's grave. Like Debra Smith Taylor's, her grave was marked only by the family stone—Roode. It was as if both young women had been swallowed up without a trace.

Instead of heading back to the house, Ed drove in the opposite direction, into Jewett City, a down-at-the-heels town of about three thousand people. He slowed down as we rounded the corner where the girls had called home to say they were running late. "They must have hung up, crossed the street, and within a few minutes, Ross picked them up," he said, "because in his confession he said it was right around here. There used to be a telephone booth on the corner here, but it's gone now."

He drove on a few more blocks. "That's the house," he told me. "That's where he lived." It was nothing like what I had imagined. I had thought of it more like an apartment complex, but it was a large boxy house that had been divided into apartments. Ed turned his car around and started back toward Griswold.

"So he picked them up in Jewett City, and they asked to be taken to a gas station in Voluntown, but he just drove past the gas station . . . and then ended up in the Exeter woods in Rhode Island?" I asked.

"Well, that's the question, isn't it?" he answered in a tone that implied he didn't believe Michael's version of the story.

"You don't think the murder scene was in Rhode Island?"

"Actually, I think the place they claimed it happened was the Arcadia woods, not Exeter. From where the girls were picked up, I believe it's twenty-three miles, and he brought the girls back and dropped them over here with a dead girl in the front seat? I don't think it happened [in Rhode Island], because when the detectives went up there, they scoured the woods because of April's shoes and the pants missing, and they couldn't find them." Ed's theory was that the two girls were killed somewhere near where their bodies were found.

Ed said he had been to the murder scene, but I wasn't sure if he was talking about the location where Michael claimed he committed the murders or the one Malchik had described in his directions. "Well, let's go see if we're talking about the same place," Ed suggested. When we passed Beach Pond and crossed into Rhode Island, I was sure that he was going to the place that Michael had described. Within a few minutes, he pulled into the exact location that I had found when I followed Michael's directions, and we got out of the car. "No way did it happen here. Somebody would have seen them," he said, pointing out that the area was too open and that someone might have seen from the road. "And it's just too suspicious that they'd come out here two years later and find pieces of cloth," he said, referring to the strips of slipcover that the defense claimed to have found.

"No more suspicious than Malchik writing down directions two years later," I reminded him.

"Maybe not. We'll probably never really know."

When I told Michael I had been to the Shelleys' house, he was curious about what they had said. I told him about our conversation. I said I'd told them that he didn't rape Leslie. He seemed shocked that I had told them that, but I wouldn't let him backpedal on the admission. "Mr. Shelley even said he had proof on the autopsy report that she had not been raped."

"That's not what I said," he argued. "You misunderstood me."

But I hadn't misunderstood. I knew what the truth was. "I asked you point-blank which story was the truth, and you said the one on the tape—the confession tape."

The next week, Michael and I talked more about the Shelleys and their feelings. "Mr. Shelley's anger—I can't blame him for not being able to forgive me. I know I caused it all. I forgive Mr. Shelley because when he is angry and says some of the things he says . . ."

"You better be careful how you say things, because saying, 'I've forgiven Mr. Shelley, but he can't forgive me' is ridiculous. What the hell should *you* forgive Mr. Shelley about?"

He started to cry. Blaming the prosecutor was one thing; blaming the parent of his murder victim was another.

Lera and I corresponded for the next several months and continue to occasionally make contact by mail or phone. Sometimes she wrote to fill in gaps, sometimes just being friendly by sending me a Christmas card or a friendly thinking-of-you kind of note. She also had questions for me about Michael that I answered as best I could.

Immediately after talking to Lera and Ed, I found it difficult to talk with Michael. In one very awkward occurrence during the summer of 2000, I was speaking to Michael on the phone when the other line rang. It was Lera. "I gotta go," I told him. "I have another call I need to take. Don't call me back today," I said, knowing he might try to call back and that I wouldn't be able to handle talking to him after talking to her. Later I explained to him who had been on the phone. "I'm glad you talked to her," he said. "I hope they're doing okay." On some level, I think he hoped that my talking to the Shelleys would make them forgive him, but I had no intention of being a go-between, and I already knew that the idea that they would ever forgive him was nonsense. If there was one thing I learned from meeting them, it was that Ed Shelley was never going to forgive Michael Ross—and I didn't see why he should, unless he believed that Michael was sincere in his remorse—and he didn't—or he felt forgiving Michael would help him get past losing Leslie.

Leslie's death had been especially hard on her sisters—her older sister, Robin, and Jennifer, who was only eight at the time. I met Jennifer during another visit to the Shelleys'. As she spoke of Leslie, her eyes welled with tears. "I kept thinking they'd come home. I never thought she was dead until I heard that they had found two bodies. Then I knew it was Leslie."

Besides reminiscing about Leslie, she also talked about the death penalty. It was clear that Jennifer had no doubts about the fact that Michael should die for what he had done, but she was also angry at the criminal justice system. "I never had a childhood," she said, sobbing. "It was like the only thing that was important was for Michael Ross to die. Nothing else mattered—every court date, every time the legislature was going to discuss capital punishment. There was hardly any time for anything else."

Even in college, she couldn't escape her sister's murder. In April 2001, Lera wrote that Jennifer was taking an English class at New England Institute of Technology in Rhode Island. She said the class was "studying . . . the death penalty. Of course she has discussed her interest in it because her sister was murdered by M. Ross!" She asked that I make copies of anything I had that she could use in writing her paper. She told me that Jennifer was thinking about getting in touch with Michael via the Internet, but "does not know what she would say to him." She didn't know that death row inmates in Connecticut had no Internet access. The Department of Correction does not want them contacting victims, convicted felons, or going on inappropriate Web sites. Lera said that if Jennifer decided to contact Michael, "it has to be her decision, and I will not try to talk her out of it. I don't know how her dad will feel about it."

I sent a few articles I had written as well as other background material from the scrapbooks or documents I had collected. Jennifer was determined to tell Michael what he had done to her life. She wanted some answers to questions that had plagued her for almost two decades, so I gave her his address, in case she wanted to write. She did.

She wrote him a short letter, saying that she was writing "to you to let you know how you ruined my life seventeen years ago when you took my sister away from my parents and I. My parents have had to live with emptiness in their lives which can never be filled." She said she had grown up trying to figure out "why this happened to my family, why my sister had to die at such a young age and why someone like you would still be alive after seventeen years of sitting on death row." She told him that she was satisfied with the outcomes of the trial "because my sister will forever haunt you. She is the girl who screws up all your lies and excuses you seem to come up with so you can have a new trial or another appeal. I am disgusted with all your excuses and reasons to explain why you killed six young ladies and how sorry you are for the crimes you have committed when you stole a life away from the family and friends of your victims. . . . The lives of the girls you stole away from us will always be remembered and for this reason you will never have peace in your life and the remorse you say you have will always fall on deaf ears!"

Jennifer told me that she would like to hear back from Michael, so I relayed the message. He was hesitant to write, but when I told him it was important to Jennifer, he complied. He ended up sending the letter to me, and I forwarded it to her, because inmates are not allowed to have direct contact with their victims or their families. Because I had a request from Jennifer to communicate with him, I didn't feel I was abetting him in skirting the rule.

He said that he was writing only because I had made it clear that she wanted and expected a response to her letter. "If I have been wrongly informed, please destroy this letter right now, for I have absolutely no desire to invade your privacy." Knowing that he could not say anything to change her opinion of him, he wrote, "I offer no excuses, because there are none. I murdered your sister. She did not deserve to die. She did nothing to provoke me to kill her, and you and your family did not deserve the ordeal that you have been through." He said he had tried to explain his mental illness for many years, but he did not mean it as an excuse for what he did. "I do not care if I am executed; in fact, part of me longs for the sweet release of death. . . . I tried to accept full and complete responsibility and I did my best to get the judge to accept a stipulation agreement which would have compelled the court to sentence me to death without dragging everyone through a second penalty phase . . . and I regret that I failed your family and all of the families in that regard." He reiterated his wish that he could undo the pain he had caused and said that every time he closed his eyes, he could see her mother, because he was haunted by "the unfathomable emptiness of her eyes. It is as if I can see straight into her soul and it is full of nothing but pain, pain that is there solely because of me." During the trial, he said he forced himself to look at Mrs. Shelley every day because he didn't want to insult her or any other family member by avoiding eye contact as he had in the first trial. "Every day I looked into those dark empty eyes and hated myself."

He said he was sorry that he could not make amends to them. "And I am sorry that you will never be able to accept the remorse that I do feel as being genuine, and that my words here—as inadequate as they are—'will always fall on deaf ears.'"

SOMERS, CONNECTICUT
MAY 2004–JANUARY 2005

"I'm not surprised. It's what I expected," Michael said when he called me to tell me that the Connecticut Supreme Court upheld his six death sentences in May 2004, four years and a month after the jury's verdict and almost two decades since his arrest. Despite his protestations, Michael was upset, more by the reasoning than the outcome. "They said that even though I'm mentally ill, it had nothing to do with the crime. That is the most idiotic thing I ever heard. If it weren't for my mental illness, I would never have hurt anyone."

Because of his reaction to the decision and his enthusiasm about his lawyers' opinion that he had winnable appeals issues, I thought that Michael would go forward with his appeals after all. For one thing, Bob Satti had died. Satti's tactics had been a big part of his reason to forgo another trial. Even if a court eventually ordered a third penalty trial, that would be years away. Why stop the process when there was a chance that a court might order a life sentence?

He had been depressed in the winter of 2002 because he had broken up with his current girlfriend, Susan from Oklahoma, the summer before. Susan had found his *Walking with Michael* newsletter on the Internet and written to him, and their correspondence soon blossomed into a romantic relationship while Michael was waiting to be sentenced for

Paula Perrera's murder in New York. But it did not take long before she became overwhelmed by his neediness and cut off the relationship on his birthday in July 2002. The following February he attempted suicide a second time, but once again he was discovered and the state of Connecticut nursed him back to health. By the time the decision came down, Michael seemed better. So I was shocked and confused when he called me in July to report that he had fired his lawyers and stopped hi appeals. I challenged him on his decision.

"What's wrong with allowing the appeals to go forward?"

He said he didn't care if he had good issues. He had made up his mind ten years earlier and he wasn't going to change it.

"You've changed your mind several times in the last ten years," I reminded him.

"I'm not changing my mind; it's done. I don't want there to be a 'Ross III,'" he said with a mix of sadness and anger, referring to a third penalty hearing. "I owe it to the families. I can't risk another trial. You know that's what would happen." He was adamant but with a note of self-pity.

"I don't get you. I don't understand why you want to throw away your life," I said.

"Life? You call this a life? I live in an eight by ten cell, hermetically sealed in a tomb. I go out for rec a couple of times a week in a dog run. I have to put up with the idiots here. The other day, Cobb [another death row inmate] left me a little love note calling me Satan and signing it 'Jesus.' I'll send it to you. The guards treat me like crap—like a worthless piece of shit. You call this a friggin' life?"

Having been inside Northern, I understood. Yet Michael Ross had committed horrendous crimes and damaged many lives. He took up a lot of my time, energy, and money, but he'd become a fixture in my life, a constant. It was in the months that followed that I really understood the extent and depth of our friendship. It had been years since I regarded my role as simply a reporter covering a story, but I never had tried to tell him what to do. When he asked my opinion or my advice—usually about legal matters—I was always straight with him. Now he had started what U.S. Supreme Court justice Antonin Scalia likes to call "the machinery of death"—and I had no idea where the off button was.

When he called on August 19, I knew something was wrong. I could barely hear Michael say hello.

"What's the matter now?"

"I can't be buried in Brooklyn," he sobbed, explaining that Tammy Williams's grandmother didn't want him buried in the same place that her husband was buried, nor did she want him to have a funeral Mass in St. John's, her parish church. "I just wanted to go home. . . . I asked if we could have it there, out of courtesy. I didn't think that anyone would have a problem. No one else had a problem." He said that may be he could have the Mass at the Benedictine Grange, the home of Father John Giuliani (the priest who succeeded Father John Gilmartin as Michael's spiritual adviser). "It's supposed to be a beautiful place," he said.

"Why don't you just get buried on the farm?" I asked. "You always wanted to go back to the farm."

"We don't even own the farm anymore," he explained. Uncertainty agitated Michael. He wanted control of his death, his funeral Mass, and his burial, and now he could control none of them.

On October 7, Michael went to court and told Judge Patrick Clifford that he had dropped his appeals. The judge set an execution date of January 26, 2005. Now his death was not just a theoretical possibility; it had a date attached. Within a few days, Michael was transferred across the parking lot from death row in Northern to Osborn

Correctional Institution, the location of the execution chamber. When Michael finally called me, he sobbed throughout the conversation. He told me that he was emotional because in the afternoon he had made arrangements to be cremated. "It was hard. It makes it very real, and it hurts."

"Are you having second thoughts?" I asked

"No, I'm not going to change my mind. You know that. Just because I'm getting emotional doesn't mean I'm going to change my mind." Then he said something that startled me. "I'm not going to trust the feelings that I'm having now because I know that for ten years I've had one goal and that was to get this over with. I can't trust my feelings now. I have to stick with what I decided because I was sure of it for so long. Every time I let my emotions take over, I make a mistake. I'm going through with this."

When Michael called on December 4, he was tearful again. He sounded more depressed every day.

"What's wrong now?" I asked.

"Have you been following what they're doing?"

"What? Who?"

"The public defenders filed motions." Michael proceeded to read me parts of the motions. He was angry that the public defenders were trying to stop the execution, but he was livid that they alleged he was not competent to make the decision to drop his appeals. It was an unusual and perhaps desperate move, because they no longer represented Michael.

"Michael, they aren't saying you're incompetent. They are saying your decision to accept death is due to your mental illness." I tried to tell him, but he wasn't listening to me.

"This is ridiculous. I'm really scared that they're going to take me across the way." Michael was petrified that he would be sent back to Northern. "Why won't they just let me go? No court will call me incompetent," he said bitterly, choking up as he spoke.

I didn't want to argue with him, but I did want him to understand what the public defenders were thinking. "You said you'd been having second thoughts but that you didn't want to trust your emotions because you had made the decision ten years ago, and you weren't going to change your mind because of emotions. That's enough to say you're not competent." I knew he would be ticked off at me for suggesting that his emotional state made him incompetent, but at that point I had to be sure I spoke my mind. I was surprised that he almost agreed with me.

"I do have mixed feelings," he admitted, adding what he would repeat a million times. "But I believe I'm doing something for a reason, a principle. I've thought about this for a long time. . . . What right does any public defender have to interfere with what I'm doing? I'm pissed." He was bitter. "They'll get me another month or six months and call it a victory, but it won't be a victory for me. Don't they understand that? Don't *you* understand that?" I did, and as long as he wouldn't change his mind and fight, he was right.

To Michael's way of thinking, there were two problems about the lawsuit. For the public defenders to call him incompetent—even if based on his mental illness, not his mental capacity—was an affront. "I'm not some friggin' moron," he said over and over. He had also written in one of his journals, "My mind is all I have left. Even though the monster resides there, I am still proud of my mind. My mind is what keeps me sane. It is my only companion, my only true friend that I can completely trust."

The second problem was the timing. He felt that they had waited

until the eleventh hour to make sure that the execution would be de-
layed. "They could have done this last summer when I fired them," he
said. By waiting until December, he charged, they were making it impossible for the issue to be resolved before the January 26 execution date.
That meant that the execution would be on hold until his competency
was resolved, which also meant uncertainty for Michael. He had planned
on taking the last month or so to try to prepare himself spiritually for
the execution, but instead he was full of the anxiety of uncertainty. I
wondered if he was afraid on some level that the delay would give him
time to change his mind, but I didn't want to suggest it, because it would
probably make him dig in his heels even deeper.

As soon as I answered the phone on November 13, I could hear that
Michael was very distraught, which was becoming the norm. "I have
only seventy-four more days of this," he cried. Although his words made
it sound as if he were looking forward to the execution, his tone made
it clear that he was afraid. "At least it's only seventy-four more days of
this crap."

"What crap? I thought you said they were treating you better at
Osborn."

"It's all the friggin' rules. I'm depressed that every time I leave my
cell I have two guards with me. When the deacon comes, we have to
do communion through the bars. Even the legal visits have been through
the glass," he said, sobbing. "Twenty years of following the rules means
nothing. They treat me like friggin' Danny Webb." (Webb was another
death row inmate, who had threatened to "take out" a few guards on
his execution day.) "I have to accept it, but I don't have to like it. But it
really pisses me off. Guards are running around the unit as if I'm Gen-
ghis Khan."

Michael's mood greatly improved after Sister Helen Prejean, author
of *Dead Man Walking*, visited him in November. "I think we really

connected. She said she would be here for me. I don't know if she meant that she would be with me inside or outside protesting. I need to clarify what she meant." Either way, Michael thought things were looking up. He had called at his usual time—6:00 A.M. on a Saturday, knowing I'd be up to take his call. He was excited and wanted me to be excited about meeting Sister Helen. Then he paused. "By the way, before I forget, I assume you'll be there on January 26."

He had intimated over the years that he might ask me to be there—maybe he even assumed I would—but he had never asked me directly or demanded my commitment. I took a deep breath, trying to fight the panic. "Can I think about it?" I asked. The sudden reality of Michael's execution was daunting.

"You *don't* have to come. There will be others there. I don't need you there. I just thought you'd want to be there so you could write about it."

"Michael, it's not that I wouldn't come if it was important to you. I have two problems. One is that I feel as if my presence would mean I condone capital punishment. I don't want to give your execution or any execution my imprimatur. The second is that . . . I don't know if I can handle it."

"You *don't* have to come," he said convincingly.

"I know, but I want to think about it."

I didn't sleep well for the next week, trying to decide what to do. Ultimately, I knew that if there actually was going to be an execution, I would be there. I owed it to him. I had started out wanting to understand his decision to accept death; now I had to see it through. Ten years of telephone calls couldn't end without a final good-bye, but I still held tight to the hope that somehow it wouldn't ever come to that. Within a week, I told him I'd be one of his witnesses.

On November 28, he called to say, "It's been a hard week. I could hardly make it through Thanksgiving," sounding as if he were going to cry.

I paused, realizing that it would probably be his last Thanksgiving. "Because it would be your last one?" I asked gingerly, in part because I had a hard time not only choosing my words, but also saying them out loud.

"No, because I think of Mrs. Stavinsky waiting for her daughter to come home and having to go identify the body. I can't deal with it anymore," he said, crying.

Michael felt ashamed of what he had done and the pain he had caused, but he also wanted sympathy. If he had been upset about the fact that it might be his last Thanksgiving, I would have tried to comfort him, but I just couldn't bring myself to let him off the hook for Robin's death because I knew what it had done to the Stavinsky family. He was not going to get sympathy for Mrs. Stavinsky's tears. That was her pain, not his.

Soon he started calling me every day, sometimes two or three times a day. Mostly he just wanted to complain about the public defenders' lawsuits to stop the execution—and eventually a few that his father filed, including one that alleged that he was incompetent and narcissistic. "Now I'm really getting upset. By him doing this, he's putting a bull's-eye on my back," he complained. "He once told me that he couldn't stand being in prison and would rather be executed. How can he go and argue against me?"

"Maybe it's because he loves you. He doesn't want to lose you."

"I know. I know, but it gets to me." Soon it seemed to Michael that everyone was in court trying to stop the execution. His sister Donna filed a suit. Some of the men on death row protested the scheduled execution by filing suit, arguing that the method of execution was cruel and unusual punishment. Then Connecticut doctors filed a suit claiming that the death penalty as administered in Connecticut was cruel and unusual. According to the doctors' suit, the method of execution that the state used was illegal for veterinarians to use to euthanize animals, so it shouldn't be performed on humans.

The protocol for lethal injection in Connecticut would be a three-step process. The inmate is given three different chemicals. The first, sodium thiopental, is a sedative, supposedly rendering the condemned person unconscious. The second, pancuronium bromide, is a muscle relaxant that makes it impossible for the person to move, even to bat an eyelash. The reason, of course, is to make the final moments appear serene. The third chemical, potassium chloride, stops the heart. Apparently, if the person is not adequately sedated, he feels the last drug seize his heart—feeling like a heart attack but much more painful, because it burns through the veins. Some autopsies indicate that the sedative can wear off if too little is given, but the second drug makes it impossible for the person being executed to say or do anything. Theoretically, that could mean he would feel the last drug—and no one would come to his aid. The condemned person's final minutes would be torture. Michael knew it and feared it.

My MCI phone bill in December for just one phone line—and I had three—was nearly a thousand dollars, but it wasn't just the cost of the calls that got excessive. It was the fact that it was eating into the rest of my life. My husband was spending a lot of time working on the East Coast or traveling out of the country, and my almost eleven-year-old twins were already feeling the impact of his absence. So Michael's new neediness was not welcomed. There was an early morning call in December that made me realize that I had to be more sensitive to the rest of my family.

With my cordless phone tucked awkwardly under my chin as I tried to listen to Michael's latest problem, I fumbled with my all-in-one multi-function printer-fax-scanner-copier. It was a little after 6:00 A.M., and my son James was telling me to hurry. He had lost his script for the fifth-grade class play and was eager for me to use his twin sister's copy to make him another. I pressed the copy button, but nothing happened. While I flipped through the troubleshooting manual, I turned my attention back to Michael, who was complaining about the uncertainty of everything. James waved his hands in front of my face. I pushed another button. All the lights suddenly flashed on the all-in-one multifunction printer-fax-scanner-copier, indicating, I believed, a total digital meltdown.

"I don't know why they can't mind their own friggin' business," Michael said, now aware that the public defenders' lawsuit would be moving through the courts for the next few weeks.

"Mom! Will you get off the phone?" James demanded.

"Tell James we're busy," Michael barked into my ear.

I didn't answer, although I would have been just as likely to tell Michael to shut up. I had not told James or his twin sister, Hannah, that Michael had an execution date set for January. They were thinking about spending that weekend skiing, and besides, I was hoping that the courts would make it go away. I took a deep breath, not wanting to scold either of them; all the players in this domestic drama knew of one another and knew how to exquisitely ply the emotions of the woman who was struggling with an all-in-one multifunction printer-fax-scanner-copier and also trying to carry on a conversation.

"You are the worst mother in the entire *world*!" James screamed. "You care more about a serial killer than your own son." He plopped down on the couch, arms folded across the chest in a full-body pout. Michael's voice cackled with laughter from the phone.

"Man, if I had ever said that," he said chuckling, "my mother would have thrown me across the room."

"Well, Michael, that's the difference between your mother and me. I'm hoping that James doesn't turn into a serial killer." He went silent. I knew that I had offended him. I had reminded him that no mother wants her son to grow up to be Michael Ross. But I also knew that he accepted my comment as an attempt at gallows humor. James was now strewn supine like a dying Garbo on the couch.

Michael decided to change the subject. His last weeks on earth centered on control of his own death. There was no detail that didn't concern him, including his final meal.

"By the way, I'm not having a last meal," he said almost boasting.

"What? Why not?"

"Because I don't want friggin' Brian Garnett to friggin' stand out there and say, 'Mr. Ross died at 2:17 A.M. His last meal was blah, blah, blah.'" Garnett was the head Department of Correction spokesman. "I don't want to give them any more to say. It's none of their friggin' business what I eat. Friggin' media. You know what it's going to be like—anti–death penalty people out there singing 'Kumbaya' and drunken yahoos all yelling for blood and revenge. It's always the same. But this time they aren't going to hear what I friggin' ate."

"Sometimes I think I know you, and then you surprise me."

"Don't worry. Lieutenant King will take care of me." William King was the head officer in the death row unit.

"What do you mean?"

He didn't want to answer me directly because we were being taped. "I mean about what we were talking about a minute ago."

I realized that King would get him the last meal.

"We're going to get cut off. And I have to get the kids ready for school," I said.

"Yeah, you better tend to James, since you don't want him to become a serial killer or anything," Michael said, indicating that he wasn't offended. "I'll call you back later." Across the room, James began to emerge from his sulk when he saw me hang up the telephone, and we grabbed our coats and left to get the script copied.

Michael continually complained that the rules and protocol for the execution were changing every day. The most upsetting change was that he would not have a contact visit before his death because he was going to be sealed behind a floor-to-ceiling bulletproof wall in the death cell. It looked like Plexiglas, so Michael referred to it as his Plexiglas coffin. The barrier had only a few small holes drilled in it to allow people to talk and also a little pass-through slot that the guards could unlock to give him meals and medications. At Michael's request, I called Major Coates, the head corrections officer at Osborn, to ask why the DOC was going to such extremes when Michael had never been a security risk, and the major told me, "It's not up to me. I gave them my opinion, and they didn't listen."

During Michael's last day, he wanted to be able to hold someone's hand, to have some kind of human contact—not be sealed in like Hanni- bal Lecter. But the state wouldn't hear of it. This was one of the many things about the machinery of death that perplexed me. Michael Ross had been a well-behaved prisoner. What harm would it have done?

When I asked a lawyer who had witnessed several executions of clients about the procedures, he said that the reason the DOC put up the Plexiglas was because they didn't want the scene to get too emo- tional. "The DOC doesn't get it. He's a human being, but the fact is that they want everything to go smoothly, and they are afraid that any level of emotion will upset that. What they don't understand is that by the time this guy is there in that death cell, he's already gone, and there's no bringing him back. They don't understand the psychology of a death sentence. There's nothing to be afraid of. By the time he's there, he's already dead."

I can't have my funeral where I wanted it. . . . I don't know when it's going to be. . . . I don't know what's going on here in terms of the rules. . . . I can't have any contact visits. . . . Sister Helen doesn't even have the right date. . . . Maybe you shouldn't come. . . . I don't know what's going on," he whined. Every call was filled with complaints and tears. "What does it matter? Just get it over with and kill me." He began to sob.

"Would you stop being so negative?"

"I can't help it. It's so frustrating—even the date of the execution. They screwed me. They picked this day [January 26] so hopefully it's going to be a freezing-cold day with a blizzard and nobody will be able to be here."

I started to laugh. It was hard to imagine a date for an execution that wouldn't "screw" the condemned person. "What day would you like it to be?" I asked sarcastically.

Without skipping a beat, he said, "I thought he'd [Judge Clifford] set it for April 6. That was sixth months from the hearing, and it would have been after Easter." He wanted it after Easter so that it would be after the anniversary of Leslie's and April's deaths, which he honored every year with a day of prayer—and to give him another Easter Sunday to celebrate.

Susan, the last of Michael's ex-fiancées, who had broken up with him just before his last suicide attempt, reappeared in January. They had developed a romantic relationship that had lasted less than a year. They hadn't communicated since their breakup a year and a half earlier, but Michael wrote to her in early January to tell her he was going to be executed. He later told me that he felt he had to say good-bye to all his friends, but it was obvious that he was hoping for one last visit with her. He still cared about her. Though I had always discouraged him from getting "involved" with women, Susan seemed to break down Michael's resolve to die, so I didn't discourage his contacting her. But still, I thought his romantic entanglements cheapened his public statements about concern for the families of his victims. "How do you think the families will feel if they hear you have a girlfriend—or worse, a wife? Their daughters didn't get that chance." I repeated this over and over, but his response was always the same, "I can't help it. I love her."

Michael was still in a bad mood when he called on January 19 because he'd had his medical exam the day before. "The physical just messed with my head." He mocked the foreign accent of the doctor, saying, "Don't worry. I won't go near the anal area." At least the humor helped lighten the mood, but that was all he could laugh about. He also announced that once again everything had changed, that the day before the execution, he might not be able to visit two at a time. "You aren't going to be on death row. I don't know where they are going to put you, but not here. They keep changing things every friggin' day." Then he announced that my visiting times would be six to eight on Sunday, ten until noon on Monday, and three to five on Tuesday—his last full day on earth. Susan would be with him the last five or six hours.

Until that moment, I had assumed that I would be with him at the end or at least sometime near the end. It upset me that he wouldn't want me there. Days before, I had received a call and an instruction booklet from Brian Garnett, the head of communications at the DOC, outlining the procedures for the night of the execution: where we would be, the order we would be taken into the viewing area of the execution chamber, what would be expected of our decorum, etc. It was becoming too real, and now he was taking away my time. "I don't believe you. I'm flying all the way from California, and you're not going to see me on the night of the execution? I'm the one who took your calls for ten years. I'm the one who stuck by you." I was pacing from corner to corner in my kitchen, following the design of the tile floor as I argued with him. The more I talked, the more I could feel myself losing control. I wanted to hang up, but that would have given in to what I saw as his uncaring idiocy.

I began to cry. "I don't believe you. I've been a friend to you, and now this? I thought you'd want me there during your last hours," I said, sobbing. "What am I supposed to do between five P.M. and the execution at two A.M.?"

Hearing me cry, he finally relented and said he would change the schedule to give me an hour in the evening, but he added, "Don't cry on me."

"What do you mean, don't cry on you? You've cried to me for ten years," I snapped back, incredulous.

"Well, I didn't think you felt that way. You're supposed to be the unemotional one. You're the strong one."

"How the hell could I have talked to you for ten years if I didn't care about you as a human being? I thought you regarded me as a friend."

A blizzard was predicted for Saturday and Sunday. Barry Butler had called and told me three different systems were coming together. He also told me that the competency issue was now in the Federal District Court in front of Judge Robert Chatigny and that there was going to be a hearing on Monday morning at 9:30. The office of the chief public defender and the Capital Defense Unit had been working around the clock to try to get a stay of execution. The hearing was about whether to stay the execution pending the competency issue.

My plane was late because of the blizzard, and I arrived at the court-house just as they were taking a short break, so Barry and I went to see Michael.

I had never been inside Osborn. In comparison with Northern, it seemed a little old-fashioned and run-down, but more human. We entered a guardhouse where a friendly officer checked IDs against the short list of people who were permitted to visit Michael. We weren't going to be allowed on death row, only in the death row visitors' booth, a small room off the main corridor. The officer unlocked a door, reveal-ing a very small cubicle, and then locked us inside. There were two plas-tic chairs, a window connecting the booth where the inmate sat, and a wall phone.

Within minutes, Michael was brought to the other side of the win-dow and locked in. His appearance was startling; he looked feminine. I hadn't seen him in a few years because of the distance from California, although we spoke more and more frequently. He had grown a pony-tail. Although he had lost more than sixty pounds to make himself more attractive to his women friends, he was fleshy and had even developed what appeared to be breasts. The years of female hormones had obviously contributed significantly to the change. I took the phone to talk.

Predictably, Michael was upset when he heard that Chatigny was probably going to issue a stay. "I don't care what he does," he said defi-antly. "I'm going in that death cell tomorrow one way or the other." We knew he couldn't force the guards to put him in the death cell, but there was no reason to argue with him. "There's no way they're going to find me incompetent now."

I changed the subject. "You know Hannah asked me if she could talk to you. She insisted that she was the one person in the world who could persuade you not to go through with this."

Tears welled up in Michael's eyes. "Why are you telling an eleven-year-old about this?"

"Michael, how can she *not* be aware of what's happening? You heard James's fit when he said I cared more about a serial killer than my own son. I had to tell them. They care. They had to know why I was so upset."

"I know, but I didn't want them to know," he said softly. "They shouldn't have to deal with something like this."

"Don't you think they'll wonder when you don't call anymore?"

He put his head down, mumbling to the floor, "They shouldn't have to deal with this."

"If you don't want her to deal with it, change your mind."

"I'm not . . ." he began, but I interrupted, knowing what he would say. We chitchatted about the snowstorm and my trip for a while, occasionally gliding back to the legal issues at hand. After forty-five minutes, it was time to go.

When court reconvened, Judge Chatigny announced that he was going to issue a stay and that he wanted to hold a competency hearing. Michael would have to go back to court, and any new sentence would have to be at least thirty days past that date.

My flight back to California was not until late Wednesday, so I was able to visit Michael two more times before I left. On Wednesday morning, he told me not to come back for the execution. "I could do it on my own." We talked about the future—as if he now had a future. "I'm a college graduate. I could also teach, maybe help them study for their GED. I think I could also be helpful to the people in mental health, because I could talk to other prisoners about depression—even about sexual disorders." He was assuming that he would be allowed in general population and that tutoring would be possible if he was given a life sentence, and I didn't want to discourage him.

"You're a smart man, and you could make a big contribution," I told him.

"I know," he said, but caught himself before the daydream went too far. "I could make a difference, but I'm not going to change my mind."

"You know I think this is crazy."

"I know. I know, but I have to," he said looking down at his feet. He took off his glasses and wiped his eyes.

I left confident that there had been a temporary reprieve of at least a month. The next afternoon when I was on my way home from picking up my children from school, my cell phone rang. It was Barry. "The Supreme Court lifted the stay. I'm out driving in my car, trying to calm down."

My anxiety levels returned to their previous elevation. "Oh, my God," I said. "Is it tonight?" I asked, knowing that I couldn't get there in time.

"No, there's another stay based on his father's suit, but now that the Supremes have spoken, the Second Circuit won't uphold it. It's probably going to be early Saturday morning," he said.

"I'm coming back," I told him. "I'll see you tomorrow morning."

The phone was ringing when I walked in the door. It was Michael. "I don't know if you heard or not," I began.

"No, what?"

"Barry just called. The Supreme Court lifted the stay. . . . It was five to four."

He joked. "I guess Rehnquist got out of his deathbed just for me so the vote would be five to four." Rehnquist, the chief justice of the Supreme Court, was dying of cancer. "He must really care," he said sarcastically.

"I'm getting on a plane tonight. Are you sure you're not having second thoughts?"

"I'm not worried. I know where I'm going and I'm going to be safe. I'm just worried about the people I'm leaving behind."

"Well you got two groups you care about, and they both want different outcomes. You've got the victims' families, and you've got everyone else."

"Tell me about it."

23

SOMERS, CONNECTICUT
JANUARY 2005

Michael had worried that no one would come to his execution because there would be a blizzard and it would be freezing cold. The blizzard had come the weekend before; now it was bitter cold. I shivered as I waited for my escort into the prison. Predictably, Barry, Michael's lawyer during the second trial, was waiting in the lobby when I got there.

"What's going on?" I asked.

"His dad's back there. I thought I'd give them some time alone. I'm here to see him and waiting in case he changes his mind." Several lawyers were standing by in the office in case anything needed to be done. The courts in Hartford and Rockville would have someone on duty all night. Throughout the evening, Barry remained in constant contact via pay phone to his office. That's the only way we could find out what was going on in the outside world. Cell phones aren't allowed inside.

"Do you think there's a chance he'll change his mind?" I asked.

"No, but I'll be here, just in case."

A few minutes later, I was taken back to see Michael. The death cell was at the very end of death row, next to the execution chamber and many doors behind the area where Barry and I had visited him. Three corrections officers were guarding the entrance to the tier. We walked past a few empty cells and went through the same ritual at the next metal door. The door opened, revealing several more cells on the right. On the left was a large window that flooded the tier with light.

There were two corrections officers guarding the two steps up to an open doorway. At the top of the steps to the left, next to another large window, a corrections officer sat at a wooden desk with a logbook. His job was to keep a constant eye on Michael and his guests and write down everything in the book, just as a guard had done when he first arrived on death row and had been placed in the same cell eighteen years before. The death cell was about ten feet to my right. Michael was entombed behind the barrier in his "Plexiglas coffin." Two plastic chairs had been put next to it for visitors. Dan Ross was sitting in the one on the left. He was tall and of a heftier build than Michael, but I knew instantly who he was, because Michael resembled him. What surprised me was that he was not intimidating at all. All I really knew about him were Michael's descriptions of a him as an "emotionless rock" and his stories about being taken to the woodshed and beaten with a stick. Dan seemed warm and friendly.

"Well, you finally get to meet my dad," Michael chuckled.

I knew Dan didn't approve of my writing about Michael, but he didn't mention it. For the next four hours, we chatted and reminisced about farming and his family—his mother, culling chicks, and even cleaning the belts that collected chicken manure. They tried to outdo each other's "mom" stories, confirming most of the stories that Michael had told me.

"That whole thing about you being a serial killer because of killing chicks is ridiculous. That's just farming," Dan said. Michael nodded in agreement—even though he had suggested the opposite many times, and he knew that psychiatrists suspected it might have contributed to his ability to kill without emotion.

He teased his father about supporting the public defenders' suit by saying that he was narcissistic and incompetent. "After all, even you think I'm crazy."

"You want to prove you're competent?" Dan snapped back. "Change your mind. Stop this. Then I'll know you're competent. This whole thing is crazy."

I laughed, but Michael sighed. "I'm not going to stop it. It's going forward," he said, looking away as his eyes welled up with tears. He had voluntarily dropped all his appeals, allowing his execution to proceed. All he had to do was file an appeal and the execution would be off.

Around 2:00 P.M., Dan and I had to leave death row because T. R. Paulding, Michael's standby lawyer, was on his way to prison to speak with Michael and have a conference call with Judge Chatigny. Dan went home; I stayed in the lobby with Barry. We had been told that we would be sitting in the prison visiting room when we weren't visiting, but that didn't happen until later that evening. It was clear that the DOC had not planned for—or perhaps wanted—us to stay there all day. They left us to fend for ourselves in the freezing cold lobby with nothing to eat or drink. Because the temperature outside was in the single digits or below, it had to have been no more that 30 or 40 degrees Fahrenheit inside, and every time the door opened, gusts of frigid air wafted through the room. So we paced around with our jackets on to keep warm as the temperature dropped. By nightfall, the temperature had fallen even more, and I needed a hat and gloves and had to keep walking around to stay warm.

When we had visited Michael earlier in the week, Barry had dropped his public defender ID when we were registering in the guardhouse. He was using an old one because he had misplaced his current ID. "I didn't lose it. I temporarily misplaced it. It happens all the time. That's why I never get rid of the old ones. Insurance." I was shocked by his photo. He had aged so much in the past decade. His hair was thinner. His face was drawn. Of course, we all had gotten older, but I wondered how much of Barry's aging was due to this case. It had changed us all—physically, emotionally, and intellectually, maybe even spiritually. I wasn't the same person who had started reporting on this story in 1995. I had always been against the death penalty, but now it was personal, not philosophical. I could put a human face on death, and the face of a human being who was also my friend.

I had also come to believe that God breathed life into all of us. No one but God had the right to take away that breath—and that included Michael Ross and the state of Connecticut. Before meeting Michael, I had been quick to judge others. Now I tried to make myself look for the good in people rather than the bad. My years getting to know Michael had been a liberating experience, because I no longer immediately attached labels to all kinds of people—liberal, conservative, intellectual, redneck, religious fanatic, serial killer.

"I'm afraid this is going to happen," I said, pausing. "And I really don't want to watch," I admitted to Barry.

"Nobody's making you," he told me adamantly.

"I know. I didn't have to come back. Michael told me not to come back, but here I am and I'm not changing my mind now. If he can be stubborn, so can I."

Barry laughed. "Yeah, I guess you're right. But what if the joke's on him?"

"On who? Michael?"

"Yeah. What if this is it? What if all this religious stuff is a sham and there's no God or no heaven? What if there's nothing after this? Then the joke's on Michael because he's doing this for nothing 'cause there's no one out there—no God, no Jesus, no heaven. I've thought a lot about this," Barry continued. "Maybe nobody's going to forgive Michael. Maybe he's just killing himself for nothing."

I didn't know what to say.

"I'm glad you didn't suggest that to him," I finally answered.

"Yeah, it might freak him out, but maybe he'd change his mind."

"That's impossible. He doesn't know how to change his mind," I said. "Although I think there already is some uncertainty there."

"You're right, but he puts on a good show. I still think he may be doing this for nothing."

I couldn't argue with that; it was the truth. Dying would stop the legal process, but none of the people who mattered would ever forgive him and none of us—even Father John—had any concrete proof that God would forgive him.

For the next few hours, state helicopters began landing and taking off on the pad next to the parking lot. Snipers were posted on the roof. The conference call with Judge Chatigny, T. R. Paulding, the public defenders, and various state officials went on for hours. Barry called the office to try to find out what was happening, but because they were on the call and using the speakerphone, all he could find out was that the judge was upset and was saying that T. R. hadn't fulfilled his responsibility as Michael's lawyer.

Although at the time we didn't know the details, Chatigny had accused T. R. of "enabling him," saying, "You are not investigating this matter and fulfilling your obligation to the court, and if you don't do something, I'm going to have your law license." He had also said something that no other judge had ever publicly said about Michael Bruce Ross—that if you look at this case "in the best possible light" Ross "never should have been convicted. Or if convicted, he never should have been sentenced to death because of his sexual sadism, which was found by every single person who looked at him [to be] clearly a mitigating factor."

When T. R. finally left the warden's office, his face was flushed and he was visibly shaken. It appeared that he might have been crying. We assumed he was upset because the judge had chastised him. However, there were myriad possibilities. He was fond of Michael. He acknowledged us with a gesture but did not stop because he needed to speak to Michael.

T. R. had taken the case pro bono as a favor to Michael, and now he found himself with an unanswerable choice—lose your law license or defy your client's wishes. Wearily, he explained his conundrum to Michael, who felt like he had been sucker punched but knew he could not go to his death thinking that he had caused T. R. to lose his livelihood. He had no choice. He told T. R. to "do whatever you have to do."

After T. R. left, I went back to see how Michael was holding up. His emotions ranged from desperate sobs to angry frustration. "They couldn't break me, so they went after T. R.," he fumed—although I wasn't sure who "they" were. In his mind, it was all the fault of the public defenders whom he blamed for starting the whole mess. As I sat by the death cell, trying to ignore the turmoil around us, I started to ask Michael some of the questions that had to be asked before it was too late—and I was thinking about my conversation with Barry.

"Did you believe in God before you got here—on death row?"

Michael stared at me. "I think so," he said in a tone that indicated anything but certainty. "I believed there must be a God or a supreme being out there. I certainly didn't believe in any form of religion. I hadn't been brought up that way."

"I remember you writing in your journal that you wish you had known Father John earlier but that you might not have wanted to listen to him back then."

"I was too angry. I blamed God for what I had done. But God didn't kill those girls. I did."

"But now you believe, and you are sure God has forgiven you."

"Yes," he said quietly, looking down at the floor.

"So does God talk to you? Do you actually have conversations with him—or her?" I was joking, but when he didn't answer, I knew what he was thinking. He was wondering if I was trying to trick him. He was wondering if I was going to use it to prove he was crazy. He didn't want to answer. "I'm really curious. I read your journals. Over and over, you pray to God. You tell him what you think. I just want to know if he talks back."

"If you want to know if I hear voices, the answer is no."

"I'm not trying to prove you are crazy. Honestly. I want to understand your relationship with God. You told me you weren't afraid. You said you would be forgiven—or that you had been forgiven by God. What I want to know is how you know that."

He was getting nervous. I sensed that I had touched a nerve. "We talked about this before once. You have to have faith. That's what the word means. You have to believe even if you don't have concrete proof like evidence in court," he said, almost challenging me.

"Okay. You can have faith that God exists. You can have faith that the Scriptures contain some truths in them and that God will forgive you because you have confessed your sins and you have atoned for them. But even you ask the question all through your journals—how do you know what is God's will?"

He sighed. He thought I was trying to use religion and logic to put him off guard. "I don't know. I just have to have faith," he told me. "If it's the right thing to do, then it should be God's will."

"If—the big if," I said. "So God hasn't actually told you that you are forgiven," I began.

"He forgives everyone. Henri Nouwen says that—"

"I don't want to hear what other people say. I want to hear what Michael says."

"God is forgiving. Like you said, I've confessed my sins. I've repented. God has forgiven me."

I looked him in the eye. "So you've forgiven Satti, and Malchik, and everyone else?"

"What's that got to do with it?"

"You know the Lord's Prayer is pretty scary on that subject. It asks God to forgive us as we forgive others. So that means if you want to be forgiven, you have to forgive everyone else. What about your mother? The public defenders for starting a suit saying you're incompetent? Because if you haven't, you are asking God to forgive you the way you forgave them."

He took a deep breath. I could see that I was annoying him at the very least and maybe even shaking him up. "I am at peace with all that. Okay? I'm not angry anymore. I carried a lot inside for a long time, but I've worked through it."

"Okay. But how do you know there's a heaven? How do you know you're going there?"

"I know it in my heart," Michael answered softly, staring at the floor again.

"I don't know if I'm sure there's a heaven; I'm becoming more and more convinced that hell is right here on earth. We have to suffer through all of this. Who knows? Maybe you're right; death may be 'sweet.'"

"I'm not going to argue with you on any of that," he said, smiling as if he had won.

By 7:00 P.M., preparations for the execution were well under way. We had been escorted into the visiting room and the lobby was buzzing with DOC officials. All sorts of prison personnel kept bringing in food trays for them—cold cuts, cookies, coffee—standard fare for a funeral reception. The staff was busily hanging curtains over every window so no one could see who was coming in and going out. "They must be bringing in the victims' families," I said.

"No, it's way too early for that. They don't want you to see the executioner," Barry whispered.

I imagined a burly man wearing a black hood and carrying a big ax trying to sneak through the lobby. I started to laugh and then realized Barry wasn't laughing. "You're serious? Why don't they just have someone from the DOC do it?"

"No one is supposed to know who actually did the killing. People apply for the honor from other states."

"You're not serious."

"I'm serious. And the pay is pretty good, too."

In another room, T. R. was trying to figure out what his legal and ethical obligations were, but State's Attorney Kevin Kane and Chief State's Attorney Christopher Morano had no doubts about what had to be done. They cornered T. R. and took him into a private room to talk. "You're in no shape to give any legal advice," they told him. "We're calling this off. It's not going to happen tonight." No one told us it was off until much later.

When I went back for my final visit with Michael, he was calmer and convinced that the execution would not happen that night. I hoped he was right, but I couldn't help but wonder whether the next time I would see him, he would be stretched out on a gurney with a bunch of tubes coming out of his arms.

Just before eleven, I was told I had to leave. I put my hand up on the Plexiglas, and he lifted his up next to mine on the opposite side. "It's been a roller coaster," I said.

"Yeah, remember? I'm a real pain in the butt."

I laughed. "And even though I hate roller coasters, I wouldn't have missed this one for the world. I'm going to miss you."

"Me too. But it ain't going to happen tonight."

As we were about to be escorted out of the prison, T. R. came out beaming. He couldn't stop to talk because he was on his way to see Michael. "I'll call you," he promised.

Because of Michael's mood shift, we were sure that the execution had been called off, but Coates, the head of the guards, nixed that assumption as we walked out. "It's off, right?" Barry asked.

"No, it's going forward. You have to go over to Cybulski. Nothing has changed."

My anxiety levels spiked. We were told to go to our cars and drive over to Willard-Cybulski Correctional Institution, another prison down the road but within sight of the entrance. The temperature had dropped below zero. I ran to my rental car. I was freezing, but even turning the heater up full blast had little immediate effect. Waiting for the car to warm up, I picked up my cell phone to see if I had any calls. It was so bitterly cold, my phone was a brick of ice. Frozen. Dead.

Our "staging area" was the visiting room, where they had snacks and coffee for us. Barry got on the pay phone to talk to his office. They knew less than we did but were constantly monitoring the television to see what was happening. I paced around the ten-by-ten entryway desperately trying to keep the image of the execution chamber out of my mind. As the time drew nearer, I doubted I could really go through with it. Waves of guilt passed over me when I considered how Michael would feel if I didn't witness the execution. I heard sirens and watched out the window as police car after police car flashed by. It was hard to see what they were doing or where they were going, but presumably they were coming together to block the entrance from the few protestors who had braved the cold, marching from Robinson Correctional Institution in Somers to the entrance of Osborn and Northern. I counted about twenty-six cars whizzing by, but it was impossible to make an accurate count, because we couldn't see all of them or the entrance—just blue flashing lights dancing on the deep white snow. *If the execution had been called off, would they bring out all this force?* From the look on Barry's face, I could tell he was asking himself the same questions.

Just before 1:00 A.M., a white van pulled up out front, presumably to take us back to the prison for the execution, and Father Anthony Bruno, the head chaplain for the DOC, got out and rushed toward the lobby. He opened the door, sending in a gust of subzero air. Barry and I shivered, both from the cold and the fact that it looked as though it was really going to happen.

"The execution has been called off. It's officially still on for Monday, but it's not going to happen. They are going to make an announcement in a little while," he told us. "I've got to get back to the prison, but you all might as well go home."

"You okay?" Barry asked.

"I'm fine. I'm just happy it's over."

"It's never over until it's over," Barry cautioned. He gave me a hug and left. Michael had taken his sleeping pill and gone to bed after we left at eleven, when T. R. told him it was off. He had no idea that we had been in limbo for two more hours.

The next morning my cell phone had thawed out, and Michael's counselor called, offering to let me visit before I went back to California. When I got to the prison, Michael had a hangdog look.

"Michael, I don't have that long with you, so let's not dwell on last night. Maybe it was fate. Maybe it was God telling you that you should rethink what you were doing."

"God had nothing to do with it."

"How convenient," I said sarcastically. "Whenever things go your way, it's God making things happen, but when it's not *your* will, it is also not *God's* will."

"That's not true," he said, defensively, but I left hoping I had planted a seed of doubt.

It took me a few days to settle down. I kept thinking about the Shelleys. I knew they would have been there waiting, so I called them that Sunday afternoon. Ed answered the phone. "I just wanted to call. I've been thinking about you. I can't imagine how painful it must have been for you to go there thinking that there would be an execution and then having it called off."

"It wasn't too bad for me," Ed said. "Lera is really taking it tough. I'm trying to stay away from everything else. Larry King wanted me on, but I wouldn't go. Then NBC parked in front of my house. We couldn't go out for days. Lera was really eaten up by it." He said that he had been "chain chewing" antacids the night of the execution, and his nerves were shot because he had quit smoking seven weeks earlier.

I told him that I didn't think there was a chance that the execution would take place anytime soon, because the court was going to appoint a special counsel to look into Michael's competency, and the state had less than one day remaining until the execution window closed.

Ed was livid. He thought all psychiatric experts were hired guns who would say anything if they were paid enough. "That's what gets me. One gives one diagnosis, and then the other gives the opposite. It's crazy and it's a waste of time and money."

I later heard that Michael had written to Susan and mailed the letter the day of the scheduled execution. She confided in me that he said he had been "putting on a brave front for everyone else" but that he was secretly troubled—deeply troubled by "needles, chemicals, seeing the victims' families. I'm terrified inside." I knew he didn't really want to die, but now I also knew he was afraid. As much as I disagreed with his relationship with Susan, I was hoping that she'd be able to persuade him to change his mind.

24

SOMERS, CONNECTICUT
WINTER–SPRING 2005

Because the United States Supreme Court sent the case back to state court, Judge Clifford was to preside over a competency hearing; he set a new execution date of May 11.

"Are you willing to talk to the psychiatrists?" Michael asked.

"Yeah, but . . ."

"I just want some people who are willing to say that I do care about the families. I don't want people twisting the facts and saying half-truths. That's how I got here on death row," he argued.

"No, you got on death row because you killed eight people," I corrected.

I spent most days and evenings for the next four months dealing with the psychiatrists and the lawyers who were trying to prove he was incompetent. Michael wanted me to tell them—and the court—that he was competent and that he was dropping his appeals because he didn't want the families to go through another penalty hearing; he wanted to give them closure. Still, there was the suicide issue. There was the fact that he was depressed and that he had told me that he suffered from death row syndrome. I knew he would rather die than go back to Northern. That alone said something about death row in Connecticut. I also knew that he saw his decision to drop any appeals as a noble act of sacrificing himself. And finally, I knew that he was stubborn and could not bring himself to change his mind once he had announced his decision publicly. It would be too humiliating. Did that prove that he was incompetent to make the decision because he was incapable of changing his mind? I wanted to cooperate, but I knew that telling the whole truth would risk Michael feeling hurt and betrayed.

Eventually I had to give a deposition because I wouldn't be able to attend the hearing. All of the lawyers from both sides were allowed to ask questions about my relationship with Michael. At Michael's lawyer T. R.'s turn, he had just one: "Doesn't Michael regard you as his friend?" I had never had to actually publicly admit to a "friendship" with Michael. However I may have defined my relationship with him, there was no doubt that he thought of me as a friend. "Yes, he does," I admitted. I was mad at T. R., because that admission took away from my credibility with the judge.

The competency hearing was held in the middle of April. Michael called only a few times, because he left very early in the morning and was emotionally exhausted when he returned to Osborn each day of the weeklong hearing in New London. When he finally did call, he was angry. He had forgotten how much he hated listening to psychiatric testimony about himself. He especially didn't like being called narcissistic.

He was mad at me because of how the doctors interpreted some of what I had said during the interviews.

"You exaggerated a bit."

"What?"

"That I am not capable of caring for anybody."

"I *never* said that. They asked me that, and I said I am not a professional, and I cannot say what emotions are real or not real."

"Well, Dr. [Stuart] Grassian based all his conclusions that I am not capable of feeling on what you and Ann told him." Dr. Grassian is an expert on death row syndrome, a depression suffered by some inmates, who was hired to say Michael was incompetent.

"That's his interpretation. In fact, if you listen to my deposition, I said that your number-one stated reason has always been that you were doing it for the families." Then I went through the litany of other reasons, ending with his pathological stubbornness.

He chuckled. "You said I was narcissistic."

"I never said that. I said I couldn't diagnose you."

Dr. Grassian had testified, "Even Michael admits, 'Martha knows me better than anyone else.' She told me this. She told me that. . . . You were all over the place."

"Jesus. I had no idea. But who would you want to be the Michael Ross expert—me or Malchik?" He laughed because he knew I was right. He was also confident that he would be found competent and the execution would go as scheduled.

"So you're going to be there? I have to send in my list." He described the execution chamber and the witness area to me and told me he wasn't sure if he would make a last statement. He also mentioned the controversy over the way Connecticut administers lethal injection—that it could be torture. "But it's not like I don't deserve it."

"Nobody deserves to be tortured."

"Tell Mr. Shelley that."

As Michael predicted, on April 22, 2005, Judge Clifford found him competent. The execution was pushed back from May 11 to May 13 to give Michael the legally prescribed time to appeal Clifford's opinion, but he had no intention of doing any such thing. I took the red-eye on May 10 so I could visit Michael on Wednesday and Thursday.

This trip was different from my trip in January, when I was frazzled and unsure about what the courts would do. Now there were no legal decisions pending, and I left California with a sense of resignation. On some level, I knew that this time it was going to happen, whether I wanted to admit it or not.

By eleven on the morning of May 11, I was sitting with Michael. In the past, he had never had a problem using the word *execution*, but as the time got closer, he referred to his execution as "it" or just used the euphemism "going forward."

"You're not scared?" I asked, realizing he might perceive the question as "going for the emotional jugular."

"No. Why should I be? I know where I'm going," he told me with conviction.

"I think I would be scared," I admitted. "What about what Father John asked you ten years ago?"

"What?"

"About meeting the girls?"

He hesitated. "I'm fine with that. I've worked through that." He didn't offer to tell me what he would say, and I could tell that he did not want me to ask.

When Michael's father arrived, he immediately asked Michael to call it off. I realized this was also my last chance to persuade him to change his mind. I was feeling desperate and began to cry. "Michael, I've never told you what to do . . ." I began.

"I know," he said quietly, avoiding my stare.

"But now I'm telling you that you're throwing your life away. Think of what good you could do." I was sobbing so hard I could barely get the words out. "You could teach inmates and help them get their GEDs. You could counsel men with sexual disorders. You could make a difference."

"Why'd you bother going to Cornell if you're not going to use your degree, Michael?" Dan asked.

"It's not going to happen. How can a decision be wrong if you're doing it for the right reasons?"

I knew I would ultimately have to answer this question, and I had to do it in a way that wouldn't offend him. I couldn't use the word *narcissistic*. "It could be wrong if it was the product of your mental illness. You know you're incapable of changing your mind. If that's because of your mental illness, then you're sticking to your decision for the wrong reason. I know you don't want to hurt the families, but I also know you don't want to die. Please don't do this," I said, still sobbing. "I hope you're not mad at me."

"No, I'm not mad at you." But I knew that he meant the opposite.

"But if I didn't try to convince you today, I could never live with myself. If I let you die without telling you what I thought, I would always regret it."

"I know. I'm not mad."

"If you change your mind, it will be the most courageous thing that you've ever done. I have always agreed with you that no jury would give you life—but I think you have a chance with appeals. Now you have to try to save yourself."

"It's not going to happen."

I felt helpless. "Why? What's wrong with trying? No one else believes that you're doing this for any moral reasons. What do you accomplish? You aren't being noble, just dumb."

He kept staring at the floor. I knew he was angry. I knew he didn't want to hear it, but I had to press him.

"Look me in the eye and tell me why you're so convinced that you have to do this."

After a long silence, he looked up. "You *know* why. It ain't going to happen. I'm not changing my mind. This is going forward."

The mood at the prison on May 12 was different than on the first execution date, which had cost the state more than $250,000. There were fewer guards and less tension.

Dan Ross arrived, and we talked for a long while. By this time, he could speak freely, not seeing me as the enemy. After an hour or so, I left the death cell to give them time alone together, because it was likely to be Dan's last chance to speak with his son. I tried to fathom what Dan must be feeling—about to lose a son who was basically letting the state execute him. It must have been excruciating as a parent to be helpless, unable to do anything to stop it.

When Dan came out, I asked him about his talk with Michael. "It was good. We said some things that we both needed to say, and I feel better that we were able to talk."

"I hope you understand now that Michael is my friend."

"Yes, I can see that," he said. "It's just that none of us wanted you writing about all of this. I was afraid it would make it never go away. When it's down on paper, it's permanent."

"It's already permanent, but I think it's important for people to understand Michael."

"Maybe. I do appreciate your being a friend to him. I'm depending on you to convince him to change his mind."

I let out a deep sigh. "He's too damn stubborn. I'll try, but I can't promise."

"I know. I've said my piece. Now it's up to him."

I sat in the waiting room for hours as others visited him. At 9:00 P.M., I was told it was finally time to have my last meeting with Michael.

"Finally," I said showing my exasperation.

"What?"

"I've been sitting in the waiting room for hours."

"Really? The time is going so fast. I didn't realize."

"When your dad left, he told me he was counting on me to change your mind."

"Oh great. Here we go again."

I tried to keep the conversation light, but inside I was repeating a prayer, "Please God, make him change his mind." I knew it was a useless and perhaps selfish mantra, but I hoped that there was something I could say or do. "So what should I be asking you, assuming this is my last chance?"

"You've already asked me all the important things—the hard things."

"Have I? You didn't always feel that way."

"Yeah, well that was then. I think we've covered everything."

"Michael, I know tomorrow and all the days after that I'm going to have questions—ones that I'll never be able to ask. I don't know what to say. I feel like I should have done more. I'm going to miss you, even though you're a royal pain in the butt."

"Me too."

I put my hand on the Plexiglas. "I wish I could give you a hug," I said. He nodded. Tears welled up in our eyes because we knew it was the last time we'd ever talk to each other. "Good-bye," I finally said, choking back the tears.

"See you in the next life."

"No comment," I said, chuckling. "I'm not getting into a discussion of the existence of heaven with you now. . . . I'll miss you."

"Good-bye. I'll miss you, too. Thanks for everything. You've been a true friend. Tell the twins . . ."

"What?"

"Tell them to keep reading *Ferdinand* and think of me."

"We'll read it together. So long, my friend."

After Father Gilmartin arrived, we chatted for a while about Michael's frame of mind. I lost track of the time and was surprised when we were told it was time for the priests to go be with Michael and for me to leave the waiting room and go to the staging area.

One other witness and I were escorted from the visiting area to a small office off the main corridor. Father John Gilmartin and Father John Giuliani joined us after sharing a final Mass with Michael and offering any support they could until it was time to take him into the execution chamber. They had also given Michael his last rites. "He seemed very calm, and he was extremely insightful about the lesson. He seems at peace. He's doing what he thinks he has to do," reported Father John Gilmartin. "Ten years, Martha, ten years. You've stood by him for all that time. You're the only one," he said.

"We all did what we had to do," I said. "But I'm going to miss my six A.M. weekend calls," I admitted.

"We're all going to miss him."

Ed and Lera Shelley and their daughter Robin had been picked up by a state trooper to come to the prison. Troopers also picked up Wendy Baribeault's three sisters—Debbie, Cindy, and Joanne. The three Stavinsky children—Debbie, David, and Jennifer—drove themselves to the prison. This time when the families arrived at the safe house, there were only three or four troopers and a few guards. "It wasn't as intense as before," Ed Shelley commented. "I think it was more relaxed because they knew that it was going to happen."

Around 1:00 A.M., the victims' families were driven by van from the safe house to the prison and taken into the parole hearing room—a long room on the left side of the corridor, just past the guard station situated across the hall from where we were waiting.

Malchik and Frank Griffin, the other officer who interrogated Michael after his arrest, were allowed to watch the execution with the families. Ed Shelley explained that the DOC had asked if the two troopers could witness the execution. "We could have said no, but we didn't." Just before 2:00 A.M. the victims' families and the two troopers were escorted into the viewing area of the execution chamber.

The viewing area is separated from the execution chamber by a large window with a blue drape that is opened after the stage is set and the witnesses are in place and is drawn when it's all over. In a weird way, as the drape inside the chamber opens and closes, the stage looks like a life-size puppet show. The victims' families had been given a tour of the area earlier and had been told that the press would go in first, then a purple curtain would be pulled to separate them from the press, and then they would be escorted in. Another curtain would be pulled, and Michael's witnesses would be brought in. We were last because we would be directly in front of Michael's head so he could look directly at us. "He'll be able to see a friendly face at the end," Brian Garnett, the DOC press spokesman, had explained to me over the phone. A guard was posted with each group to make sure there was no interference or indignity.

The staff and officials had rehearsed and rehearsed the procedures, but no amount of rehearsal made it easy. One official described the scene as "surreal. We just don't have it in us to kill people—at least I don't. But if you are going to have a death penalty, you are going to have executions. It's going to happen. We'll see what happens when the next one comes up. It might not be as easy as killing a Michael Ross."

Ironically, late in the afternoon, Garnett briefed the press, telling them that Michael had gotten up early, eaten oatmeal and juice, and had not asked for a last meal but had settled on the same fare that the other prisoners were eating—turkey à la king with rice, mixed vegetables, bread and butter, and coffee. Michael didn't hear Garnett talking about what he had eaten—and of course, Garnett didn't know the truth and had it all wrong. Lieutenant King had gotten him what he wanted. I've omitted it here out of respect for his wishes. In the end, Michael would have chuckled at Garnett's gaffe. I did.

It was just after 2:00 A.M. when Michael's witnesses were finally escorted into the viewing area on the side of the tier opposite the death cell. Instead of turning left after the hallway door was opened, we went to the right and walked all the way down the tier. We were on the mirror side of death row, except this side had a death chamber instead of a death cell. I looked at the draped window leading to the execution chamber. I could see Ed Shelley's reflection front and center—almost like a ghost. We waited for several minutes, wondering what was causing the delay. Had Michael changed his mind? No. The truth was that they had trouble finding his veins, one of the things he feared most.

Finally the curtain was drawn, revealing Michael lying on the gurney. His arms were stretched out on either side of him, tied down with four strips of black Velcro and connected to tubes. His fingers were tied together with what looked like ace bandages. I was surprised that his eyes were shut, but I knew why. He didn't want to look at the anger in Ed Shelley's eyes or the tears in Lera's. That was even more frightening than death.

Warden David Strange took a microphone and stood next to Michael. "Inmate Ross, do you have a final statement?"

"No, thank you," Michael said, not opening his eyes. I felt cheated that he didn't at least look over to say good-bye.

"He doesn't have the balls to say anything," whispered one victim's family member.

The warden then went to the red phone on the wall that was connected to Commissioner Theresa Lantz's red phone. She picked it up and reiterated the well-practiced script. "Chief State's Attorney Morano, are there any legal impediments to carrying out this execution?"

Having just checked with his office, he took a deep breath, knowing that this would be as close as he would ever come to ordering an execution. "No, Commissioner, there are no legal impediments."

Lantz told the warden to proceed with the execution. The warden then went to the end of the room, where he crossed his arms in front of him, signaling to the executioner—who was behind a one-way mirror—to proceed at 2:13. Seconds later, Michael shuddered. It's impossible to know whether it was a reflex triggered by the sedative or whether he was reacting to feeling the first solution enter his veins. He also could have been scared.

"Feeling some pain?" whispered a female voice. Ed and Lera later told me it was Debbie, Robin Stavinsky's sister.

Then a few minutes later, Detective Frank Griffin, one of the arresting officers, whispered, "It's too peaceful."

I watched his chest heave up and down, wondering which breath would be his last. It didn't take long for his face to turn gray and his arms to be mottled with purple. At 2:21, nine minutes after it had begun, the curtain was drawn. We all stood there silently waiting for the official word. At 2:25 the warden's announcement came over the loudspeaker.

Michael Bruce Ross was dead.

I didn't cry when the warden made his announcement because I felt as though I was going to be sick. I had been holding everything in all day, and I finally let go. I was numb. I didn't know what to feel. I just knew I wanted to get out of the prison as soon as possible. The last thing I wanted to do was break down in front of any of the prison officials or staff.

We were the first to be taken out and led back to the office, where we were to wait until the media and the families had left the prison. Father Bruno was standing outside the viewing area in the hallway. "I don't know how you did it," he said. "I don't know how you got through it."

I lost control. Tears welled up in my eyes. I didn't know how I had gotten through it, but I made it. It was over. I remembered what a lawyer friend told me about how she reacted after witnessing an execution. "I walk around with a hole in me." Now I knew what she meant. I had watched the state of Connecticut kill a person, deprive someone of his life with a deadly mix of three chemicals. My friend was dead, and I would never be the same.

We weren't allowed to leave the prison until after 3:00 A.M. While we waited, Father Bruno said almost apologetically, "You know, I was talking to the commissioner today, and she said, 'I never thought it would come to this.' None of us did, and I hope we never have to do it again."

"If you have a death penalty, you have executions. What did you think would happen?" I asked incredulously. He had no answer.

Of course, Michael couldn't go out without sending his own mixed message. On his next-to-last day, he had written to Susan. "It is difficult for me to write this today, as I know this will be the last words that I write to you. I know that I should stop this. I know that this is wrong, but I can't stop it. I can't deal with all of this anymore; it is just easier to let it all end right now. To stop this now would lead to more craziness that will never stop. The families will hate me even more, the press would crucify me, and going back to Northern would be totally unbearable (I'd never hear the end of it from both the guards and the inmates). I'm so tired of all this. I look forward to tomorrow night—finally this 20 years of hell will be over."

The rest sounded almost as if he were trying to convince himself. "So many people hate me. I am not totally evil. I am capable of doing good. This *will* help the families; this is good. So while I *am* scared, I *will* get through this. I won't back down. I am not a total coward. Then I can rest."

I had an early morning flight back to California, so I drove straight from the prison to Kennedy Airport. I cried for the first hour and then finally had no tears left. The adrenaline was gone, and I began to have trouble staying awake. I opened a window to let the cold air blow in my face and then stopped for coffee. After boarding the flight, I ordered a Bloody Mary and slept most of the way back. Five months of anxiety and ten years of telephone calls had ended. Michael was dead and I was exhausted.

I was home before noon.

My son greeted me at the door.

"Mom, are you okay?"

"Yes," I said. "I'm fine." I couldn't tell him how I really felt.

Two days later, Barry called. "You okay?"

"Yes. No. I don't know. I should sit down and write, but I can't because I just realized something."

"You thought the book would save him," he said assuredly.

"How did you know?"

"I just knew. You weren't writing it to describe an execution. You were writing it to save a life."

A week after I got back, my sister called to say that my almost eighty-four-year-old father was not doing well. My mother had been sick from October until her death in February. He had visited her every day, and it had taken a toll on his already frail health. Until her hospitalization, his colon cancer had been under control, but the worry and stress had weakened him. Just after her death in February, an MRI revealed that his tumors had grown significantly and the prognosis was not good. He decided that he did not have the strength to go through another round of chemotherapy, and having seen that other treatments had almost killed him, we didn't press him. I had been planning to visit him Memorial Day weekend, but my sister said he might not be alive by then, so I flew out that day.

I knew that my father was proud of me for being a friend to someone on death row, and he was also sensitive to the fact that I had witnessed something that neither of us wanted to happen. He didn't ask about the details but simply inquired, "Are you okay? It must have been hard."

"I don't know if I'm okay. I'm still in shock."

"I can understand that, but if he wanted you to be there, you did the right thing."

"Would you have done it?"

"I'd like to think so; I know it would have been a hard decision. Maybe for me it would have been easier because I've been at so many bedsides as people died."

"But you were holding a dying person's hand, not watching through a window as someone was actually killed."

"I can't even imagine."

He had been hoping to come for a visit to our cottage in Maine during the summer, an annual pilgrimage of renewal, but by early June it was clear that he wouldn't make it. So I brought Maine to him. I cooked him a lobster the night before he died. "Just close your eyes and imagine you're eating your lobster, listening to the loons as you sit on the porch in Maine," I told him.

"Oh, my, this is so delicious," he said. "It's paradise." He also had a piece of his favorite strawberry rhubarb pie, baked by a close family friend. The next morning, he was very confused, so I called my sister to join me. When she saw how weak he was, she went to get our brother. The rest of the day, the three of us stayed at our father's bedside with Michael Catlett, his minister and a close friend who was like a son to my parents. Occasionally my father would wake up, and we'd retell old family stories. Sometimes he would initiate the memory; sometimes it would be one of us. By late afternoon, his breathing became slower and he stopped waking up. We waited and watched each labored breath, wondering if it would be his last. He died around 6:00 P.M.

I couldn't help but compare my father's serene death, surrounded by loved ones who could soothe him and touch him, with the one that I had witnessed less than a month before. His was peaceful and private; Michael's had been painfully public, and he had not been able to hug us good-bye or share a last meal with his family and friends. Of course, my comparison is flawed. My father was a compassionate pacifist who had spent his life helping people. The monster in Michael had destroyed many lives, and both Michael and the monster paid the ultimate price.

25

SUMMER 2006

I visited the Shelleys a year after the execution. We met in a noisy McDonald's in Old Saybrook, Connecticut. Ed, dressed in a sleeveless shirt, was sitting in a booth when I walked in. Lera was outside having a smoke. Both of them had put on a little weight; they were more relaxed, more at ease. Ed's anger had always been palpable; Lera's piercing blue eyes had always been filled with sadness and tears as she talked of her daughter.

When I mentioned that they seemed more relaxed, Ed said, "I mean, it's all over and done with. We are getting along with our life, and we've found peace."

"You seem more at peace," I said to Lera.

Tears welled up in her eyes, "Well, it's easier now. Before the execution, from October to May, I was very depressed. I didn't want to see anybody; I would cry. It was horrible going through the final thing— 2004 to 2005." Near the execution dates, TV remote trucks had camped out in front of their house, waiting for one of them to come out.

"It was terrible. My daughter would go out and say, 'Leave my father alone,'" Ed said. "Then they would go to the top of the hill and call the house. They were going to our neighbors' houses. They were going to stores and everybody in town and asking, 'What do you think?'

They asked people who didn't even know us. It was just totally ridiculous."

"But now it's no longer an issue in your life."

"Right," they both answered.

"Do you think the execution needed to happen in order for you to mourn?"

"Oh yes, yes, oh yes. It had to be over, because he would have been in the limelight. He would have made sure of that," Ed said.

They said the execution hadn't been difficult for them. If anything, they were disappointed that Michael didn't open his eyes. Lera said she thought it was because he didn't want to see her cry. "In *Walking with Michael*, who does Michael mention? He mentions my face over and over." Lera surprised herself by calling him Michael. "I guess you must have made him seem a bit more human to me." But she was right about Michael's motives; her hurt, her tears had haunted him. Ed insisted that Michael was also afraid to look him in the eye. "He knew Mr. Shelley would be there front and center," Ed said proudly. "I thought it was cowardly of him."

Some of their views had changed. Ed and Lera now admitted that he was sincere about accepting execution, since he had gone through with it, but Ed added that he thought he had done it for himself because he couldn't stand to be on death row anymore. "He knew he was guilty, and it got to him." However, Ed made it perfectly clear that he still did not believe that Michael was mentally ill. "Mentally ill? No. Evil? Yes."

And he was also still adamant about another thing. Ed Shelley had no intention of ever forgiving Michael Ross for killing Leslie. "Of course I'm not going to forgive him. He thought I was going to forgive him? Good grief." Lera didn't answer; at that point there was no reason to say more.

———

Jennifer Tabor Carcia, Robin Stavinsky's little sister, was one of the few other family members who spoke to me. I was in Maine sitting on my porch; she was at home in Connecticut. The night of the execution, she had carried her favorite picture of her sister into the viewing area—despite the fact that they had been told not to do that. She had hidden it in her bra and held it while she watched Michael die. "I found him to be nonhuman. I had no emotion about it at the time. I didn't cry. I wasn't angry. I don't remember much."

She was surprised that he hadn't made a final statement and was curious why, so I explained that he "was afraid that it would be too trite. He had given a long apology at the sentencing, but what could he say in a minute other than 'I'm sorry'? He thought that would be more hurtful. And he was not sure he could get through it without crying."

"Well, that makes me feel a little better."

She said it bothered her that he didn't open his eyes because he didn't acknowledge that the families were there. "Seeing him die didn't affect me as much as when I had to put my cat down. He was a monster and so manipulative. He chose when to kill and when to die. He could have called it off. I remember the anxiety of thinking that he might call it off, but he took the easy way out. I know I sound a little callous, but his little bit of suffering was nothing compared to these girls and our families. Maybe in ten years I'll be in a different place."

"So you think the death penalty was the proper penalty for what he did?"

She took a deep breath. "A family member said, 'Did the state do us any favor by pursuing the death penalty?' And I said, 'No.' The death penalty hurts everybody. It didn't do us any favor, but it took us a long while to understand it. There are so many different situations. I can't say I am against the death penalty or that I am for it." She said when there's a death penalty, the system punishes the families. "After a trial, the families have to wait and wait, left to wait for decades as the legal process slowly plays out."

"Now that it's over, do you feel you have closure?"

"Closure? What does that mean?"

When I told her that the Shelleys told me they had moved on, she said, "To me, *closure* is just a word. Robin's death still haunts me. How can there be closure? Nothing is changed. My life has evolved around this. I am who I am because of this. If that hadn't happened, I would be a different person. I would have a sister. I would visit her, and I would have nieces and nephews." She said, for her, Michael Ross's execution was just one step along the path, but it would never be over. "I have grieved my whole life, and to watch one human being die did not make that go away. I'll never have closure because I will never get Robin back. It was just one event in a long series of events that I have had to go through," she said, sounding as if she were about to cry. She heaved a deep sigh. "You knew him as a person and you lost that. You started this same journey at his death. Do you see how it runs so parallel to us? It all runs around together."

I never thought that any family member would ever think of Michael's death as a loss to anyone other than his immediate family. "But I didn't lose a sister or daughter. I can't even define my relationship with Michael. It evolved into a friendship. I was totally afraid of him when I first met him—petrified—but over time that changed, and when he was able to trust me, he became a friend. He was already on medication when I met him, so I never knew the monster; he was just Michael."

"I feel a little better talking to you, knowing that there was a human side to Michael." She paused for a second. "I called him Michael. Maybe he is less of a monster now to me since I talked to you. In a way, it's good to know he had humanity."

"All he wanted was forgiveness—something that he knew he could never receive in life. He thought that by agreeing to die, he was proving that he was sorry," I explained. "He didn't know any other way to prove it."

"That takes me another step forward in my journey," Jennifer said thoughtfully, "knowing that he was trying to say he was sorry."

Lera called me on November 26, 2010, to tell me that Ed tragically took his own life. Wanting to spare Lera or his family the horror of finding him, he called 911 to tell them what he was about to do. His body was found in the woods just behind the Shelley house minutes later. Perhaps Ed was Michael's tenth victim—if one counts his own death as his ninth.

EPILOGUE

In a sense, Michael died for the monster's deeds. The monster never would have made that sacrifice, but Michael was ready and willing to give up his life as punishment for his crimes. In a twisted way, he saw himself as a martyr, dying so that others could get on with their lives. He wanted to make his last act proof that he was sorry for what he had done so that maybe someday even one member of his victims' families would finally forgive him. There was also an element of control in the decision—he, not the state of Connecticut, set the timetable. He knew he was going to die in prison. All he did was move up the date. Michael was pragmatic about the role of politics in criminal justice. He didn't think any judge or jury would ever give him a life sentence, and he didn't think the legislature would abolish the death penalty as long as he was on death row, and I think he was right in that assessment.

On April 4, 2012, the Connecticut State Senate passed a prospective death penalty abolition bill, and the State House of Representatives followed suit on April 12. Governor Dannel Malloy signed it into law on April 25, making Connecticut the seventeenth state to repeal its death penalty statute. The Connecticut law replaced capital punishment with life without parole, but it is a prospective abolition and does not apply to the men already on death row. Some anti–death penalty advocates believe that Michael's execution made abolition possible in Connecticut; the reality of death had shocked people into realizing that if a state has a death penalty, ultimately it will execute someone.

But Michael Ross was no hero or martyr. Michael murdered eight women and inflicted unbearable pain on nine families, including his own. He would want me to remind everyone of that fact. He didn't want to be remembered as a monster, but he also didn't want anyone to forget the monster's deeds.

My job has been presenting the two pictures of Michael Ross. I met a serial killer on paper and through his memories, and I saw all too clearly the incredible damage he had done. For ten years, I also got to know a man who would have done anything to have changed the course of his life and undone that damage. He was a man who believed that when it is in your power to do what you believe is right, it is your moral obligation to do it no matter what the consequences. He was convinced that he had only one moral option—to forgo appeals and accept death. Anything less would have violated his own moral code. Intertwined with his Christian beliefs were transcendentalist tenets. It didn't matter that man's law gave him the option to file appeals for decades; he was following both his own conscience and his higher power. The right thing to do was to die and let the families move on. In that regard, Michael did accomplish the one thing that he always said was his primary goal: Mrs. Shelley will never again cry in court.

Michael's case not only gives us a glimpse of the myriad factors that led to his becoming a serial killer, but also poses important questions about mental illness and the death penalty. I believe our justice system understands mental illness as well as nineteenth-century doctors understood bacteria. Justice is often wantonly and disproportionately meted out when the psychiatric bases of horrendous crimes are decided by juries and even judges.

No doctor offered the definitive reason why Michael killed. It remained a question that tormented him. All the psychiatrists who examined him agreed that he was a sexual sadist, however. Dr. Borden even felt his illness went beyond sexual sadism and concluded that he had a sadistic personality disorder. Because of that diagnosis, Dr. Borden said it wasn't the rape that was the ultimate sexual release; it was the murder. How much of his mental illness was genetic and how much of it was environmental could not be determined. Some tragic alchemy of his genetics, brain structure, and body chemistry, coupled with his childhood experiences, created a sadistic serial killer. I am certain that he did not choose to be violent, as Dr. Lonnie Athens would have us believe, nor did he have murderous intent. This is key to understanding Michael. He desperately needed people to believe that he did not *want* to rape and murder and that he could not control his behavior.

He was not a sociopath devoid of emotions or remorse. He had a conscience. What made him unable to control his murderous impulses? As I told the Shelleys, I don't think anyone could commit the horrific acts that Michael did without being mentally ill. Until we have a fuller understanding of mental illness, we'll have to wonder whether we are executing people who could not control their behavior. They may not have been "insane" at the time of the murder, given the specifics of the legal definitions that legislatures write and judges interpret, but there are impulses that some of us can't control. Michael Ross's story illustrates the devastation caused by unsuccessful attempts at diagnosing and treating mental illness. At least nine lives could have been saved if he had been given early and competent help to keep him from raping and killing.

Mental illness is often seen as an excuse used by a defendant, not a real medical condition that needs to be considered by the jury. Perhaps part of the problem is that the balancing act that jurors are asked to perform is sometimes actually a moral dilemma rather than a legal or medical one. They are told to balance the crimes and circumstances against the mitigating factors. They are put in an impossible position, playing God. Michael Ross's case is a perfect example of the flaws in that process. The very facts that should have spared Michael's life—like the number of bodies, proving his sexual sadism and mental illness—were at least part of the reason that caused two juries to decide on death. When there are so many victims, juries are not usually willing to believe the psychiatric evidence and spare a life—even when doctors on both sides agree that the defendant is mentally ill and give him the same diagnosis. There is no doubt in my mind that Michael should not have been put to death by the state of Connecticut.

Even Michael Ross believed the monster was evil, but I believe he would have done anything to cut the monster out of him if he could have. He detested it as much as anyone. Depo-Provera and Depo Lupron were as close as he came to chemotherapy or exorcism, but he couldn't rid himself of the guilt or the culpability. The man I came to know was not evil; he was sick and tormented.

Had Michael Ross been given life without the possibility of parole, his case would have been over in 1987. Even though Ed Shelley might have been disappointed that Michael's life was spared, he would have been spared nearly twenty years of court hearings. The state of Connecticut would have saved millions of dollars; the average death penalty case costs $2 million more than housing a prisoner for life. In Michael's case, the two execution dates alone totaled nearly a half million dollars, and the state paid for defense and prosecution lawyers, judges, security, transportation, and court personnel for two trials and mandatory appeals. I am left wondering what his death actually accomplished.

I realized after his execution that I never told Michael that knowing him helped me get over my demons, perhaps because I didn't fully comprehend it until he was gone. He was often irritating and demanding, but there were many of us who grew to like or even love him. I know he was thankful to have me as a friend, and I have to admit I felt the same way. Perhaps what I learned most from Michael Ross is that even the person who is supposed to be the worst of the worst is still a human being. Michael Ross taught me that profound Quaker tenet— all of us have a little of the divinity within us.

But ultimately Michael's story is about everyone's need to find forgiveness. I often catch myself thinking about Father John Gilmartin's question, about what Michael would say to the women he murdered when he met them in heaven, and I'm sure it would be "Please forgive me."

ACKNOWLEDGMENTS

Many people supported me during the nearly twenty years I was reporting and writing this manuscript, including my parents, Clara and Jack Elliott, who passed away before this book could become a reality. They provided me with the moral compass and courage to be willing to get to know Michael and be his friend. I am very grateful for the support of a few friends and family members who read drafts or kept me going in many ways: Lina and John Paul Beltran, Michael and Tracy Bollag, Rebecca Ditmore, Susan Elliott, the Reverend Rob Fischer, Ruth Friendly, Jack Hitt, Cynthia McFadden, Harry Sims, Joyce and Don Sipple, J. B. Stewart, the Reverend Ann Symington, and Dana White. I need to especially thank my dear friends Jenifer Stewart and Dede Lavas, who gave me their unwavering love and support.

Essential to this project was the cooperation and assistance of the people who were part of Michael's story and helped me to understand it—Dr. Walter Borden, Jennifer Tabor Carcia, Ann Cole, Fred DeCaprio, Father John Gilmartin, Karen Goodrow, Dr. James Merikangas, Paula Montonye, Susan, Dan Ross, Peter Scillieri, Jennifer Shelley, and Pete and Frances Wolak. Special thanks go to Dr. Fred Berlin, Barry Butler, and Ed and Lera Shelley, who spent countless hours helping me.

This manuscript would not have become a book had it not been for the support of my agent, Wayne Kabak, as well as the vision of Ann Godoff, president and editor in chief of Penguin Press. My editor, senior editor Virginia Smith Younce and her former assistant, Kaitlin Flynn, gave me invaluable critiques and kept me working on the manuscript until I got it right. William Carnes, who later succeeded Kaitlin as Ginny's assistant, was a crucial guide in getting this book to press. Thank you to the countless others at Penguin Random House who worked behind the scenes to make this book a reality.

My three children, Hannah, James, and Hadley Cornell, gave me loving support and almost always understood when I took Michael's calls at all hours of the night and day or worked on the book during weekends and holidays. I am especially in debt to Hadley, who has her doctorate in clinical psychology and read several drafts of the book.

Of course, ultimately I am most grateful to Michael Ross, who spent ten years confiding his innermost thoughts to me. Without his trust, his story could never have been told.

SELECTED BIBLIOGRAPHY

American Psychiatric Association. *Diagnostic and Statistical Manual of Mental Disorders*, III (1980), III-R (1987), IV (1994), and IV-R (2000). Arlington, VA: American Psychiatric Association.

Berlin, Fred S. "Issues in the Exploration of Biological Factors Contributing to the Etiology of the 'Sex Offender,' plus Some Ethical Considerations." *Annals of the New York Academy of Sciences* 528 (Aug. 1988): 183–92.

Berry-Dee, Christopher. *Talking with Serial Killers: The Most Evil People in the World of Their Own.* London: John Blake, 2003.

Blume, John H. "Killing the Willing: 'Volunteers,' Suicide and Competency." *Michigan Law Review* 103 (2004–5): 941–1009.

Capote, Truman. *In Cold Blood.* New York: Random House: 1965.

Clarke, Karen. "Life on Death Row." *Connecticut,* Mar. 1990, 51–67.

"Criminal Law—Constitutional Law—Due Process—Equal Protection." *Tulane Law Review* 2 (1947).

diGenova, Joseph E., and Victoria Toensing. "Bringing Sanity to the Insanity Defense." *American Bar Association Journal* 69, no. 4 (Apr. 1983): 466–70.

Elliott, Martha J. H. "Why a Killer Offers to Die." *Connecticut Law Tribune,* Apr. 29, 1996.

Friendly, Fred W., and Martha J. H. Elliott. *The Constitution: That Delicate Balance.* New York: Random House, 1984.

Freund, Kurt. "In Search of an Etiological Model of Pedophilia." *Acta Psychiatrica Scandinavica* 62, supplement 287 (1988): 1–39.

Furman v. Georgia, 408 U.S. 238 (1972).

Greg v. Georgia, 428 U.S. 153 (1976).

Greenfeld, Lawrence A. *An Analysis of Data on Rape and Sexual Assault.* U.S. Bureau of Justice Statistics, Feb. 1997, 1–40.

In Re Kemmler, 136 U.S. 436 (1890).

Klausner, Lawrence. *Son of Sam: Based on the Authorized Transcription of the Tapes, Official Documents and Diaries of David Berkowitz.* New York: McGraw-Hill, 1980.

Krueger, Richard B. "The DSM Diagnostic Criteria for Sexual Sadism." *Archives of Sexual Behavior* 39, no. 2 (Dec. 2009): 325–45.

Mailer, Norman. *The Executioner's Song.* New York: Hutchinson, 1979.

Meager, Bruce J. "Capital Punishment: A Review of Recent Supreme Court Decisions." *Notre Dame Lawyer* 52 (Dec. 1976): 261–89.

Merikangas, James R., ed. *Brain-Behavior Relationships.* Lexington, MA: Lexington Books, 1988. See especially 155–56.

Morris, Norval. *Madness and the Criminal Law,* University of Chicago Press, 1982.

Newton, Michael. *The Encyclopedia of Serial Killers.* New York: Checkmark Books, 2002.

Peters, Kimberly A. "Chemical Castration: An Alternative to Incarceration." *Duquesne Law Review* 31 (1993): 307–28.

Prejean, Helen. *Dead Man Walking.* New York: Vintage, 1994.

Powell v. Texas, 92 U.S. 514 (1968).

Ramsland, Katherine. *The Forensic Psychology of Criminal Minds.* New York: Berkley, 2010.

———. *Inside the Minds of Serial Killers: Why They Kill.* Westport, CT: Praeger, 2006.

Rhodes. Richard. *Why They Kill: Discoveries of a Maverick Criminologist.* New York: Vintage, 2000.

Ross, Michael. "It's Time for Me to Die." *Northeast* magazine, *Hartford Courant,* Mar. 1995.

———. "My Journey Toward the Light." *Medjugorje Magazine*: Summer 1996.

———. "Reflections from Death Row." *Sexual Addiction & Compulsivity* 4 (Nov. 1, 1997).

———. Select correspondence.

———. "Thoughts on Forgiveness." *The Monthly Aspectarian*, November 1997.

Rule, Ann. *The Stranger Beside Me.* New York: Norton, 2000.

Sacks, Oliver. *The Man Who Mistook His Wife for a Hat.* New York: Touchstone, 1998.

Stone, Alan. "The Insanity Defense on Trial." *Harvard Law School Bulletin* 33, no. 1 (Fall 1982).

Vronsky, Peter. *Serial Killers: The Method and Madness of Monsters.* New York: Penguin, 2004.

West, Donald J., and Alexander Walk, eds. *Daniel McNaughton: His Trial and the Aftermath.* London: Gaskell, 1977.

Winchester, Simon. *The Professor and the Madman: A Tale of Murder, Insanity, and the Making of the Oxford English Dictionary.* New York: Harper, 1998.

Winslade, William J., and Judith Wilson Ross. *The Insanity Plea: The Uses and Abuses of the Insanity Defense.* New York: Scribner, 1983.

INTERVIEWS

Some of the people who agreed to talk to me asked that they not be quoted directly or mentioned as a source. The following is a list of the people I interviewed who agreed to be identified as sources:

Dr. Fred Berlin

Dr. Walter Borden

Barry Butler

Jennifer Carcia

Ann Cole

Fred DeCaprio

Father John Gilmartin

Karen Goodrow

Michael Malchik

Dr. James Merikangas

Paula Montonye

Michael Ross

C. Robert Satti Jr.

Peter Scillieri

Ed and Lera Shelley

Jennifer Shelley

Susan

Pete and Frances Wolak

UNPUBLISHED ARCHIVAL SOURCES

It would be impossible to list every unpublished document used for this book. What follows is a list of the major sources referenced in the manuscript.

Autopsy reports in the deaths of Wendy Baribeault, April Brunais, Leslie Shelley, and Robin Stavinsky.

Connecticut State Police reports investigating attacks of "Carol" in North Carolina, summarizing reports of state and local police.

Connecticut State Police reports investigating attacks of "Priscilla" in Ohio, summarizing reports of state and local police.

Connecticut State Police reports investigating the deaths of Wendy Baribeault, April Brunais, Leslie Shelley, Robin Stavinsky, Debra Smith Taylor, and Tammy Williams.

Connecticut State Police reports investigating the deaths of Dzung Ngoc Tu and Paula Perrera.

Cornell University Campus Police reports investigating rapes on campus 1980–81 and the death of Dzung Ngoc Tu.

Crime scene photos concerning the deaths of Wendy Baribeault, April Brunais, Leslie Shelley, and Robin Stavinsky.

Ithaca police reports investigating rapes at Cornell and the death of Dzung Ngoc Tu.

Journals of Michael Ross, vol. 1–4, May 12, 1977–October 18, 1998.

Johnstown, Ohio, police reports investigating the attack on "Sharon."

Illinois police reports in connection with the attack on "Priscilla."

Letters from Michael Ross to Martha Elliott, 1995–2005.

Letter from Michael Ross to State's Attorney C. Robert Satti Sr.

Letters from Michael Ross to Susan, 2005.

Letters from Michael Ross to various family members.

Letters from Lera Shelley to Martha Elliott, 2000–2011.

Letter from Dr. Robert Miller to State's Attorney C. Robert Satti Sr.

Letters to Michael Ross from members of his family.

Letter to Michael Ross from Jennifer Shelley.

Letter from Jennifer Shelley to Michael Ross.

Psychiatric evaluations by Dr. Fred Berlin, Dr. Walter Borden, Dr. Raymond DuCharme, Dr. Michael Eligenstein, Dr. John Cegalis, and Dr. James Merikangas.

State v. Ross, trial transcript, Mar. 1987–June 4, 1987.

Transcript of closed hearing before Judge Seymour Hendel.

Transcript of taped confession of Michael Ross.

Videotapes, psychiatric evaluations by Dr. Howard Zonana, 1985, tapes 1–6.

Walking with Michael, newsletters from Michael Ross to people all over the world, 1996–2005.